THE
CROWNED
CANNIBALS

THE CROWNED CANNIBALS

WRITINGS ON REPRESSION IN IRAN

Reza Baraheni
With an Introduction by E. L. Doctorow

VINTAGE BOOKS
A DIVISION OF RANDOM HOUSE
NEW YORK

A Vintage Original, June 1977
First Edition
Copyright © 1976, 1977 by Reza Baraheni
Introduction Copyright © 1977 by E. L. Doctorow

Library of Congress Cataloging in Publication Data

Baraheni, Reza, 1935–
 The crowned cannibals.

Includes bibliographical references.
 1. Iran—Politics and government—1945–
2. Baraheni, Reza, 1935– —Biography.
3. Poets, Persian—Biography. 4. Political
prisoners—Iran—Biography. 5. Torture—Iran.
 I. Title.
DS318.B335   320.9'55'05   76–62496
ISBN 0–394–72357–0

Portions of this book were first published in *Intercontinental Press,
Penthouse, Mother Jones,* and *The New York Review of Books.*

*Grateful acknowledgment is made to the following for permission to reprint
previously published material:*

  Grove Press, Inc.: Ten lines of the poem "The Dictators" by
Pablo Neruda. Reprinted from *Five Decades: A Selection* by Pablo
Neruda, translated by Ben Belitt. Copyright © 1974 by Grove Press,
Inc. Translation copyright © 1961, 1969, 1972, 1974 by Ben Belitt.
Spanish text copyright 1933, 1935, 1937, 1939, 1947, 1950, 1954,
©1956, 1957, 1958, 1959, 1961, 1962, 1964, 1967, 1968, 1969, 1970
by Pablo Neruda (Editorial Losada, S.A., Buenos Aires).

  Jerzy Kosinski and P.E.N. International: Excerpts from letters
written by Jerzy Kosinski to the Prime Minister of Iran.

  Le Monde: Excerpts from an article written by Eric Rouleau which
was published in the October 5, 1976, issue of *Le Monde.*

  Princeton University Press: "Walls," by C. P. Cavafy. Reprinted
from page 3 in *C. P. Cavafy Collected Poems.* Translation copyright
©1975 by Edmund Keeley and Philip Sherrard.

Summoned to give evidence regarding what was a sort of crime, he has exercised the restraint that behooves a conscientious witness. All the same, following the dictates of his heart, he has deliberately taken the victims' side and tried to share with his fellow citizens the only certitudes they had in common—love, exile, and suffering. Thus he can truly say there was not one of their anxieties in which he did not share, no predicament of theirs that was not his. . . .

. . . Dr. Rieux resolved to compile this chronicle, so that he should not be one of those who hold their peace but should bear witness in favor of those plague-stricken people; so that some memorial of the injustice and outrage done to them might endure; and to state quite simply what we learn in a time of pestilence: that there are more things to admire in men than to despise.

None the less, he knew that the tale he had to tell could not be one of a final victory. It could be only the record of what had had to be done, and what assuredly would have to be done again in the never ending fight against terror and its relentless onslaughts, despite their personal afflictions, by all who, while unable to be saints but refusing to bow down to pestilence, strive their utmost to be healers.

—*Albert Camus*
THE PLAGUE
(tr. Stuart Gilbert)

CONTENTS

INTRODUCTION
E. L. Doctorow

> Whatever [the writer] beholds or experiences comes to
> him as a model and sits for its picture.... He believes that
> all that can be thought can be written.... In his eyes a
> man is the faculty of reporting and the universe is the
> possibility of being reported.
>
> —*Ralph Waldo Emerson,*
> *GOETHE; OR, THE WRITER*

Some of us who are writers find the universe in our marriages and affairs, in the inadequacies of our parents, and the antagonism of our peers. We produce heroes and heroines of private life. What is possible to report is the exquisite sensibility we have for the moral failings of those around us. This is not necessarily a misuse of the faculty, but neither is it the only use. There is a kind of writer appearing with greater and greater frequency among us who witnesses the crimes of his own government against himself and his countrymen. He chooses to explore the intimate subject of a human being's relationship to the state. His is the universe of the imprisoned, the tortured, the disfigured, and the doleful authority for the truth of his work is usually his own body. Thus we have Solzhenitsyn's *Gulag Archipelago,* an account of the vast Soviet system of secret police and labor camps. And because it is set in a part of the world to which we have tenuous connection, we can be safely righteous about the prisoners freezing and dying there.

What can we do for them short of beginning World War III on their behalf? Hope that through the weird, stiff maneuvers of international diplomacy—treaty signings and commodity sales and cultural exchanges—some relaxation, some loosening of the seized soul, some ease, will come to the murderously rigid Soviet state paranoia.

Yet we have living among us, in exile, another of the writer-witnesses, and his name is Reza Baraheni. His country is Iran, and he is chronicler of his nation's torture industry and poet of his nation's secret police force. In this case our aesthetic response must be a shade less righteous because Iran, by all responsible accounts, is a country whose ruler we installed ourselves and to whose health and well-being we have been devoted in all the usual ways —with our planes and tanks and computers. "Azudi has shattered the mouths of twenty poets today," says Reza Baraheni, speaking in a poem of one of the Shah's torturers. And how do we, who as aestheticians know that politics makes bad art, judge a line like this? And which of our critics who believe that words are a tapes-try, and of no value except in the pretty designs they make, can deal for art's sake with the embarrassing, unobjectified, uncor-related bitterness of a writer whose spine has been burned with an acetylene torch? What do our literature teachers say who do not grant art a political character but who would speak to their stu-dents of The Human Condition? For Baraheni or Solzhenitsyn or Gloria Alarcon in Chile or Pramoedya Ananta Tur in Indonesia or Kim Chi-Ha in South Korea, it turns out that The Human Condi-tion is first of all to be made of flesh that can be torn, organs that can be violated, bones that can be fractured. In America it is or should be every writer's dream to give literature back to life. The writer-witness of state assaults on human beings in the twentieth century has the corollary problem: How to communicate to those who insulate themselves in literature, the terrible inadequacy of aesthetic criteria as applied to human suffering. A problem of craft: How does the novelist, as he describes a scene of torture, keep us from closing the book—or from making patronizing distinctions between what is aesthetically successful and what is only sensa-tional?

Reza Baraheni is not unacquainted with the demands of high criticism. He received his Ph.D. in English literature from the University of Istanbul, Turkey, in 1960. His dissertation was a

comparative study of Tennyson, Matthew Arnold, Swinburne and
Edward FitzGerald. Before his arrest in Iran he was a professor of
English and Dean of Students at the University of Teheran. He is
a novelist, a poet, a translator of Shakespeare, T. S. Eliot, Pound,
E. E. Cummings, Camus, and is considered by many of his colleagues in Iran to be the virtual founder of modern literary criticism in that country.

Somehow, in the inverted logic of tyrannies, achievements
such as these threaten the state. And so it came to pass that
Baraheni was imprisoned and tortured for one hundred and two
days in 1973, before public opinion, generated by Amnesty International, the American PEN and the Committee for Artistic and
Intellectual Freedom in Iran, secured his release and his exile to the
United States. Baraheni emerged with a new credential—he'd become one of the writer-witnesses. And in a poem called "Our
Mission in Arras," in reference to the river between Iran and the
Soviet Union where dissidents of both countries are rumored to
have been drowned, he writes:

> A dissident poet from Russia whispers to me
> I whisper back
> We smile. We depart
> Soft pieces of ice pass between us . . .

So let us propose discussion of the idea that a new art, with
its own rules, is being generated in the twentieth century: the *Lieder*
of victims of the state. It sings of regimes so repressive as to be
fun-house mirror images of civilization. It recounts years of solitary confinement. It tells of pliers for pulling fingernails, it speaks
of electric currents sent into sexual organs, it describes prison cells
in which a person can neither stand up nor lie down. True, this is
a necessarily small range of subject. There is a limit to the possibilities of metaphor. The subtext always has to do with the
degrees of death in life. But within these strictures the poet is
entitled to sing with his or her own voice.

One feels a certain amount of curiosity—let's call it that—for
the individual who gives his life and loyalty to secret police organizations, but especially for the trolls in that netherworld who do
the actual raping, breaking and maiming of poets. From all reports
they look like ordinary human beings. One presumes, therefore,

that in order to do what they do they perform an act of excommunication, so that the victim of the abuse cannot be considered human and the rights of his or her person cannot be thought of as human rights. Hundreds of years ago such emotional preparation for torturing invoked the name of God. In our century it takes the name of Caesar. But quite clearly what is involved, always, is the inability of the torturers to accept their own mortal designation. The knowledge of flesh, of the terrible vulnerability of the flesh, and of the mind, of the fragile psychosocial constructs which support it, is a knowledge too great to be contained. Someone must be punished—mortality, the pride of the brain and the grace of the body, must be driven back into itself. The prisoner, that pretender to life and thought and self-possession, must be taught what a broken, crawling, pleading piece of excrement he really is.

Surely, then, such hate of self, of the very idea of oneself, is the root of the torturer's being. Yet there is a limit to our curiosity, as much as for the common roach of whom we are similarly aware for his ability to adapt and survive. There are others afflicted with self-hate who do not torture—common maniacs at the worst, who rampage and kill and are apprehended and treated by one or another means society has for them. But the torturer is distinguished by being accredited by society. He is that maniac whose inhuman instincts are educed, paid, titled and granted solemn rank with uniform and working hours and pensions for his future. That is what current political analysis must mean by the phrase *banality of evil*— the appropriation of evil by the state, its incorporation into law, the lifting of the dark spirit of the individual from its own responsibility, leaving it shining with belief and rectitude.

Thus the new poetry can bring to us character as well as event. Of course, a major technical problem is that the torturers all have the same speech, the same rationale usually worked out for them by their superiors (who might themselves be too delicate to witness what they do). It goes this way:

"If you do not torture, you do not find the terrorists. Do you think they would talk if you gave them a cigarette and a cup of tea? We ourselves are family men. We have wives and children at home, and it is not pleasant for us to slice off women's nipples or hang men by their testicles. But you must appreciate our enemies: they are out to bring down civilization as we know it. They would incite the population with lies printed in newspapers (if we allowed newspapers to be published) or with speeches in public places (if we allowed people to gather). They will stop at nothing. And that is why we interrogate in our prisons writers, artists, intellectuals, lawyers, doctors, teachers—or anyone, in fact, who might show signs of thinking like them."

There is not much an artist can do with that—like the form of the sonnet, very strict. Nevertheless, it is always a wonder to see how a government which proposes itself as a means of creating a civilized life for people maintains itself at the expense of the people. This peculiar moebius strip of logic leads us in its twisted way to the thought that in the twentieth century all people are, by definition, the enemies of their own governments. Thus we see today in every part of the world and under every ideology, from the most left or the most right, a citizenry brought to its knees by its protectors.

The organization known as Amnesty International quietly investigates and records cases of political imprisonment and torture around the world. It is one of the newer organizations we have, along with the Wildlife Conservation Fund, Save Our Shores, Ban the Nuke, and so on, that together indicate the wide front of the losing battle human beings are today waging against their own destructiveness. According to Amnesty International, in its report on torture published in 1974, no less than sixty countries of the world were systematically practicing torture on their political prisoners. All, presumably, are members of the United Nations, which in 1966 unanimously adopted the Universal Declaration of Human Rights, including the right of prisoners not to be tortured.

One can find little justification for the concept of progress and the perfectibility of humankind in such grisly hypocrisy. It is true that slavery in the sense of its widespread practice in the nineteenth century and before is not now an endorsed custom in most recognizable societies. That might be considered progress. But one could make the case without too much difficulty that political imprisonment of a few is the symbolic and pragmatically effective slavery of the whole. Or that just as everything in our century has speeded up—our travel, our means of dispensing information—torture might be a kind of speeded-up slavery, a life of slavery in instant form, condensed for the sake of economic convenience so that the slave victim does not have to be supported for an entire lifetime. Thirty-five or forty years of unendurable labor under abominable conditions can be accelerated by means of modern technology and delivered in a year or less of intolerable pain and debasement.

In our country, of course, we do not commit atrocities upon each other in any systematic national way. There is no federal policy in existence that calls for torture of dissidents or protesters —or indeed, without distinction, the contrasting majority who do not dissent or who are silent. We are a democracy. But if, like me, you live in a quiet house in a pleasant neighborhood where trees grace the yards, I can show you that if Reza Baraheni were to ring your bell, or mine, and recite one of his poems to your astonished face, or mine, he would have come to the right door. You and I might by nature avoid stepping on insects, but the torturers of Iran and of Chile are as close to us as the child is to the parent. They are our being, born from our loins. Look, a terrible connection is made with these dark, exotic faraway places, these barbaric civilizations who do not have our tradition of freedom, of justice: they are ours. We made them with our Agency for International Development and with our Office of Public Safety. We made them with our Drug Enforcement Administration and our Military Assistance Program. With our genius for acronym, we made them.

How worrisome that we who claim democracy for ourselves have to protect it by refusing to extend it to other people. One would think that the idea of partial democracy was a logical impossibility. One could as well speak of being only partly murderous. But the impossible is what we believe—logic that falls apart the instant we try to put it together—when we construe certain kinds of tyrannies in other places to be necessary to what we think of as our freedom.

Perhaps we are not free and the reasoning here is actually consistent. Perhaps there is no freedom anywhere—a kind of domino theory, as it were, the serial connection and collapse beginning with the first imprisonment without trial, and torture, of some obscure foreigner whose thoughts are too dangerous to endure and who is imagined, in his agony, to benefit the state. Perhaps we are not tortured because we are safely docile and cheerfully buy shares in business firms who distribute with the encouragement of our government weapons of containment and devices of technological repression used by the thugs the new poets tell us of.

In *Democracy in America,* Tocqueville describes what tyranny would be like in a democratic nation. "It would degrade men without tormenting them. . . . it seeks, on the contrary, to keep them in perpetual childhood. . . . the will . . . is not shattered but softened, bent, and guided; men are seldom forced by it to act, but they are consistently restrained from actions. Such power does not destroy, but it prevents existence. . . . it stupefies people and all the nation is reduced to nothing better than a flock of tamed and industrious animals." Perhaps in this, as in so much, the canny old Frenchman is right: If you or I do not condone torture, who among us does? If we abhor gangsters and tyrants and dictators, who among us installs them in their power? Let us have their names, who act in ours.

One reads Baraheni and wonders with a peculiar chill why there is not an ongoing national cry of protest and outrage on behalf of all tortured people everywhere. Why do we not hear from the pastors of our churches, our college presidents, our statesmen? Where are our community spokesmen and our intellectuals and artists, our Nobel prizewinners, our scientists, our economists? Why do we not hear from our businessmen, doctors, lawyers, our labor leaders, our police chiefs? Why is there not some great concerted refusal to condone, assist, endorse or do business with those who practice torture? Surely here is one moral issue which cannot be obscured by language or compromised by political point of view. In the push and pull of diplomacy, the manipulation of public opinion, the granting or withholding of money and of arms, why, with our immense power, can't we put an end to torture—at least in those states, construed as our friends, that are under our influence? Surely the torture of individuals extends beyond the limit of our own barbarism, the hungers of our corporations and our own paranoid sense of security, so that we can safely say: Not this far—at least not this.

Or must we continue to watch, unconnected and stupefied, the rise of a new art form? And shall we wager how long it will be before we produce our own native practitioners? Or must we wonder with Samuel Clemens if the human race is a joke? And if it was devised and patched together in a dull time when there was nothing important to do?

THE
CROWNED
CANNIBALS

TERROR
IN IRAN

Iran is a country of stupendous figures. When buying arms, she negotiates in billions; when her army, air force and police are sent for training in the United States, they come in detachments of thousands; when she prepares to step up oil production to meet the requirements of a deficit budget, it is a matter of billions of dollars and millions of barrels; when ships loaded with arms and cargo become jammed in the ports of the Persian Gulf, and trucks carrying food and spare parts from Europe and the Soviet Union line up for weeks on end on the borders of the country, the economic waste is again counted in billions.

Three years ago Mohammad Reza Pahlavi, the Shah of Iran, told the news media in America that he was driving his countrymen to the portals of "The Great Civilization." One would have thought that he had rational statistics to prove it. Instead, he solved the problem with yet another colossal contrivance of numbers. Back in Iran, he simply changed the Iranian calendar by decree, from the solar Hegira year of 1355 to the year 2535—what he grandiosely declared to be "the Calendar of Cyrus the Great."

Like everything else in Iran, this too was imposed overnight. Now we Iranians live not in a crudely conceived Orwellian utopia of 1984, nor in the dashing odyssey of Stanley Kubrick's 2001, and no less in a crass science-fiction fable haphazardly proposed for, say, 2200. Rather, we have been ordered into the majestic year of 2535(!), concocted, computerized and processed in the wayward imagination of His Imperial Majesty, the Shah of Shahs, Light of the Aryans and the Shadow of God on Earth.

Thus we live on the precipice of a gargantuan doomsday. Those Iranians who have refused to believe it are tormented and shot. The infernal hours of this mad doomsday have become part and parcel of every Iranian's daily life. There are a million cars in Teheran, a city originally built for people using camels, mules and horses. Now nearly everyone spends hours every day sitting and sweating in cars or buses on the small crossroads of the city, hooting and swearing at countrymen in other means of transportation. All the payments for these cars are pocketed by members of the Royal Family and those close to the inner court. The whole circus of Iranian monarchy operates on the basis of profiteering and exploitation.[1]

The Shah and the Queen are flown in helicopters to the sites of the multiple companies they own or to the airport, from which they fly to St. Moritz and to their summer and winter resorts on the shores of the Caspian Sea and the Persian Gulf. Very rarely do they ride in cars through the streets of Teheran. Separate from everything, they are alienated as well from the pattern of city life in Iran. They peer at their distant mist-covered city from behind shuttered windows, meditating on hundreds of young men and women who await the day when they will have the chance to tighten the noose around the necks of the self-declared "Father and Mother" of the nation. The marble and mirrors of their numerous palaces reflect everything in the guise of their future killers. These tyrants are also prisoners, the prisoners of their own blind arrogance and ambitious tyranny.

Outside the city of Teheran there are another million cars,

[1] "A U.S. Senate study, having revealed among other things that a member of the royal family received gifts from the Northrop aircraft firm, resulted in the transfer, dismissal or incarceration of hundreds of intermediaries of all types and of civil servants at all levels of the Iranian government. Admiral Ramzi Attai, commander-in-chief of the navy, whose wife committed the imprudence of exhibiting, in front of the royal court, a diamond valued at more than one million dollars . . . was convicted last February, sentenced to five years' imprisonment and fined 3.7 million dollars. . . . With respect to corruption, everyone agrees that it has hardly been reduced. 'The only difference from the previous situation,' we were told by a representative of a large foreign company, 'is that we now must pay to the people holding still higher positions in the country's hierarchy.' They [the Iranian bourgeoisie] are nevertheless quite uneasy about the political regime which is based on personal power and which has excluded the bourgeoisie from centers of decision-making, while preferring arbitrary decision processes." Eric Rouleau, Le Monde (October 6, 1976).

buses and trucks which funnel frantically into three narrow roads, streaming out of the capital into the open unknown. Thousands of people die through accidents on these old mule and cart roads, broadened several feet and asphalted thinly to satisfy the Shah's sad notion of "The Great Civilization," outlined in his abortive, if aptly named "White Revolution." Ancient cities have been subjected to the opprobrious indecencies of a tinsel westernization, despoiled by the vulgarities of a regime which neither values nor understands the living attainments of the East or the West.

This Woolworth mentality has been aptly summed up by one of the great intellectuals of the country, Jalal Al-Ahmad, as "Westomania." The worst taste in architecture is complemented by a sickening dosage of cheap Western goods and commodities, even as gaudy pictures featuring the cheery, frozen smile of the Shah and his queen hang everywhere, further mocking and disfiguring our ancient, historic cities. It is even worse in the smaller towns. A half-mile street, inevitably named after the Shah, cleaves them into two equal halves. These anemic towns, surrounded by dusty, neglected villages and winding hills, are inhabited by equally depleted people. A pained if time-worn indignation smolders in the eyes of every man and woman in these rural areas, and the peasants are beginning to leave their villages.

To witness the collective dispossession of the nurtured tradition and way of life in an entire nation, travel to Iran. The people of the country are being alienated from their cultural and ethnic roots and thus from their identity. They have been denied all that is of merit in the West while their own values are corroded. The cultural denuding thus involves a double alienation which gnaws at our vitals like a cancer. The Shah is carrying out the total annihilation of our art, literature, music and national languages. How did this come about? How did he attain this stupendous power? A short explanation is in order.

No historian of the Middle East and Iran will deny that in August, 1953, the CIA overthrew the legally elected government of Dr. Mossadeq, brought back to the country the Shah, his wife, his brothers and sisters who had run away earlier, and reinstalled the present monarch. Imagine a more tyrannical George III being crowned 6,000 miles away by the very descendants of George Washington and Benjamin Franklin with money raised by the American taxpayer. The CIA re-created the monarchy, built up

SAVAK—the Shah's secret police—and trained all its prominent members, and stood by the Shah and SAVAK as their powerful ally, making way for the police state which Iran has become. The Americans involved included Richard Nixon, Allen Dulles, John Foster Dulles, Kermit Roosevelt and General Norman Schwartz-kopf.

Among the Iranians involved were Shah Mohammad Reza Pahlavi, his twin sister Princess Ashraf, the notorious Nazi General Fazlullah Zahedi, whose son is the present Iranian ambassador to the United States, the infamous mafia-type thug Sha'ban the Brainless and a selected assortment of muscle men, mere brutes, prostitutes and pimps.[2]

Millions of American taxpayers' dollars were spent to overthrow Iranian democracy. Richard Nixon and the CIA Watergated first Iran and then, on the basis of this and similar experiences in the Third World and Europe, moved into Washington and Watergated their own democracy. Dozens of Watergates abroad paved the way for illegal entry into the Democratic Party headquarters in Washington. E. Howard Hunt called the 1954 CIA coup in Guatemala a "duplication" of what Kermit Roosevelt had performed in Iran in 1953. Watergate was a sequential continuation of other duplications. And the end is yet to come.

Thousands of men and women have been summarily executed during the last twenty-three years. More than 300,000 people are estimated to have been in and out of prison during the last nine-

---

[2] Concerning the American involvement in Iran see: David Wise and Thomas B. Ross, *The Invisible Government* (New York, Vintage, 1964); Leonard Mosley, *Power Play* (New York, Random House, 1973); Fred Haliday, *Arabia Without Sultans* (New York, Vintage, 1974); Anthony Sampson, *The Seven Sisters* (New York, Viking, 1975).

"General Fazollah [Fazlollah] Zahedi, the man the CIA chose to replace Mossadegh [Mossadeq], was also a character worthy of spy fiction. A six-foot-two, handsome ladies' man, he fought the Bolsheviks, was captured by the Kurds, and, in 1942, was kidnapped by the British, who suspected him of Nazi intrigues. During World War II the British and the Russians jointly occupied Iran. British agents, after snatching Zahedi, claimed they found the following items in his bedroom: a collection of German automatic weapons, silk underwear, some opium, letters from German parachutists operating in the hills, and an illustrated register of Tehran's most exquisite prostitutes." David Wise and Thomas B. Ross, pp. 110–11. For General Zahedi's Nazi connections see Fitzroy Maclean, *Escape to Adventure* (Boston, Little, Brown, 1951), pp. 198–207.

Sha'ban Ja'afari was given the title "Brainless" by both the populace and the intellectuals in Iran for his beastly extortion from the people in the Bazaar of Teheran.

teen years of the existence of SAVAK; an average of 1,500 people are arrested every month. In one instance alone, on June 5, 1963, American-trained counterinsurgency troops of the Iranian army and SAVAK killed more than 6,000 people. According to Amnesty International's *Annual Report 1974/75*, "the total number of political prisoners has been reported at times throughout the year [1975] to be anything from 25,000 to 100,000."[3] Martin Ennals, secretary general of Amnesty International, reports in his introduction to the above book: "The Shah of Iran retains his benevolent image despite the highest rate of death penalties in the world, no valid system of civilian courts and a history of torture which is beyond belief."[4]

I believe the number of political prisoners in Iran is still on the rise. The number of announced executions in the first five months of this year (1976) is more than eighty, while the number for the whole of last year was less than forty. Assuming a proportional rate of increase, the number of political prisoners this year must have at least quadrupled, since the number of officially announced executions will have risen fourfold.

Nothing could be further from the truth than to say that an Iranian prison looks like a garden, or that Iranian writers are held in better prisons than the other prisoners. All prisoners have a common destiny. With twenty-six books to my name I was kept in a dark solitary confinement cell four feet by eight. There was nothing on the floor except a dirty old blanket. There was no bed, either.

There were days when seven prisoners of diverse backgrounds were pushed into this cell. We got ourselves accustomed to sleeping while standing. Some had dysentery because of bad food and fear. Some could not stand because of sore feet or burned backs or pulled-out toenails. We breathed into each other's faces. All of us had been kidnapped by SAVAK agents; none of us had seen any warrants. Nobody outside knew where we were. We didn't know ourselves where we were, because we had all been brought to the prison blindfolded. The seven of us could have easily run a school, or a supermarket, or a factory. Imagine tens of thousands of educated men and women in prison while 75 percent of the

[3] Amnesty International, *Annual Report, 1974/75* (London, AI Publications, 1975), p. 129.

[4] *Ibid.*, p. 8.

whole nation is illiterate! Imagine hundreds of doctors in prison when every fifty villages in the country have only one doctor! Imagine roads awaiting construction while engineers are rotting in jails! The number and the extent of my government's crimes against its people have no end.

At least four agents of SAVAK are used to kidnap each suspect. There have been occasions when 5,000 people have been kidnapped on one day. This puts the number of such kidnappers in the thousands. Sometimes even tanks are used in order to get a suspect out of his lodgings. No one knows exactly the total number of SAVAK officials and its informants. At a press conference in 1971, a SAVAK authority said that there were, in addition to full-time employees, informants "in various segments of society—workers, farmers, students, professors, teachers, guild members, parties, and other associations."[5]

The Shah's claim in a recent press conference that the number of SAVAK agents is between 3,000 and 3,300 is entirely wrong.[6] The Shah could not hold his grip on the population if that were so. The given number is fictitious. The actual army of agents and informants has been reported during the last five years to number from hundreds of thousands to millions. Of the fourteen people I met in prison cells during my imprisonment in 1973, at least two had been asked to become members of SAVAK, and upon refusal they had been tortured. Everything I had said during my stay in the United States in the academic year of 1972–1973, before my imprisonment, had been reported to SAVAK, which operates on a global scale.

The Shah's despotic regime has not only rendered the whole legal and constitutional process of the country meaningless, but it has also moved to brainwash a whole nation. Last year the Shah suddenly abolished all the existing parties and decreed a new "Resurgence" party whose membership is compulsory to the entire adult population. But even this one-party system is meaningless to the Shah, because, for him, Iran is a one-man nation. Members of the royal family are at the heads of the news media, the Ministry of Information, and the Ministry of Culture. All information passes through these ministries before reaching the people.

[5] *Iran News and Documents,* a publication of the Ministry of Information, Vol. III, No. 8 (April 12, 1971), p. 16.

[6] *Kayhan* (August 18, 1976).

The Shah has closed down all the major press in the country and created others which are in the hands of the members of SAVAK. Ninety-five percent of all the available press in the country is in the hands of two families who take their orders from the Shah and the police.[7] There isn't a single piece of paper in the hands of those who don't want to write the way the Shah tells them to write. There is only one paper factory in the country, and this runs at the whim of the authorities. A best-seller in Iran means a book that sells 3,000 copies. According to the Iranian papers, every Iranian studies books only twenty to thirty seconds a year.[8]

Every schoolteacher with experience will tell you that in some villages schoolchildren are taken out to graze the grass for their lunch. In many villages people still exchange their daughters for a cow because they can milk a cow and till the land with it but they can hardly do that with their daughters. A half-skilled laborer in Tabriz, the second or third biggest city in the country, gets even less than twenty-five cents an hour, while a pound of meat costs more than two dollars, onions—if found at all—are priced at fifty cents a pound, and potatoes are not to be had at any price.

In Quri-Chai, the northern slums of Tabriz, there is only one school for 100,000 schoolchildren. In most of the cities of Baluchestan, there is only one bath for the entire population (in the city of Bampour, for instance), but since people are so poor that they cannot afford to pay the nickel required to go to the bath, it has fallen in ruins.[9] People have frozen to death in winter in this great oil-producing country.

Yet the Shah and the Iranian government claim that Iran will have reached the standard of living of the industrially advanced nations in a matter of a few years!

We need schools, jobs, food, health facilities, democracy, freedom of the press, a revolution in our legal system. We are one of the richest countries of the world. We should be able to do wonders with our wealth. But the Shah has grabbed that wealth, is arming us to the teeth and helping the whole Middle East arm itself to the teeth. Meanwhile, the majority of the

[7] The Mesbahzadeh and Mas'udi families, who, respectively, run *Kayhan* and *Ettela'at* publications.

[8] Foreign edition of *Daily Ettela'at* (February 3, 1975).

[9] Ahmad Borgheiee, *Nazari be Baluchestan* (Teheran, Mazyar Publications, 1973), p. 15.

people of my country stay poor, uneducated and sick.

Iran is the country of the poorest of the poor and the richest of the rich. The lot of the majority of the people in Iran has not moved forward even an inch during the last fifty years of the Pahlavi dynasty's reign, though the seven-year-old middle-class boy of fifty years ago, namely, the present Shah of Iran, has grown to be one of the richest men on earth.

The reason most of my countrymen would tell you that they carry a grudge against the United States is that the U.S. government has given its unconditional support to a monarch who has terrorized a whole nation, plundered its wealth and bought billions of dollars' worth of military equipment which neither he nor our nation knows how to use. Iran is a dangerous quagmire in which the United States is sinking deeper and deeper. The future will speak for itself. But if Iran becomes the new Vietnam, we can be sure that it was the inhumane and irresponsible policies of the U.S. government, the excessive greed of American arms corporations and the extreme stupidity and adventurism on the part of present Iranian authorities that led to the creation of that crisis in the history of humanity.

THE POSITION OF IRANIAN WRITERS AND WHY THEY ARE TORTURED

In a country where all political institutions are subjected to the vanities of a dictator, literature and the creators of literature turn into the voice of the nation's conscience. Iran's contemporary prose and poetry speak of the physical and spiritual poverty of humanity dominated by terror. They also articulate the spirit of protest against the injustices of despotism. Indeed, Iranian writers substitute for the political leaders who have either fallen prey to the ruler, emigrated or been imprisoned. In the past, SAVAK had no literary sophistication. But recently spies and informants have turned into critics of literature who dissect a literary image to find a political truth hidden in it.

The government encourages sexist or lukewarm mystical literature, but if you speak about life in the streets of Teheran today, you go to jail. Almost all the prominent writers and poets of the country have suffered incarceration and torture at the hands of SAVAK agents in recent years. The government searches houses one by one for books by these writers and others like Jack London,

Bertolt Brecht and Maxim Gorky. If they catch someone reading *The Call of the Wild*, they give him seven years in prison, calling him a terrorist. Last year the members of a theater group were given between two and eleven years in prison because they had tried to rehearse Maxim Gorky's *The Lower Depths*. [10]

No book in the country is published without the censors' authorization. It sometimes takes years to get permission for the publication of a book that has already been printed. All copies of a novel of mine have been confiscated by SAVAK. And I could cite hundreds of similar situations. In Iran one cannot stage *Hamlet, Richard III* or *Macbeth* because no Iranian should see the death of a prince or a king on the stage. He might jump to conclusions, as if contemporary Iranian history itself is devoid of attempts at regicide.

THE PROBLEM OF IRANIAN NATIONALITIES

The present population of Iran is thirty-four million. There are only fourteen to sixteen million Persians in the country. Of the rest, ten million are Azarbaijanis, four million are Kurds, two million are Arabs and two million are Baluchis. There are other ethnic minorities too, such as Christians, Jews and Zoroastrians. But only one language is the official language of the country. The Shah considers all Iranians to be Aryans, thus overlooking the ethnic diversity which exists in the country. Everyone has to learn one language, Persian. This is a great injustice to the other nationalities.

I belong to the Turkish-speaking Azarbaijani nationality. The men and women of my generation were told by the Shah to forget about their language and to read and write everything in Persian. We did so under duress and learned Persian. When I write a poem or a story about my parents, my mother, who is alive and doesn't know how to read or write or speak Persian, cannot understand it. I have to translate it for her so that she can understand.

The Shah's efforts to Persianize the Azarbaijanis and the Kurds and the Arabs and the Baluchis have failed. But his cultural

[10] "Fact Sheet" by the Committee for Artistic and Intellectual Freedom in Iran, December 25, 1975. Nasser Rahmani-Nejad, the director of the play, has been given eleven years in prison; Saeed Soltanpour, five years; Mohsen Jalfani, five years; Mahmoud Dowlat-Abadi, two years. They are also prominent Iranian writers and critics.

discrimination still prevails. For instance, the 3,000 American children brought to Iran by their parents working for Grumman can go to an English-speaking school. Yet millions of native Iranian children born to Azarbaijani, Kurdish and Arab parents do not have even one school in which they can study everything in their native languages. This is only one aspect of the Shah's racism.

Another aspect lies in the fact that the Shah is purging the Persian language of all that is Arabic and Turkish. This makes learning Persian even more difficult for those whose native language is Arabic or Turkish. In doing so, the Shah is also purging the present Persian language of 40 percent of its vocabulary. Arabic, though a Semitic language, stands in relation to Persian, an Indo-European language, as Greek and Latin do to English, from the standpoint of vocabulary. Imagine eliminating all Latin and Greek words from English because the two ancient languages are alien in spirit to English. In passing, let me note the ironic fact that the Shah himself speaks Persian very badly; he is more at home with French and English.

The Shah is destroying not only the cultures and languages of the Iranian Azarbaijanis, Kurds and Arabs, but he is also mangling the linguistic and cultural identity of the Persians themselves. He is destroying the traditions of a whole civilization. Of this whole tradition and civilization he wants to preserve only the worst part, that is, the crown placed upon his head by the CIA and protected through the auspices of former President Richard Nixon and Ambassador Richard Helms.

THE PROBLEM OF TORTURE AND MY PERSONAL STORY

Iranian monarchs have always been unrestrained torturers. But torture acquired new dimensions in 1920 with the emergence of Reza Khan as the strong man of the country backed by the British. He became king in 1925 and abdicated in 1941 because of his Nazi and fascist tendencies. In his time no books of history were written to show his attitude toward the dissidents.

After 1941, however, documents began to emerge. Children had been beaten in front of their parents; boiling water had been pumped into the rectums of dissidents; the mouth of a poet had actually been sewed up with needle and string. Several men had been throttled in a peculiar way. The torturers would take them to respectable cells with a bed and several cushions, knock them down on the bed, put the cushions on their mouths and simply sit on the cushions until the victims underneath breathed their last. Or they would first torture them with what was called *dastband-e qapani,* a handcuff which tied the hands together from over the shoulder and the side. Then they would start to beat them on the chest with a stick until they confessed. One would confess to anything under that torture. Physician Ahmadi, a most hideous name in the torture industry of Iran, was called in to inject an air bubble into the veins of the victim.

Such abominations were performed a few years before Hitler started the massacre of the Jewish people. I am sure the two regimes would have loved, in the spirit of Aryan brotherhood, to make a few experiments together, but time was not ripe for that. The torch of torture passed into the hands of the present shah, not immediately, because such things require some experience, but after the CIA coup in Iran. Since August, 1953, we have been under constant torture.

Let me tell you briefly why I was arrested.

A book of mine had been published in 1972 when I was in the United States as a visiting professor of English and comparative literature. The book was called *Masculine History,* and it dealt with the causes of social and historical disintegration in Iran, the oppression of women, the problem of Iranian nationalities, and ways through which some of the crises in our culture could be solved. Upon returning to Iran, I published three other articles dealing with the same problems. One of them was called "The Culture of the Oppressor and the Culture of the Oppressed," which discussed the problem of alienation and nationalities. I was arrested on September 11, 1973, and tortured the next day, and I stayed in the Comité prison for 102 days. I found out later that I was released because of international pressure, especially from American writers and poets.

The torture on the second day of my arrest consisted of seventy-five blows with a plaited wire whip at the soles of my feet. I was whipped on my hands as well, and the head torturer took the small finger of my left hand and broke it, saying that he was going to break my fingers one by one, one each day. Then I was told that if I didn't confess my wife and thirteen-year-old daughter would be raped in front of my eyes. All this time I was being beaten from head to toe.

Then a pistol was held at my temple by the head torturer, Dr. Azudi, and he prepared to shoot. In fact, the sound of shooting came, and I fainted. When I opened my eyes, I was being interrogated by someone who called himself Dr. Rezvan. The interrogation, combined with psychological torture and sometimes additional beating, went on for 102 days until I was let out.

The account of my arrest, torture and release has become public record in this country and Europe. I quote from a description I wrote of the torture instruments for a British magazine and for my book *God's Shadow*.

There were also two other iron beds, one on top of the other, in another corner of the room. These last two, I later learned, were used to burn the backs, generally the buttocks, of the prisoners. They tie you to the upper bed on your back and with the heat coming from a torch or a small heater, they burn your back in order to extract information. Sometimes the burning is extended to the spine, as a result of which paralysis is certain. There were also all sizes of whips hanging from nails on the walls. Electric prods stood on little stools. The nail-plucking instrument stood on the far side. I could only recognize these devices upon later remembrance and through the descriptions of others, as well as by personal experience. The gallows stood on the other side. They hang you upside down and then someone beats you with a club on your legs, or uses the electrical prod on your chest or your genitals, or they lower you down, pull your pants up and one of them tries to rape you while you are still hanging upside down. Evidently great rapists, with very ingenious imaginative powers, have invented this style to satisfy their thirst for sadism. There were in the other torture rooms worse instruments which other prisoners would describe: the weightcuffs that break your shoulders in less than two hours of horrible torture: the electric shock instrument, apparently a recent introduction into the Iranian torture industry; and the pressure device which imposes pressure upon the skull to the extent that you either tell them what they want or let your bones break into pieces.

Most of the horrible instruments were located on the second floor. I was not taken there, but the office of my interrogator, Dr. Rezvan, was next to this chamber, and one day when he was called to another office for some sort of consultation, I walked into the room, glanced round it and then went back. It resembles an ancient Egyptian tomb and is reserved for those suspected of being terrorists or accused of having made attempts on the life of the Shah or a member of the Royal Family. Not every prisoner goes through the same process, but generally this is what happens to a prisoner of the first importance. First he is beaten by several torturers at once, with sticks and clubs. If he doesn't confess, he is hanged upside down and beaten; if this doesn't work, he is raped; and if he still shows signs of resistance, he is given electric shock which turns him into a howling dog; and if he is still obstinate, his nails and sometimes all his teeth are pulled out, and in certain exceptional cases, a hot iron rod is put into one side of the face to force its way to the other side, burning the entire mouth and the tongue. A young man was killed in this way. At other times he is thrown down on his stomach on the iron bed and boiling water is pumped into his rectum by an enema.

Other types of torture are used which have never been heard of in other despotic systems. A heavy weight is hung from the testicles of the prisoner, maiming him in only a few minutes. Even the strongest prisoners have been crippled in this way. In the case of the women, the electric baton is moved over the naked body with the power increased on the breasts and the interstices of the vagina. I have heard women screaming and laughing hysterically, shouting, "Don't do it, I'll tell you." Rape is also a common practice. Thirteen-year-old girls have been raped in order to betray their parents, brothers or relatives. Once, looking down from Dr. Rezvan's office, I saw a five- or six-year-old girl placed in front of several prisoners in handcuffs to disclose their identities. Anytime she resisted she was slapped or her ears were pulled hard until she cried and screamed. She seemed to have no knowledge of what was happening, and she seemed to know none of the men.[11]

---

[11] Reza Baraheni, "Index on Censorship," Vol. 5, No. 1 (Spring, 1976), pp. 16–17, and *God's Shadow* (Bloomington, Indiana University Press, 1976).

SAVAK'S HARASSMENT
OF DISSIDENTS ABROAD

I came to the United States with the intention of exposing the Shah's repression. I immediately joined the ranks of Americans and Iranians who had formed the Committee for Artistic and Intellectual Freedom in Iran (CAIFI), which had been instrumental in releasing me from the Shah's jail.[12] My firsthand account could be especially useful. Other Iranian writers had been in prison and tortured, and had managed to get out of the country. But they had kept silent, and ironically some of them had been imprisoned again. I had no intention of going back so long as the present regime endured. I wrote and published and lectured and read my poetry on the atrocities committed by the Shah's regime.

As soon as my voice proved effective, I had libels and slanders thrown at me in some of my public meetings. At a meeting in Austin, Texas, a few months ago, I was threatened with death by suspect elements in the audience. On one occasion in California, I was told by San Jose State University Campus Police Chief Ernest Quinton, in the presence of Professor Kay Boyle, Professor Jessica Mitford and Daniel Ellsberg, that there was "information from a reliable source" that I would be killed if I took part in the panel. I was advised by the three other panelists not to participate.

On August 5, 1976, I was told over the phone by Professor Richard Cottam of the Department of Political Science at the University of Pittsburgh in Pennsylvania that he had heard from a most trusted friend of his in the State Department that the Iranian government had dispatched several assault squads from SAVAK to Europe and the United States who were to exploit the cooperation of mafia elements in this country to eliminate those Iranians who had raised their voice against torture and repression in Iran. "These men," the professor told me, "will appear as ordinary muggers and kill the Iranians one by one." Although he had no idea of the identity of the intended victims, he told me that my name could definitely be on the "top list."

I held a press conference at the office of PEN on August 11 to

[12] CAIFI has also been instrumental in releasing Dr. Ali Shariatti and Dr. Gholamhossein Sa'edi, two prominent writers, from prison. Recently, Ferèydoun Tonokaboni, a leading short-story writer, was released from prison, thanks to international pressure built up by CAIFI, PEN and Amnesty International.

inform the public of the danger of the arrival of such squads of SAVAK thugs. I also quoted in this press conference from *The Times*[13] and *The Sunday Times*[14] of London how SAVAK agents had been ordered to take over all the affairs in the Iranian embassies and consulates in connection with dissident Iranians abroad. I mentioned the cases of two British MP's, Mr. Stanley Newens and Mr. William Wilson, who had discovered from documents made available to them that they were being subjected to SAVAK surveillance because of their outspokenness against repression in Iran. I discovered from these two newspapers that SAVAK had ordered its operatives to break into the homes of Iranians abroad, collect material, steal documents, take pictures of dissidents, tap their telephones and keep them under strict surveillance.

In connection with the reported arrival of these SAVAK squads in the United States, I have written letters to the U.S. Attorney General, the director of the FBI, Mayor Beame and the police commissioner of New York. So far, I have received no answers.[15]

But the harassment of my family by SAVAK doesn't stop with me. My niece Narmin Baraheni was arrested in January, tortured by SAVAK agents and given seven years in prison for charges which are not yet known. The Iranian government is spending millions of dollars on American universities with one aim in mind: to keep Iranian dissidents out of them. This has made it very difficult for me to get a job in these institutions.

The Shah has thus exported his policy of bribery and co-optation to other lands and many centers of learning. While terror goes on at home and Iranians both abroad and within the borders of Iran live in fear, the Shah uses the services of former Secretary of State William Rogers and former U.S. Ambassador to Teheran Armin Meyer to persuade the American public that he is only a "benevolent despot," as if such a paradoxical creature could possibly exist. Mr. Rogers is deeply involved, both as director and

[13] The London *Times* (July 23, 1976).

[14] The London *Sunday Times* (August 1, 1976).

[15] After parts of this chapter appeared in an article in *The New York Review of Books*, I received a letter from the office of the U.S. Attorney General telling me I could not be given protection. Two FBI officials also visited me in January asking for additional information. Meanwhile, I received information from Iran via travelers to Europe that SAVAK was planning to kidnap my children.

lawyer, in the Pahlavi Foundation of New York, a tax-exempt organization set up by the Shah's multimillion-dollar Pahlavi Foundation of Teheran. The funds for this foundation were extracted from the Iranian peasants by the Shah and his father. Both the former Secretary of State and Congressman John Murphy of New York, another director of the Pahlavi Foundation of New York, are thus serving the interests of one of the most horrible dictators in modern history.

I would like to end with a quotation from a statement delivered on August 11, 1976, by former U.S. Attorney General Ramsey Clark in the press conference held at PEN concerning the arrival of squads of SAVAK thugs from Iran:

> A single death threat cannot be tolerated for the desire of profit from fifty billion dollars in trade.
>
> The Congress and the Executive should act to prohibit all military and economic aid and trade with Iran while it tyrannizes and tortures at home and threatens life abroad. America's friends must be those nations that respect the fundamental human rights of all people.[16]

[16] "Statement by Ramsey Clark" from documents of the press conference held at the office of PEN, August 11, 1976.

Parts of this chapter were delivered as a statement to the U.S. Congress in September, 1976, by Reza Baraheni.

MASCULINE HISTORY

The "Khwarenah" is a concept of fortune or destiny of primary importance in Persian mythology and without equivalent in related mythologies. . . . The national "Khwarenah" (charismatic fire) of Persia is as important as that of the heroes, for this it is that gives the nation its superiority over others. The "Khwarenah" of the Kaya-nids [legendary Persian kings] and the "Khwarenah" of the Iranian nation helped to promote an extremely strong sense of possessing hereditary gifts. . . . Zarathustra is hindered in his work by men and demons, and . . . he has need of temporal aid, a secular champion who appears in the form of King Vishtaspa. Here we have the prototype of the alliance between throne and altar that is character-istic of the Iranian concept of kingship.[1]

"You've never even produced a good chef."[2]

Iranian Monarchy, Myth and History

About 570 B.C., according to Herodotus, a ritual of horror took place at the court of the King of Medes, who ruled over what is now known as Azarbaijan, Hamadan and Kermanshah.

[1] *Larousse World Mythology*, Pierre Grimal, ed. (New York, Putnam's, 1965), pp. 191, 193, 197.

[2] Oriana Fallaci, *Interviews with History* (New York, Liveright, 1976), p. 272.

A few hours before the ritual was to begin, the King ordered his minister to send his son to the court. The minister's son was supposed to play with Cyrus, the king's grandson, whose life had been saved by the minister himself in defiance of the King's order to dispose of him. When the minister arrived, he was seated next to the King. He was puzzled and honored at the same time when he was served his meal before the King. Why, he wondered, while not daring to question the awesome majesty's reason for the honor. He ate—and with great appetite, as one should eat all meals brought by the servants of the King.

The others, a few ministers and advisers, the young, sturdy grandson and the King himself, ate nothing. They watched until the minister had finished his meal. Then the King clapped his hands.

A gold pot was brought in, covered with a gold lid. The lid was lifted. Lying in the pot was the head of the minister's son. The body had been cooked and spiced according to the customs of the court cuisine and fed to the father.

The minister had been ordered to kill Cyrus at birth because it was prophesied that Cyrus would overthrow his grandfather. The King was afraid that Cyrus, a Persian on his father's side, would usurp the monarchy from the Medes and hand it to the Persians. Since the minister had disobeyed the King, he had to be fed the body of his own son.[3]

Cyrus, the reason for this grim ritual of cannibalism, lived to found the Persian monarchy. In less than a decade he ran away from the court of his grandfather, assembled all the Persians around him, fought the Medes and invaded Babylon. By the time he met his death at the hands of the northern tribes, he was the most powerful king in the whole Middle East. His son Cambyses took the army to Egypt and invaded a great part of Africa, but on the way back he died mysteriously.

Then rose Guamata, the Magi, whom people considered to be the man destined to liberate all. In fact, he liberated the farmers, distributed the wealth accumulated in the court among the people and moved to bring universal happiness. But in 522 B.C. the Persian aristocracy, headed by Darius, mustered all its forces, plotted against Guamata, killed him and, through further conspiracies,

---

[3] *The History of Herodotus,* trans. by George Rawlinson (New York, Modern Library, 1928). See entire section on Iran.

enthroned Darius, who traced his lineage to Cambyses and through him to Cyrus himself. The seven men who assassinated Guamata tore his body to pieces. Then they decided to restore their own version of peace and order in the land.

Of the conspirators against Guamata, Otanes, who happened to believe in democracy, was the wisest. He told his friends: "We should no longer have a single man to rule over us. . . . How indeed is it possible that monarchy should be a well-adjusted thing, when it allows a man to do as he likes without being answerable? . . . He sets aside the laws of the land, puts men to death without trial, and subjects women to violence. . . ."

Megabysus, the second speaker in the conference of the conspirators, came out in favor of oligarchy: "Let the enemies of the Persians be ruled by democracies; but let us choose out from the citizens a certain number of the worthiest, and put the government in their hands."

Darius was the next speaker. He assailed the views of both men with a sharp criticism of democracy and oligarchy, and finally concluded: "Monarchy far surpasses the other two. . . . What government can possibly be better than that of the very best man in the whole state? . . . We ought not to change the laws of our forefathers when they work fairly; for to do so is not well."

The rest of the conspirators had nothing to say and went over to the side of the powerful Darius, thus ratifying the bill for the reestablishment of monarchy in the country. But since there were seven men in the conference, and not all seven could be kings, a tricky method was initiated to choose one of them as monarch. In his great *History*, from which all the above quotations have been drawn, Herodotus describes the plan: "They would ride out together next morning to the skirts of the city, and he whose steed first neighed after the sun was up should have the kingdom."

Darius solicited the assistance of his ingenious groom, who solved the problem by bringing together Darius' horse and his mare on the very spot where a few hours later all the conspirators would ride out to meet each other. Darius' horse, reminded of his earlier pleasure, gave out a loud neighing. The crown was immediately placed on his owner's head.[4]

4 *Ibid.*, pp. 177–80.

Sometime later, on the stones of a mountain, an inscription was carved which read in part: "I am king; Ahura-Mazda gave me the kingdom."[5] Such ironical distortions are plentiful in the history of Iranian monarchy. What Darius did more than 2,500 years ago resulted in the re-creation and strengthening of a ruling pattern in Iran which, for the purpose of simplification, I have called Masculine History.

It is not my intention to give a detailed outline of Iranian monarchy. I will speak of its prevalent structures and patterns, and then attempt a theoretic restructuring of objective data. Here are some of the highlights of the monarchy's inherent brutality.

About 1,400 years ago, an Iranian king named Anooshiravan invited to his court 12,000 adherents of the cult of Mazdak, a new political religion. Mazdak, who was among his own followers in the court, advocated such changes as abolition of the aristocracy and the caste system, establishment of equal rights for all and acceptance of both male and female polygamy. Female polygamy had been prohibited since the advent of patriarchy about the beginning of the first millennium B.C., but male polygamy had continued to thrive and still persisted after the conversion of the Iranians to Islam in the seventh century.

The King had pretended acceptance of the new religion's practices. Instead, he buried all 12,000 people, along with the new prophet, upside down.[6] The name "Anooshiravan the Just" was given him at this time, apparently as a bribe, so that he would be ashamed to continue killing at a speed that would surely decimate the nation.

A thousand years later Shah Abbas the Great was actually flanked by cannibals whenever he held open court. When the Shah did not like a minister, a poet or a writer, he would simply turn to his right or left and say: "Eat him!" The ritual would take place there and then. The King's orders could not be delayed.[7] In fact, one of his courtiers at this time told the French traveler Chardin that whenever he left the court he would go home and

---

[5] *Larousse World Mythology,* the section on Iran. Also see *The History of Herodotus,* entire section on Darius.

[6] Khajeh Nizam-al Mulk, *Siyasatnamah* (Politics) (Bongah-e Tarjomeh va Nashr-e Ketab, 1969).

[7] Nasrullah-e Falsafi, *Zendegane-ye Shah Abbas-e Avval* (The Life of Shah Abbas the First) in four volumes (Teheran, University of Teheran Press, 1955).

stand in front of the mirror to see "whether his head still stood on his shoulders."[8]

The Iranian historian Bastani-ye Parizi relates even more horror stories of the shahs of Iran. When Ya'qub-e Leyth, the founder of one of the early Iranian dynasties after the Arab invasion, fought with Ratbil, "he massacred the people of the city of Kabul, had their heads severed from their bodies, and sent them over the River Hirmand to his province Sistan. There were more than two hundred ships carrying the heads of the dead."[9] Shah Esmail, the founder of the Safavi dynasty, held his enemies in iron cages for months, had ovens to burn human beings, drank wine in the skulls of his enemies and had his orders to his commanders inscribed on the dismembered bodies of his adversaries.[10] Agha Mohammad Khan, the founder of the Qajar dynasty, plucked so many eyes out in the city of Kerman that when placed together on a scale they weighed twenty-three kilos.[11] After the invasion of the city of Kerman, Agha Mohammad Khan "ordered his men to behead 600 captives. The heads were mounted on the shoulders of 300 other captives, two heads on each captive, and they were all sent to the city of Bam. These poor and miserable captives walked forty leagues in front of the horses with the heads hanging from their shoulders. At a written order from Agha Mohammad Khan, the governor of Bam killed these three hundred men, and built with the heads of all nine hundred men a *kalleh-menar* (minaret of skulls) which still stood in Bam 17 years later when the British traveller Pattinger saw it with his own eyes in 1812."[12]

Hossein Makki, another historian of the present era, speaks of the horrors perpetrated by Reza Khan, the founder of the current Pahlavi dynasty, before he became shah. Boiling water was pumped into the rectums of the members of the opposition; seven-year-old children and seventy-year-old-men were subjected to torture; women were beaten to death; Reza Khan himself beat the deputies of the parliament. In one case Reza Khan ordered his men

[8] Mohammad Ebrahim Bastani-ye Parizi, *Siyasat va Eqtesad-e Asr-e Safavi* (Politics and Economy of the Safavi Period) (Teheran, Safi-Alishah Publications, 1969), pp. 86–88.

[9] *Ibid.*, p. 23.

[10] *Ibid.*, p. 24.

[11] *Ibid.*, p. 23.

[12] *Ibid.*, p. 306.

to behead the poet Bahar, but they mistook another man, Vaez-e Qazvini, for the poet and beheaded him in the courtyard of the parliament.[13] He was no better when he became king. After his abdication in 1941, when one could write freely about his reign, the press called it *dowre-ye tarik-e bist-saleh* (the dark period of twenty years), describing in full his torture chambers, his torturers and his inquisitions.

Characteristic of this long line of kings is the mythical quality ascribed to their murders. Almost all of them relate, in their inscriptions, chronicles, or books of history written at their command, that they have seen God, Zoroaster, Mohammad, Ali, his sons or other significant religious leaders, in their dreams or in reality, before they either became kings or took off on a mission that resulted in the massacre of thousands of men, women and children. They invoke the Almighty to drink wine in the skulls of their victims.

The historian Parizi relates the mythical accounts of a dozen dictators who believed they had missions outlined by God that they must fulfill before they died or the whole country would be doomed to extinction. Accordingly, the present shah has made his divine mission the most important theme of his reign. Gerard de Villier explains some of the visions and dreams the Shah claims to have had when he was a child. These include the Shah's rescue by Imam Ali from the clutches of the deadly typhoid and by Hazrat-e Abbas, a favorite of the Shi'ite sect of Islam, from a headlong fall on a solid rock, as well as the appearance of a man "with a halo around his head," which others in the palace could not see, that consequently let the Shah assure others that a divine hand was choosing him for the future.[14] The Shah also told Oriana Fallaci in an interview: "I am not entirely alone, because I'm accompanied by a force others can't see. My mystical force. And then I get messages. Religious messages. . . . I've lived with God ever since the age of five. That is, since God sent me those visions."[15] Several anthologies of speeches and writings of the Shah put out by the Iranian government are decorated with accounts of

[13] Hossein Makki, *Tarikh-e Bist-Sale-ye Iran* (Twenty Years of Iranian History), Vol. III (Teheran, Mohammad Ali Elmi Publications, 1945), pp. 109–10, 126, 418–20.

[14] Gerard de Villier, *The Imperial Shah* (Boston, Toronto, Little, Brown, 1976), pp. 37–38.

[15] Oriana Fallaci, p. 267.

these visions and his "mission." Earlier anthologies had been embellished by similar visions of earlier kings.

What is the nature of these visions? Where do they come from, and how can we relate them to the past and present socioeconomic structure of Iran? To answer these questions we must go back in our study to the origins of Iranian history, which are also the origins of the Iranian monarchy.

The Shah considers monarchy to be the "natural regime" of Iran. In the summer of 1961 he told France's Press Club: "Only those regimes are in danger which are not natural. The Iranian regime is a natural regime which has stayed with us for the last 2,500 years. This regime was not imposed on us by foreigners; monarchy is not the creation of the colonialist powers."[16] In other speeches and books he considers monarchy to be the pillar of Iran's natural identity, the irreplaceable structure of its existence.

What is the truth behind this claim? It must be traced back to the accumulation of wealth in the hands of the ruling fathers at the origins of what has been termed "Oriental Despotism." How did the accumulation of wealth take place in the early phases of Iranian history? What were its immediate effects?

> Until the lower stage of barbarism, fixed wealth consisted almost entirely of the house, clothing, crude ornaments and the implements for procuring and preserving food: boats, weapons and household utensils of the simplest kind. Food had to be won anew day by day. Now, with herds of horses, camels, donkeys, oxen, sheep, goats and pigs, the advancing pastoral peoples—the Aryans in the Indian land of the five rivers and the Ganges area, as well as in the then much more richly watered steppes of the Oxus and the Jaxartes, and the Semites on the Euphrates and the Tigris—acquired possessions demanding merely supervision and most elementary care in order to propagate in ever-increasing numbers and to yield the richest nutriment in milk and meat. All previous means of procuring food now sank into the background. Hunting, once a necessity, now became a luxury.[17]

[16] *Bargozide-i az Neveshte-ha va Sokhanan-e Shah-an-Shah Aryamehr* (A Selection of Writings and Speeches by the Shah of Shahs, Light of the Aryans) (Teheran, Pahlavi Library Publications, 1968), p. 35.

[17] Karl Marx, Frederick Engels, *Selected Works*, 2nd printing (New York, International Publications, 1972), p. 493.

This increase of wealth was connected with the downfall of matriarchy and the rise of patriarchy:

> Thus as wealth increased, it, on the one hand gave the man a more important status than the woman, and, on the other hand, created a stimulus to utilize this strengthened position in order to overthrow the traditional order of inheritance in favor of his children. But this was impossible as long as descent according to mother right prevailed. This had, therefore, to be overthrown, and it was overthrown. . . . We know nothing as to how and when this revolution was effected among the civilized peoples. It falls entirely within prehistoric times. . . . The overthrow of the mother right was the *world-historic defeat of the female sex.* The man seized the reins in the house also, the woman was degraded, enthralled, the slave of the man's lust, a mere instrument for breeding children. . . . With the patriarchal family, we enter the field of written history.[18]

This theory of the downfall of matriarchy and the rise of patriarchy, outlined first by Morgan, reinforced by Engels and molded into a convincing document on the rise of various classes in the dawn of civilization, was augmented by later research on the part of many anthropologists, and mythologists in the West. None of these studies, however, provides specific examples from the culture and history or prehistory of Iran. Let me clarify a few points.

All Iranian myth, legendary history, religion and religious cults start with the supremacy of men over women. Kayoomarth, the first king and the first great father, was a man who had tamed the animals of the earth. Later, Zoroaster, whose religion is one of men and with whom we enter the era of patriarchy, sought temporal aid in the form of Vishtaspa, a man. This does not mean that there was no matriarchy in Iranian prehistory: "At present archaeology has discovered the existence of indigenous (non-Aryan) matriarchal cults in Iran and Central Asia. All the archaeological researches of the Soviet Union speak of the existence of these cults before the arrival of the Indo-Iranians in these regions."[19] And

[18] *Ibid.,* pp. 495–97.

[19] Mehrdad Bahar, *Asatir-e Iran* (Iranian Mythology) (Teheran, Iran Cultural Foundation Series, 1973), p. 57 of Introduction.

certainly there are significant reminiscences of these cults and rituals in the literary works, sculptures and objects dug out of archaeological sites. Moreover, there are undeniable examples of matriarchal culture in the folklore of the various nationalities and tribes living in Iran today.

According to the scholars of Iranian mythology, there are documents to prove that the sacrifice of young men to the Mother Goddess took place, and continued to exist in vestigial forms, in the Iranian plateau. The tragic death of Siyavash, the legendary hero of Iran who also symbolizes spring vegetation and fertility, is one of the outstanding examples of vestigial forms of youth sacrifice. Later, such sacrifices became ritualistic and only a matter of cult or decorum. On the first day of spring, in lieu of actual sacrifice, the king or the governor of the city would temporarily resign from his position and a nominal governor would take his place. The governor could give orders, arrest people and punish them, but he had to resign in a few days to surrender his place to the original ruler.[20]

The historian Parizi tells us how Shah Abbas, one of the kings of the Safavi dynasty, invited one of his enemies to become king, then subsequently removed the nominal king and, in fact, killed him. In another historical incident King Mahmoud of Ghazneh commanded his slave-boy Ayyaz to sit on his throne so that he, the King, might stand in front of him in the manner of a slave. But as the mythologist Bahar says: "Matriarchal societies of the Iranian plateau and Western Asia had given their place, because of the increase in production, to patriarchal societies, and the rule of women had given its place to the reign of men, and it was no longer possible to sacrifice men for the fertility of the land."[21]

The increase in level of production, the accumulation of wealth, the soaring power of men in both family and society, and the concentration of all productive forces in the male domain led also to the concentration of all art, literature and culture in the hands of men. This, one may say, happened elsewhere in the evolution of society from savagery to barbarism to civilization, and therefore my definition of Masculine History is in no way different from the Western modification of historical patriarchy.

[20] *Ibid.*, p. 56 of Introduction.

[21] *Idem.*

It is here that I take exception to the views of most of the Western and Eastern scholars who either lump the East and West together, dogmatically compartmentalizing Eastern objectivity into Western theories (such as the present Stalinist Orientology of the Soviet Union), or see in the whole of the East—especially in some of its philosophy and poetry, such as Sufism and mysticism —a kind of ethereal salvation for their bourgeois boredom.

Stalinist Orientology, based on a vulgar dogmatic Marxism, claims for both the East and the West one identical pattern of historical evolution, from slavery to feudalism to capitalism. Such a doctrine overlooks, on one hand, the later observations of Marx on the Asiatic Mode of Production and disregards, on the other, the objective situation in the East itself. Stalin threw out the Asiatic Mode of Production in a 1931 meeting in Leningrad, and since then Soviet Orientology has not been able to look at the history of the East with open eyes. Stalin thought of the three stages of historical evolution as a suprahistorical law, which every nation in the world had to go through, one at a time and phase by phase. China had to go through the same stages as Germany, and, historically, India and Britain were subjects of the suprahistorical law of revolution by stages. No nation in the world could by-pass any one of these stages. This iron-clad theory forms the basis of Stalinist Orientology even now, although to a lesser degree than in the Stalin era itself. The East is bored with this Stalinist conception of history, because, as we shall see in the case of Iran, there is a variety of stages and situations in these countries, rather than one fixed stage at any given moment in time.

Equally abhorrent to the East is the typical salvational attitude of the bourgois West, because of its romantic escapism into a heaven which simply does not exist. Most of these escapists, intrigued by the virgin deserts in the Middle East and Africa, the temples, the pyramids, the mosques, the caves and even the deserted streets of Oriental nights, and fed up with the war of the capitalist machine, stretch their legs in the same cafés, caravanseries and teahouses which their fathers and forefathers—Arthur Rimbaud, Oscar Wilde, André Gide, Pierre Loti, John Galsworthy, Somerset Maugham, E. M. Forster, Hermann Hesse and a dozen others—visited before them. But the East is no longer as virgin as it was for Hermann Hesse, and the modern escapist is not as talented as his predecessors. These present-day tourists fill their poems with Eastern names, images and undigested inspiration and intuitions, forgetting that they are clinging to something buried deep in the past of the East itself, which has been covered—not once, but many times throughout the last five hundred years—by generation after generation of colonialists who were, in fact, their very fathers and forefathers. They go back to their homes in California or Massachusetts, Paris or London, with copies of the Koran and Avesta and works on Zoroaster, Buddha and Confucius, and stand on their heads in the morning, invoking the lost spirit of the East. The poverty, both physical and spiritual, of the present East, the greatest heritage of Western imperialism, is completely overlooked by these men and women of high adventure.

There is a third group of people with whom I do not share a common ground: the Western Orientalists and social scientists of the Middle East. Orientology is the cultural superstructure for colonialism. The typical Orientalist generally worked under the auspices of his government; in the United States the Orientalist–social scientist, succeeding and integrating the Orientalist, is an adviser to the Pentagon, the CIA, the State Department, the think tanks of the big corporations. A few exceptions aside, these scientists are at the service of imperialist exploitation of all the peoples of the East. We cannot adopt and successfully use their theories and practices.[22]

The Economic Structure of Masculine History

The lands, the waters, the gold, the mines, the beasts, the men, women and children, the seasons and months—in sum, all things that are on the earth or that fall from the sky—belong to the Shah of Shahs of Iran. He is the absolute possessor of everything both objective and subjective. He is God himself walking on earth.

The great poet Saadi (1215?–1292) said in the first chapter of his *Rosegarden,* dedicated to "The Nature of Kings," that: "To want anything contrary to the wish of the Shah, would be equal to playing with your life. If he calls day, night, you should simply say, Behold the moon and the Pleiades." The epic poet Ferdowsi

[22] See *Middle East Studies Network,* No. 38 (Washington, D.C., Middle East Research and Information Project [MERIP] Reports, June, 1975).

(935–1020) said that the Shah was one who "drove wolves and sheep together to the watering area." In fact, there are thousands of lines of poetry, and certainly thousands of pages of prose, in which the Shah has been praised as God and sometimes as even more powerful than God. The panegyrics of the Khorassani school of poetry from about 950 to 1200 are full of such laudatory phrases that the exaggerations would be acceptable now only as absurdities. The poet Onsori (d.1039) said: "Many a man has denied the existence of his creator, but they have all admitted his [the Shah's] greatness and wisdom." Farrukhi (d.1037), another poet of the same period, wrote a passage describing the Shah's crossing over the sea: "the sea appeared to be saying, Your Majesty, you are the sea, I am only the dry spring." In another line, the poet likened him to Jesus: "If the King sheds its shadow on a dead man, the charisma of the shadow will bring him back to life."

This "charisma," arising from the depths of the barbaric period, during the transformation of matriarchy to patriarchy, lies at the root of Iran's Oriental Despotism. Add patriarchy and the Asiatic Mode of Production (which we will discuss in the following pages), and you have the secret of Masculine History in Iran.

First, the charisma: "One other sign of tribal life is the existence of *farreh.* . . . *Farreh* is that magical, celestial power which used to belong to the witch-ruler, and since the witch-ruler appears in Iranian mythology in the form of the priest-shah, he carries along this power and rules over people's body and spirit with its help."[23]

The concept of Zillullah, or the Shah as God's Shadow, which was used by most of the shahs of Iran to give their rule a certain religious legitimacy during the Islamic era, should be studied in the light of the mythological definition of the word *farreh*. As soon as the man gains supremacy over the woman and matriarchy is overthrown, and as soon as he gains control of the productive powers of both society and the family, he turns his objective economic power into an abstract divine halo, thus claiming to be the sole representative of God on earth. This halo acts as the moral, religious and divine justification of his economic power. The Shah's words to Oriana Fallaci about his "visions" are only an invocation of the divine *farreh*, or, as *Larousse World Mythology* has called it, the *Khwarenah*, which seems to be a variation of the word. Whatever

[23] Mehrdad Bahar, p. 39 of Introduction.

the name of the concept, there is no doubt that the man's economic status lent him the courage to consider himself God's agent on earth.

"Considering the fact that magicians were the first rulers among Iranians—and this we see very clearly in Iranian mythology—and taking note of the fact that these rulers considered themselves gods incarnated, or God's messengers or God's Shadows, we can think of the concept of *farreh* in its more developed form to be that celestial power which is with the Shahs, and if they make a mistake, or do not come from royal blood, *farreh* turns away from them."[24]

The Book of Kings, Ferdowsi's great narrative, tells of *farreh* turning away from several kings who made mistakes or who were not of royal blood; however, this was not the case with all such kings. The present shah is a very good example. His father was not born of royal blood. British imperialism put the halo around his head and gave him the specific *farreh.* The current shah got the power first in 1941 through the intervention of the Allies, and then in 1953, when he was about to lose it to the much more charismatic figure Premier Mossadeq, the foremost world power, the United States, interfered and bestowed the Shah with a "divine gift."

This is no exception. Almost always, the *farreh* has been the outcome of a power struggle, national or international, and the one who has gotten the upper hand has exalted himself as God's Shadow. The present shah has very definite ideas about power, as well as a special conception of Western democracy:

When you don't have monarchy, you have anarchy or oligarchy or dictatorship. And anyway monarchy is the only way of governing Iran. . . . To get things done you need power, and to keep power you shouldn't have to ask permission or advice from anybody. You shouldn't have to discuss your decisions with anyone. . . . I can't separate the man from the king. Before being a man, I'm a king. A king whose destiny is swayed by a mission to be accomplished. And the rest doesn't count. . . . A king means first of all duty, and I've always had such a strong sense of duty. For instance when my father told me, "You're to marry Princess Fawzia of Egypt" . . . I agreed at once because it was my duty to agree at once. One is either

[24] *Ibid.,* pp. 60, 61.

a king or one isn't. . . . But I don't want that kind of democracy!
. . . I wouldn't know what to do with such a democracy! . . .
Freedom of thought! freedom of thought! Democracy, democracy! with five-year-old children going on strike and parading
through the streets. That's democracy? That's freedom?[25]

With very minor changes we can hear the voice of King Darius
through these words. In fact, the comparison is apt, not because
the Shah resembles Darius in grandeur—we know he doesn't—but
because of what happened right after the two kings took power.
When Guamata was killed, farmers demonstrated all over Iran to
commemorate the reforms he had accomplished during his short
rule. Darius abolished those reforms, and when people reacted
with riots he responded with massacres. When Mossadeq was
arrested, all his reforms, among them the nationalization of Iranian
oil, were abolished, and the massacre of all the members of his
following began.

The Shah has spoken of his ancient and divine *farreh* in Christian terms, too, but the comparison calls up the spirit of some of
the best scenes in Samuel Beckett and Eugene Ionesco. The following dialogue is drawn from a very pro-Shah book, thus making the
absurdity more meaningless than usual:

"Well, yes," he said. "They call the king the Shadow of
God . . ."

"Wasn't that title abandoned some years ago?"

He nodded. "A long time ago. I never use it, but there are
people who still do."

He considered the subject for a moment, and then asked:
"Incidentally, what does it mean when the Pope washes and
kisses the feet of the people?"

Briefly, I reported the origins of the ceremony. Christ had
washed the feet of his disciples before his passion.

"Why did he do it?"

"To symbolize his humanity. The Pope now similarly
dramatizes his equality with men when he holds power to the
keys of the Kingdom."

"All right, could I not say that these people kiss my feet
because they want to make me feel equal to them?"

[25] Oriana Fallaci, pp. 265–75.

I replied: "I think not. Theirs is an act of homage. However, if you were to wash their feet . . ."

"Yes?"

". . . then that could relate to the Pope's ceremony."

"But if they do it to me . . . ?

"Perhaps," I suggested half seriously, "such a symbolically humbling act might serve for the coronation. Your present image as a reforming king suggests that it might not be altogether out of character."

"Yes, perhaps." He hesitated almost imperceptibly and then continued. "Well, we could not copy the Christian formula."[26]

Indeed, the Shah tells E. A. Bayne in the book from which the above was taken that whoever kisses his feet becomes free, and that those who kiss his feet do so because they see in this action the realization of their dreams as free people. He also declares that the Iranian Constitutional Revolution (1906–1912) had anti-Iranian elements in it because it was an effort to limit the traditional authority of charismatic kings, and that the reason the Iranian people revolted against Mossadeq in 1953 was that they could not stand the affront to the Shah of Iran, who is the father of the whole nation. These assertions amount to the pronouncement that Oriental Despotism is the everlasting identity of the Iranian people.

A few selections from Western writing on production under Oriental Despotism might help the reader understand the genesis of this unmitigated despotism.

> . . . Bernier rightly considers the basis of all phenomena in the East—he refers to Turkey, Persia, Hindustan—to be the *absence of private property in land.* This is the real key, even to the Oriental heaven. . . .[27]

> The absence of property in land is indeed the key to the whole of the East. . . . But how does it come about that the Orientals did not arrive at landed property, even in the feudal

[26] E. A. Bayne, *Persian Kingship in Transition* (New York, American Universities Field Staff, 1967), pp. 41–42.

[27] *Marx, Engels on Colonialism,* 5th printing (Moscow, Progress Publishers, 1974), Marx to Engels, London, June 2, 1853.

form? I think it is mainly due to the climate, taken in connection with the nature of the soil, especially with the great stretches of desert which extended from Sahara straight across Arabia, Persia, India, and Tartary up to the highest Asiatic plateau. Artificial irrigation is here the first condition of agriculture and this is a matter either for the communes, the provinces or the central government. An Oriental government never had more than three departments: finance (plunder at home), war (plunder at home and abroad), and public works (provision for reproduction).[28]

. . . 1) the public works, were the business of the central government; 2) beside this the whole empire, not counting the few larger towns, was divided into *villages*. . . . I do not think anyone could imagine a more solid foundation for stagnant Asiatic Despotism.[29]

In a very exceptional and profound article on comparative history between the East and the West, the Iranian scholar Mohammad-Ali Khonji outlines the serious mistakes made by almost all the living Orientalists and social scientists of the past forty-five years when Stalinism held sway in the Soviet Union and elsewhere. He reiterates that all Western scholars of Iran should pay attention to the almost totally forgotten concept of the Asiatic Mode of Production, which could, all ideological prejudices aside, throw more light on the aforementioned areas than any other Western conception of the East.

According to Khonji, the paramount difference between the East and the West lies in the former having "to grapple, from neolithic times up to the present with two big problems: either the scarcity of water or its excess in floods." The Western people received their water free from the clouds and the rivers, and all they had to do was learn how to sow and reap. This discovery, according to Khonji, was a revolution itself. "But in order to realize this, the Eastern man needed another revolution of equal significance, and that was artificial irrigation."[30]

Thus water becomes a factor of life and death, and whoever

[28] *Ibid.*, Engels to Marx, Manchester, June 6, 1853.

[29] *Ibid.*, Marx to Engels, June 14, 1853.

[30] "History of the Medes and the Origin of Diakonov's Theory," *Rahnema-ye Ketab* (September, 1967).

has this natural resource will use it as an instrument of economic and political power. Those who were assigned in the beginning to the task of administering the distribution of water turned gradually into the owners of water, subjecting others in the territory to their authoritarian mandates. Here, land was an extension of water. Even today, the more water one can possess and keep and distribute, the better one can freely grasp lands and make them his own.

In this way, human administrators of the divine water became *arbabs,* or *maleks,* the owners of land and water, miniature gods walking on earth, eventually rulers and kings. Public workers became exploiters of the populace. According to Khonji's interpretation of the Asiatic Mode of Production, civilized society in Europe is first divided into classes, and out of class antagonism the bureaucracy of the state is created. In the East, however, first a state is created, composed of public workers and administrators, and then the division into classes takes place.

The smaller governments, and subsequently the larger ones, either build and own artificial irrigation systems from which they sell water to the peasants and the cities or actually possess the available natural canals. In this case, they exchange water and land for physical labor at the cost of the absolute pauperization of the whole population. The peasantry becomes that "solid foundation" on which "stagnant Asiatic Despotism" erects itself to its ultimate heights. Whatever happens to the society, the burden falls on the starving, sweating, toiling populace. All taxes mean the plunder of the populace; war means the death of the populace: The victory of a king means the massacre of the population of the other king's territory, along with the expropriation of all his gold and money, wives and slave-boys.

But the people who make that victory possible gain only their chains. If their king is defeated and killed, massacre—or at least fresh taxation—awaits them. No wonder people rioted when they found out that Guamata had been killed; no wonder the king responded the way he did.

Another work crucial to the understanding of the Asiatic Mode of Production in Iran is a book called *Boneh, the System of Collective Agricultural Production in Iran* by Javad Safi-nezhad. The writer makes no reference to any Western scholar or document. He undertakes an in-depth study of the structure of the labor system in Iranian villages. He speaks of the vital importance of water and its relation to the production arrangements of the village, and analyzes the whole framework of exploitation. He does not indulge in any form of theoretical explication of his subject matter. Nevertheless, it is certainly true that his innocent description of Iranian villages would have been a source of inspiration for Marx and Engels, who did not actually have enough substantial evidence to finalize their thoughts on Asia, and of great interest to Max Weber, with his theory of patrimonialism, and Karl A. Wittfogel, whose concept of hydraulic society is treated in his *Oriental Despotism.*

Southern, central and Eastern villages of Iran are villages in which there is very little water. The scarcity of water in these areas is the main obstacle for the growth of agriculture. . . . The assembling and settlement of villagers depends on the water. The greatest assembly of villagers, and consequently the largest assembly of villages occurs in places where there is either a spring or an irrigation system. The quantity and the quality of the crops in these areas are dependent on the variant of water. . . . The stinginess of nature in these areas had led to the adoption of production methods through which, under unsuitable natural conditions and the present production relations, the best use can be made of the land. . . . *Boneh* is an independent agricultural unit, composed of a number of peasants, with distinct social positions and with a division of labor based on social and economic privileges, who cultivated one or several pieces of land for one year in a village with the help of a definite amount of water and tilling power (cow-worker) and with work tools belonging to the Boneh.[31]

Safi-nezhad goes on to explain the degree to which water is significant, who the landowner, the tenant and the peasants are, and what percentage every member of the *Boneh* receives. It is surely a miserable life of sweat and toil, starvation and anxiety, with an uncertain future. Water is distributed by the day of the month and the week, and only for very short hours. The central element is water; then comes land, followed by the rest of the elements. Thirty-three percent of all crops in the village of Taleb-

[31] Javad Safi-nezhad, *Boneh, the System of Collective Agricultural Production* (Teheran, Toos Publications, 1964), pp. 3, 9.

abad, for instance, went to the peasants and 67 percent to the landowner.[32] The landowner could have many other *Bonehs*, but the toiling peasant had only his hands and his meager share of the total percentage.

It is not surprising that when in 1946 the Democratic Government of Azarbaijan (which is not as dry as the areas mentioned above) initiated an extensive land reform in the province, most of the villagers joined the government supporters and the landowners left. They came back only after the Shah overthrew this democratic government and introduced his dictatorship.

The pyramid of the *Boneh* social structure resembles, on one hand, that of the patriarchal family and, on the other, that of the above state. The father exploits the family, his wife and children; the landowner, or the *arbab*, exploits all the fathers and their families; the charismatic ruler exploits the whole nation. The fathers, the landowners and the shahs have their circles of *farreh* around their head. Wives and children suffer most of all, and if they work —which they generally do—the father grabs everything and takes it for himself. The *arbab* does this in relation to the workers in the *Boneh*, and the shahs receive their tributes from the landowners. Thus is Oriental Despotism also masculine.

Although there is nominal possession of property, in reality no one securely possesses anything. The Shah can take away anything from anyone at any given moment. "Oriental Despotism therefore appears to lead to a legal absence of property." If there is surplus labor, it "belongs to the higher community, which ultimately appears as a *person*. This surplus labor is rendered both as tribute and as common labor for the glory of the unity, in part that of the despot, in part that of the imagined tribal entity of the god."[33] In Iran the despot and the god are the Shah, who, in spite of the miserable poverty of an entire nation, is the richest man on earth.

How does he manage this throughout the ages? A writer of the last century in Iran interprets the phenomenon in his memoirs:

If one explains the government system of the Iranian provinces to the people of other countries, nobody will believe

[32] *Ibid.*, p. 52.

[33] Karl Marx, *Pre-Capitalist Economic Formations* (New York, International Publishers, 1975), p. 70.

him. At first one or ten or a hundred prominent men or courtiers ask for the government of one of the provinces. The King
and the Prime Minister auction it, say, for 100,000 tomans.[34]
One proposes more and another less, until the person who has
offered to pay the most gets the government of that province,
regardless of his ability, suitableness, wisdom and knowledge.
For instance, if the Shah gets 200,000 tomans, the Prime Minister, the exclusive servants of the Shah, an influential priest
of Teheran, the influential harem of the Shah, and his children
and relatives, receive another 200,000 tomans, according to
their positions and ranks. Sometimes the power of the liaison
and the proximity of his position to the court lead to his
preference to others. This transaction actually means the selling of the bodies, the souls and all the properties of that
province to the governor. The governor picks out 500 or 1,000
men from among the greedy, the wolves and the pitiless—as
his assistant governors, the commander of his soldiers, the
head of his personal servants, his stable master and chief cook,
and etc . . . —almost uncountable in number and takes them
to that province in full majestic glory. Now, he has the duty
to obtain from the people of that region, in addition to taxes
and thousands of other financial impositions, so much money
and in so many different ways that he will not only get his
400,000 tomans and pay for all the luxuries of his house and
men, but he will also have at least another 400,000 tomans in
addition, to save. His men save as much as half, one-fourth,
one-fifth or one-tenth of the governor's savings—each according to his rank and position. This young, vain and ignorant governor is not only the governor of the province, but
also its chief of the Justice Department, chief of Finance, the
head of the Education Department, the chief of trade. . . .[35]

The writer continues by saying that the governor has an agent
in the capital who bribes the authorities so that no complaint from
his province will reach anyone's ears. He tells us how, when a man
was appointed governor of Fars, ten mules were needed to carry

[34] In Iranian currency, one toman now equals ten rials. One U.S. dollar equals
approximately seven tomans, or seventy rials.

[35] Sayyah-e Mahallati, *Khaterat-e Hadji-Sayyah* (Hadji-Sayyah's Memoirs) (Teheran,
Ebn-e Sina Publications, 1967), pp. 479–84.

his torture instruments. And in the following pages he tells us how all the ministries are actually purchased from the Shah in this fashion. The historian Parizi relates how a Qajar king gave the whole province of Fars to his twelve-year-old son Zellossoltan (the Shadow of Shah), who ended up possessing the best lands of the provinces of Mazandaran, Guilan, Fars and Isphahan, with hundreds of thousands of herds. This man was so insolent, even to the dignitaries around him, that he never went to the toilet to urinate. His head servant would bring a golden bowl, unbutton the pants of the Shah's Shadow in front of everyone, take out his organ and hold it until he urinated, wash it, put it back and button up the pants.[36]

Every province in Iran had one of these tyrants as its governor, and the people who surrounded them were of the same nature and caliber. When one of the governor's units passed through a village, the people had to provide not only food and lodging, but also women and young boys for pleasure. Parizi tells how a woman who had just given birth beseeched the commander of the governor's unit not to flog her because she was not ready for him; she begged him to take her from the back. Fortunately, the man forgave her this one time.

Taxes on women and boys were so common that another historian, Rahim-Rezazedeh Malek, writes of a letter from Fathali-Shah to his son Abbas Mirza, a nineteenth-century governor of Azarbaijan: "My dear son, our catamite slaves have gradually grown old, and are no longer suitable for the required services. You should get hold of a good number of beautiful boys and send them over to us."[37] Almost all the historians of the last hundred years agree that another Qajar king, Nasseraddin-Shah, deflowered young girl-children in the intervals of his cabinet meetings. Parizi tells that Khosrow-Parviz, a king of the Sassanide dynasty, had more than 12,000 wives.[38] If this was the case with a king of olden times, the situation was little different in the nineteenth century, during the reign of Fathali-Shah. One historian sums up his preoccupations in the following seven categories:

[36] Mohammad Ebrahim Bastani-ye Parizi, pp. 448, 453.

[37] Rahim-Rezazadeh Malek, *Soosmaroddoleh* (Count Lizard) (Teheran, Donya Publications, 1975), p. 36.

[38] Mohammad Ebrahim Bastani-ye Parizi, p. 417.

1) What beautiful girls are to be found in the provinces to be presented to our Majestic presence; 2) When and how to make love to each of these women; 3) To measure our blessed beard and see how long it is, and to have it combed and rose-watered; 4) To write poetry under the pen name of Khaqan; be after unique themes and rare rhymes; 5) Write letters to the provinces, asking the governors to send over beautiful, un-bearded slave-boys; 6) To play knuckle-bones with the boys in the harem; 7) Ask the provinces to send money for the expenses of our Saturnian court.[39]

According to the same historian, this shah had 786 children and grandchildren, all of whom were provided for by the money raised from the provinces of Iran. And each one of them lived like a petty king or queen.

Money from everywhere poured into the court. According to Malek, "the salaries of the harem, delivered every month to the Trustee of the Harem, came from the Customs Department. The Trustee sent the money to Nasseraddin Shah's wives (eighty-five women) according to contract."[40] The Shah himself had all the provinces, as well as gifts from the governors and princes. And all the wealth of the country was plundered in this way by people who called themselves God's Shadows, or Shah's Shadows. These shadows sold titles in exchange for money to other shadows, thus turning the country's history into a nightmare of shadows.

According to Parizi, Darius III, who was defeated by Alexander the Great, had 360 wives, and "six hundred mules and three hundred camels carried his treasury." His tents even had full gardens in them.[41] Ya'qub, an Iranian king who revolted against the Arab Caliph, had "eight hundred thousand thousand dinars in his treasury,"[42] and Shah Abbas, the king who was flanked by cannibals, had a treasury that was forty feet square.

All this wealth came from the plunder of the people, war spoils and expropriation from those who had become rich through means other than the court. This pattern, broken by the Constitutional Revolution of the middle classes against the ruling monar-

[39] Rahim-Reza Zadeh Malek, pp. 25–26.

[40] Ibid., p. 75.

[41] Mohammad Ebrahim Bastani-ye Parizi, p. 410.

[42] Ibid., p. 422.

chy, was rehabilitated in 1925 by Reza Shah and kept serving the interests of both the monarchy and the colonial powers. The monarchy in this period became the fountainhead of British colonial interests in the country. In just a few years, counterrevolutionary forces killed all the leaders of the revolution, eliminated all its manifestations and crowned a new dynasty, more treacherous than the one before.

In less than sixteen years, Reza Khan augmented his three-bedroom house in the red-light district of Teheran, where he had originally lived, with almost all the best lands in Mazandaran, Gorgan and Guilan, and almost all the major factories in the country. The light industries developed during his reign only served his own interests in his factories. The monopoly of imports and the stock exchange by the government, at the head of which the dictator stood, promoted the new shah's assets to millions upon millions of dollars. He kept Britain quite satisfied by building the Iranian north-south railway, which was simply a strategic line for the British: it was distant enough from India, making the colony inaccessible to the Soviets, and it was close enough so that the British army could launch an attack on the U.S.S.R. in less than thirty hours. He also extended the oil treaty with the British, to their ultimate satisfaction. The money for the railway was paid through taxes imposed on the sale of sugar and tea, though it was quite evident that, if the people of the country needed railways, it should have been an east-west rather than a north-south line.[43]

When he abdicated in 1941, Reza Shah owned more than 2,000 villages (which his son, the present shah, inherited along with other assets). He had a very ingenious method of obtaining land from its owner. He would stand on the farm and ask for the landowner to come to him. The landowner would stand in front of him, nervously looking at his shoes. The Shah would wield a thick stick, bringing it down hard where his own pants opened, which understandably would terrify the other man. "Whose lands are these?" the Shah would ask. Trembling, the man would murmur: "They are mine, but they are *pishkesh*—a gift presented to you." The Shah would say: "Send the deeds for my signature."

[43] *Gozashteh, Cheragh-e Rah-e Ayandeh* (The Past Is the Light Showing the Road to the Future), from Djami Writers, 1976. The authors, place and publishers are not given. This is the most comprehensive study of the period 1941–1953 in print in Persian.

And this was the only transaction that took place. The Shah was thus using a traditional *ta'arof* (false compliment) to usurp people's property.

If the man was foolhardy enough to challenge the Shah, he would be sent to the "Deeds Room" in the "Ministers' Cave," the last station before he either freely signed over his lands or accepted suffocation by cushion or the fatal injection of an air bubble by Physician Ahmadi. In order to receive the air bubble, he would generally be sent to Alimoddoleh, a hospital rented by the Department of Police.

For those intellectuals who raised their voices against his economic plunder, Reza Shah kept cells with typhus lice in them. If some of the recalcitrant intellectuals continued to live, and the story of their resistance reached his ears, he would ask in rage: "You mean he is still alive. Ten years wasn't enough for him to die. Have I made a hotel for him?"[44]

When the present shah inherited his father's easily obtained wealth, he was at first too weak to resist the insistance of the parliament, the peasants and the opposition parties to give up these lands. During the next fifteen years, the deeds changed hands several times, mostly between the monarch and the government. The 1953 coup gave the Shah's deeds permanent independence from government control. Gradually, some of these lands were deeded out to the peasants. With the money collected, numerous tire, cement and shipping companies, a bank, several hotels (including concessions in the Teheran Hilton), gambling casinos and cabarets were bought, and the Pahlavi Foundation—which has in its possession most of what the Shah owns—was set up on a tax-exempt status, answerable to none but the Shah himself. (Later, former U.S. Secretary of State William Rogers helped create a branch of this foundation as the Pahlavi Foundation of New York.) The Shah's assets in some of these projects amount to billions of dollars. Now Princess Ashraf and Queen Farah—the Shah's sister and wife—are starting their own independent foun-

[44] *Ibid.,* p. 55. See also Jack Anderson, "CIA Profile: Shah of Iran, Dangerous Megalomaniac," Boston *Evening Globe* (July 11, 1975). Anderson said of the Shah's father: "Reza Shah began his career as an illiterate soldier and battered his way to the throne. Possessed of an explosive Cossack temperament, he was known to slay dogs that dared bark in his presence, to hurl offending subordinates bodily through windows and to string up enemies by their heels and kick in their teeth."

dations. They want to carry all their money abroad before the curtain falls for the last act of the Iranian monarchy.[45]

The Shah's wealth at present equals that of the ancient kings thanks to the kickbacks, bribes and percentages received from the sale of arms, the embezzlement of millions of U.S. aid dollars, and the consistent plunder of the workers, peasants and middle-class Iranians. He is now one of the two or three richest men on earth. Princess Ashraf has become one of the richest women on earth by exacting bribes from every truck and bus company in the country. Prince Shahram, Princess Ashraf's son, owns more than twenty factories and contract firms, and has been involved in payoffs by American corporations to the Iranian authorities. The Shah himself is busy buying whole courses in such prestigious American universities as MIT, Harvard, UCLA, Georgetown and a dozen others. Rich and glamorous festivities are held every day of the week in Teheran and in all the other cities of the world with an Iranian embassy or consulate. If he doesn't publicize his power and wealth, he believes the world will come to an end.[46]

Although she has witnessed the rise of a bourgeoisie during the last fifty years, Iran has not yet been able to oust the Shah and attain independence either from the venal monarchy or from world imperialism. At this moment in history the Iranian people are caught in a bizarre situation—a state of high tension in which the weight of the past traditions presses down on the new that are striving to be born. The prominent features of this situation are:

(1) the existence of a compradore system in which Iranians act as agents of foreign companies, pretending they are carrying

[45] *The Pahlavi Foundation,* No. 40 (Washington, D.C., MERIP Reports, September, 1975), pp. 14–15; Anne Crittenden, "The Shah in New York," New York *Times* (September 26, 1976); Eric Pace, "In Iran: It's Alms to the Poor and the Rich," New York *Times,* same date.

[46] This is what MERIP Report No. 40 says about Ashraf: "On November 17, 1960, Geneva police had arrested Princess Ashraf for being in possession of two suitcases containing some $2 million worth of heroin. *Time* gave the story highly critical coverage, which evidently must have upset the Shah." Mike Wallace, quoting to the Shah from a piece in the Washington *Post,* reads: "A wealthy Iranian businessman says, 'Not a truck can move anywhere in this country without a payoff going to Princess Ashraf.' " (New York *Times,* October 22, 1976). On reported bribes paid to Prince Shahram *Time* magazine (June 23, 1975) says: "Northrop paid $705,000 to Iranian Prince Charam [Shahram] Pahlavinia, a member of the imperial family, for services such as helping the company find a good Iranian architect. At the time, Northrop was part of a consortium that received a $200 million contract to build a telecommunications system in Iran."

forward the industrialization of the country;

(2) a superstitious monarchy glutted with wealth and luxury, standing on the peak of the pyramid of the ruling classes;

(3) the existence of a potentially explosive situation among the workers and students, without a political party that will bring them together under the rubric of an objectively conceived set of demands;

(4) the rapid migration of the peasantry to the urban areas and their desperate and usually unsuccessful efforts to join the ranks of workers, which generally results in their becoming either soldiers in the army or unskilled laborers on the verge of pauperism;

(5) a landlordism and waterlordism based on the Asiatic Mode of Production not yet entirely gone, with an industrialism not yet arrived;

(6) a racism based on Persian chauvinism, with 60 percent of the country's population (Turks, Kurds, Arabs, Baluchis) deprived of the use of their own national and ethnic cultures and languages;

(7) the existence of inhuman inequalities between men and women, a condition in which women could be considered second-class citizens;

(8) the costly militarization of the country topped off by the amalgamation of a primeval apparatus of repression and bestiality with a sophisticated and modern structure of torture, repression, inquisition and censorship.

The abortion of the Constitutional Revolution in the second and third decades of the twentieth century and the failure of a combination of democratic and nationalist movements in the fourth and the fifth decades have made Iranians, in this post-coup counterrevolutionary period of their history, acutely aware of the shortcomings of past values, parties and groupings, and the traditional methods of challenging the Shah and his allies in the Western world. The diversified opposition in the country is keenly aware that it has to wage battle on its own and cannot rely on any help from the parties outside. In the face of détente, both Eastern and Western blocs maintain absolute silence in relation to Iran because of their mutual interests in the region, particularly in the Persian Gulf. Muzzled and hounded as it is, the opposition has to prepare and wait for its turn to overthrow monarchy and foreign rule in Iran and introduce democracy at all costs, on all levels. In these endeavors, the Shah is the first and foremost target. The total overthrow of monarchy, this last bulwark of Asiatic Despotism in its final stage of corruption and decomposition, this patrimonial structure of Masculine History, will be only the beginning of a great series of social and political changes which will eventually lead to the rule of the popular masses in their own right.

Women and Their Position in Masculine History

Early in October, 1976, the largest women's magazine in Iran published the story of an illegal affair in the city of Qazvin between a forty-year-old Iranian priest and a girl of fourteen. They slept with each other in the mosque for three years. When the people of the city came to know about it, the priest was beaten up and the girl underwent trial—not by the authorities but by the family members who acted as judge, jury and executioner. It was decided that the girl should be killed by being struck by a car. Her brother and uncle executed the verdict.[47]

In the summer of 1972 a woman was hanged, the first such occasion in the past half-century of Iranian history, for the murder of the two children of her husband's second wife. She had kidnapped them but with no intention of killing them. All the men she asked to help her were interested only in sleeping with her. She could not keep the children alive, and ultimately she was convicted of murdering them.

Are we dealing with Medea and Jason's children? The revenge of the ancient mythological hero doesn't hold water here. We must examine the roots of the matter.[48]

An extremely keen observer from the United States traveling through Iran wrote this of the sexual relations in Teheran:

> Women are seldom seen with men; there are few couples, no lovers, and at dusk Tehran becomes a city of males, prowling in groups or loitering. The bars are exclusively male; the men drink in expensive suits, continually searching the room with anxious eyes, as if in expectation of a woman. But there are no women, and the lugubrious alternatives to sex are apparent: the film posters showing fat Persian girls in shortie paja-

[47] Editorial, *Zan-e Rooz* (Today's Woman) (October 2, 1976).
[48] *Ettela'at* (June 22, 1972).

mas; nightclubs with belly dancers, strippers, kick lines, and comedians in ridiculous hats whose every Farsi joke is a reference to the sex the patrons are denied. Money pulls the Iranian in one direction, religion drags him in another, and the result is a stupid starved creature for whom woman is only meat. Thus spake Zarathustra: an ugly monomaniac with a diamond tiara, who calls himself "The King of Kings," is their answer to government, a firing squad their answer to law.[49]

I could hardly disagree with this assessment of the typical Iranian male. If one is a villager in Iran, one's mouth stays wide open when he encounters an unveiled woman in the street. A worker can barely keep from touching his crotch when he sees a woman. If the typical government official admits a woman to his office, it is only to swallow her body with his eyes. The typical university professor raises his head from his book only to let his glance float avariciously to the area between the legs of his female students. Almost all the jokes in Iran are about sex, the majority about women and some about young boys. Two men stand in the corridor having a conversation; a female colleague says hello and stands with them for a few minutes; the men's eyes immediately become foolishly dreamy; when the woman walks away, they both follow the movement of the fleshy parts until she disappears from view; they exchange a few jokes about her buttocks. The conversation of men becomes totally absurd when a woman joins them. They compete with each other in attracting her attention. But they have only one thing in mind: to mate with that meat standing in front of them.

In the middle of the street, a man suddenly takes off in full speed toward a woman walking a few yards ahead of him, thrusts his hands into her lower parts and, before anyone can raise any objections, disappears into the crowd. All women will assert that at some time in their lives they have been assaulted, raped or nearly raped by men. In justifying this, with the most bestial judgment on women, men say: "You start to rape her, she joins you in the middle, and by God! What a pleasure!"

Yet sleeping with a woman is, in itself, viewed as a defiling action—not for the man, of course, but for the woman. If a woman

[49] Paul Theroux, *The Great Railway Bazaar* (New York, Ballantine Books, 1975), pp. 62–63.

sleeps with a man without marrying him, she is considered to be a prostitute, even in her own eyes, in many cases, because she judges herself according to the values of males. But if a man sleeps with a hundred women, he is no prostitute, even in the eyes of his wife, wives or the other women with whom he has had relations. They, too, judge him according to the dominant values of males.

Thus the body and mind of a female begins to take shape based on the male's conception of women. She becomes a sub-dued, slavish, subhuman sex object even in her own mind, and her body rises high on the buttocks to satisfy the homosexual whims of the man. She turns into the sodomized boy; she virtually changes her sex, surrendering herself to the vanities of her man and even taking pleasure from such dislocated intercourse, forget-ting the natural function of her vagina.

Indeed, she becomes alienated from her female nature—even from the center of her womanhood, her vagina—and she looks at her organs through the eyes of the man who is satisfying himself as if he were simply sleeping with a young boy. A man and a woman are united in Iran in a sort of male homosexual marriage, but at the expense of the woman and to the benefit of the man. After all, a woman could not be homosexual in that bed, even if she wanted to be, or were, a homosexual. And the man's homosex-uality in that bed is satisfactory as long as he is active by penetra-tion of the woman through the anus; otherwise, his homosexuality is deficient.

Man, the ruling sexual force, creates a social atmosphere which is totally male and which conditions women according to male peculiarities. In this subhuman world of alienation and reifi-cation, the woman begins to possess the image which men have thrust upon her. She is supposed to believe that rape is good for her, penetration of the anus is marvelous for her and submission to men is an ideal feminine quality because the virtue of a woman lies in her capacity to become the man's *Kaneez*, which simply means a slave-girl. The man comes to think that her vagina is no longer good because she has given birth to children, who inciden-tally carry the husband's name and have the total identity of the father rather than the mother. Thus she becomes an object, a mere thing, worthy only to cook and clean and take care of the hus-band's sons and daughters.

Female homosexuality in Iran is hushed up in such a way that no woman, in the whole of Iranian history, has been allowed to speak out for such tendencies. A lesbian is considered to be far worse than a prostitute. To attest to lesbian desires would be an unforgivable crime.

There is the other side of the coin: a brave or radicalized woman, one who is politicized and asks for her own rights in this tyrannical universe of men, is looked upon as having something of the criminal about her. She is immediately labeled by the male-oriented society as a lesbian or prostitute.

For a man to have a female supervisor is unthinkable. He will look at her as a miscreant who has sold her body to obtain the position. Yet no woman would think of the thousands of male bosses in the country as people who have sold their bodies to get ahead. Even a woman would regard a female doctor as someone who was not the kind of person she should go to for consultation and treatment. The image of degradation created by man and his masculine society has now become a part of the psychology of women. Their achievements do not have the same stature as those of men. The belittled woman actually becomes the little woman, even in her own eyes.

All men know about the social contract of absolute possession of females by males. I remember once listening to the conversation between a colonel and a lieutenant:

> *Colonel:* "Why do you keep sodomizing the soldiers?"
> *Lieutenant:* "I promise it won't happen again."
> *Colonel:* "You have already broken your promise a dozen times. Why don't you get married? Then you can sodomize your wife."
> *Lieutenant:* "As soon as I have money, I will get married."

The cure for male homosexuallity in Iran is thought to be marriage to a woman. The woman is never asked whether she wants to be sodomized or not. The social contract, understood by all parties concerned, dictates that the man can do anything to his wife without her consent. If she deceives him, or even raises her eyes to look at another man, he has the right—even under the present laws, in which some lip service has been given to women —to kill her without receiving the kind of sentence generally given a murderer in Iran. He has committed a *qatl-e namoosie,* which means a murder with the intent to make up for his loss of prestige through her betrayal. So many examples of such murders are printed in the Iranian papers that there is no need to record a particular example here.

A woman becomes only the man's *namus,* his good name in the society of men. Paradoxically, the word *namus,* originating from the Greek and arriving in the Persian language through Arabic, means "genitals" in colloquial Persian. If a man's wife deceives him, he has virtually lost the use of his genitals; if he kills her, he can regain it. In colloquial language, she is his genitals, a mere possession of his lower parts; the official language establishes her as an instrument of his good reputation. The husband says in his defense: "She was my wife, wasn't she? She betrayed me, didn't she? I killed her. I've a clear conscience, and it's nobody's business!" He possesses her even after her death. He comes out with a clear conscience and marries another woman with the understanding that she too will be killed if she betrays him.

In most villages of the country, if a father or his son finds out that his daughter or sister was not a virgin on the night of her wedding to a man picked out by them, she may face death or at least banishment from the village and from the sight of her father and brother. Virginity is considered that secret, sacred part of the body to be held in great veneration by the male society, whose decency, prestige and reputation depend so much on repression of all that is good, honorable and respectable in women, that is, all her emotions and instincts and her superb capacities for love and affection. A man does not touch a girl's virginity because then he may have to marry her; thus penetration of the anus is supposed to be the natural way of sexual intercourse in the premarital days of a woman.

In fact, there are very distinct differences between a girl and a woman: a woman is no longer a girl because she loses her virginity when she marries. As in many cultures, a husband *gets* or *takes away* the woman, while a woman *goes* to him. All the verbs of command belong to the husband. A husband "fucks" *(kardan,* or *gua'eedan)* a woman, but the reverse is never applied to the woman: she "is fucked." She is the passive verb of society. If her husband divorces her, she is doomed to a miserable existence. If she is not rich, either she forgets about her sexual life altogether to keep the family reputation from being tainted or she becomes the *sigheh* of one man after the other, under an unwritten contract of temporary marriage and a religious cover for legalized prostitution. If she is rich, men marry her because of her wealth; in fact, they marry her wealth.

There is a great difference between the widow and the widower. If the widow—who normally does not remarry—works in an office, she is a deer caught in a jungle full of lions. Men who might succeed in sleeping with her do so only to take pleasure from a piece of meat and to try and pass her on to others. In all these transactions, her pleasure, her emotions and instincts, are things about which no man cares. But the widower who remarries takes another virgin, very exceptionally a widow, and the ceremonies are the same as for a first marriage.

The wedding night is of special significance for most Iranian families. The bride carries to the bedroom a white handkerchief called *dastmal-e-zofaf* (a defloration handkerchief) which is soaked in the defloration blood and handed to the women and men waiting outside. This is evidence that the girl had not been touched by any man before her husband. The handkerchief is examined by everyone to testify that the girl is from a decent family and has protected the *namus* of her parents, brothers and sisters. The girl's mother keeps the handkerchief for years.

The girl who does not prove to be a virgin is faced with immediate cancellation of the marriage contract. If she is poor, she joins the ranks of thousands of Iranian prostitutes in Teheran and other large cities. If she is rich, the man has probably deflowered her so that she will have to be his wife. She may marry him, but if she or he, for some reason or other, doesn't want to marry, she has plastic surgery done and her virginity is sewed up so that penetration by the ideal husband will soak the handkerchief with blood. There are famous surgeons for this purpose. Modern medical science is at the service of Masculine History.

If no husband comes along, the girl must remain a girl for as long as she is waiting, which means that she has to preserve her virginity indefinitely. An unmarried woman should be buried as a virgin. When a girl over twenty-five is offered to a man of, say, forty, he will immediately react with a sentence like: "I want a virginity, not a piece of leather."

Marriage is a contract through which one man, the husband, buys the woman from another man, the father. The father generally gets some cash, called *shirbaha* (milk money), from the future husband, plus a contract in which the husband promises to pay the wife a prearranged sum of money, called *mehr* (marriage portion). The husband owes this money to his wife, though it is generally only payable to her upon his death or upon divorce. But married life can be such a hell that the woman often says: "I release you from the bond of *mehr;* divorce me and set me free!" All men who want to get rid of their wives force them to finally declaim that sentence.

After marriage, the wife belongs to the husband, but the husband does not belong to her. He can marry another wife, even under the present laws. (In fact, I know many courtiers who have had two wives. The Shah's father married four times, and there is a rumor that the Shah himself has a second official wife; yet both men have claimed that they are liberating Iranian women.) In addition, there are all the women he can have under temporary marriage regulations, which are just added means of accommodating the sexual pleasures of the man.

A married man immediately becomes a patriarch, the head of the family, and from then on all the other members will take orders from him. On the wedding night he is called *shah-damad* (the Shah-groom); in the cities of the province of Khorassan, he is called the Shah; in the province of Azarbaijan, he is called *khan-damad* (the Khan-groom). Thereby the Shah has parceled out his supreme power to the groom, the husband and the father of the family. The house is called *khaneh,* and, although the word *khan* is Turkish and Mongolic, and the word *khaneh* is Persian, one may actually assume that *khaneh* is the place in which the Khan of the house has the same absolute authority as the national or tribal Khan and the Shah of Shahs have over the kingdom. The word *khanom* (wife, lady and mother) is the feminine form of *khan.* Even linguistically, the woman and her attributes are mere extensions of the father-shah.

The majority of Iranian husbands do not mention the names of their wives in any gathering. They use the word *manzel,* which is the Arabic word in Persian for "house." They say, for instance: "My house told me that you had come looking for me, but I wasn't home." Or sometimes they use male names, such as Hassan or Hossein, or even insignificant objects such as shoes and hats. My father used to call my mother *bashmagh,* the Turkish word for "shoes," in the presence of other men. It sounded very funny:

"Tell shoes to bring a cup of tea for Mr. Mohammad." A man walking into someone's house will cough several times, then use all kinds of masculine names, calling out for Hassan and Hossein without there being any such males in that house. All this time, he may be quite aware of the name of the housewife, but he dare not use it.

A woman's face and hair should not be seen by any man, except the husband, the father, the brothers and the uncles. The social situation in the country has been such during the last fifty years that this has changed to a degree. But all the women in the villages and most of the women in the cities still cover their faces with a *chador* (veil), so that physically they are not in the open.

In the mid-thirties Reza Shah tried to unveil the Iranian women by brute force. Whenever a woman walked outside, his police would tear the veil from her face and figure. Women, not yet ready socially or psychologically for such an action and as a result of their economic, political and legal subservience to a masculine society, were forced to stay home. But difficulties arose. Since there were no showers in Iranian homes, women had to go to a public bath. The husband would put his wife in a large sack and carry her like a bale of cotton to the bath.

I remember from my childhood, when my father would carry his mother in the sack, empty his load in the bath and then come back for his wife, my mother. He once told me that Reza Shah's policeman had asked him what it was that he was carrying. He had improvised an answer: pistachio nuts. The policeman said, "Let me have some," and started tickling Granny. First she laughed, and then she wiggled her way out of the sack and took to her heels. My father was arrested.

The situation of the majority of women has not changed substantially from the time of Cyrus, the founder of the Iranian monarchy, 2,500 years ago. Here is what one writer says of the peasant woman in Iran:

> The peasant woman is not to appear in public eyes or to be consulted. She must go to the public bath unseen by the people so that no stranger sees her face. At home, she must fear the man and consider herself below him. She must see it rightful for the man to beat her and throw her out of the house. But she does not have the right to go to her father and

complain. She must suffer and prove that she is a decent and good wife. The husband's cursing and beating of the wife is necessary and deserved to keep the wife at home and not to spoil her. When the daughter reaches the age of two or three, she has also to wear a veil and hide her face from strangers and avoid them. She must speak little in front of her father and brothers, eat little at meal times, not speak at all in front of guests, stand up when her father or brothers come or leave, not touch the food before them, pray and fast regularly; in short she must imitate her mother. This is the peasants' education and social manners and it will never disappear by just a little advice and big words.[50]

The situation of women living in the cities is little better. One of the best novels of the country, *Ahu Khanom's Husband* by Mohammad Ali Afghani, portrays in the most indisputable form the horrors to which the husband, Seyyed Miran, the head of the guild of bakeries in the city of Kermanshah, subjects his wife.[51] A few quotations from the book will suffice to show the whole picture.

Many people believe that a woman has no rights in her husband's home other than money for the bathhouse, and whatever she brought with her from her father's house. If she spends a few coins as alms for the salvation of the spirit of the dead, the husband will have to forgive her, otherwise it is theft. (p. 73)

When the husband is beating her, she says, "calmly":

"Hit me, hit me! May God keep suffering away from your hands, Seyyed Miran! You are hitting me, hit me." (p. 335)

When he beats her, there is an unsurpassed brutality on his side and an unspeakable tenderness on hers:

When he arrived above the woman, he raised the stick high in the air and brought it down on the crown of

[50] *Kand-o-Kav dar Masa'el-e Tarbiati-ye Iran* (A Search into Problems of Education in Iran) (Teheran, Bamdad Publishers, n.d.), pp. 95–96; also quoted in Azar 'Asi, "Women in Iran," *International Socialist Review* (April, 1971).

[51] *Ahu Khanom's Husband* (Shorah-e Ahu Khanom) (Teheran, Amir-Karir Publications, 1962).

her head unconcerned, as if the head was a heap of wool. (p. 338)

When he marries a younger second wife, the complaint of the first is:

> What had I done to deserve such an unkindness. I suffered in his house for fifteen long years. . . . I gave birth to a girl who is simply a darling, and three sturdy boys. Was I sterile, or ill-omened, or lame or deaf? What was wrong with me, after all, that he married this woman? What had I done that was frivolous or disobedient? What secret of his had I disclosed? What laws of his had I violated? (p. 352)

She hears her husband speak about her to the second wife in these terms:

> "I don't want to hear her breathing. I get the creeps when I see her. When I am with her my soul is in prison." (p. 353)

When she asks him to clarify the situation and tell her what to do, the husband speaks like the typical Middle Eastern male chauvinist:

> "Your duties have been outlined by God. What task and commitment can be more sacred and important for a woman than being preoccupied with raising her children. Haven't you heard the proverb that paradise lies at the feet of mothers." (p. 507)

And in the next pages, when he becomes angry, the husband says very frankly to her:

> "You have neither deceived me, nor stolen anything from me. I hate you, that's all. You force me to speak my heart and I do so. . . . I have neither broken away, nor can I break away from my kids. But I hate them all the same for having your blood in their veins." (p. 511)

> Her cruel husband, after fifteen years of married life, wanted to throw her out the window like a worn-out object which had served its time and was of no use now. (p. 513)

And when another woman tells the husband who has just thrown Ahu Khanom and her kids out of the house,

"She doesn't know anyone in this city. Where can she go? What can she do?"

the answer is:

"She can go to the whorehouse. And if that's impossible, or they won't let her in, she can go get buried in the grave-yard." (p. 620)

Though the novel deals with the Reza Shah period, the social relationships explored in its pages outline the existing exploitation of women by men. There is a Persian expression: "As soon as a man gets an additional pair of pants, he thinks of another wife." Behind the exploitation and brutalization of women by men lies economic exploitation.

A woman is limited nowadays in several ways. Her husband is polygamous, while she must be monogamous. He can marry a foreigner, but she needs a special permit from the government to do so. A girl inherits half of what a son does from the family assets; upon the death of her husband, she inherits one-eighth of his wealth. If she wants to work, she must obtain the consent of her husband and choose a profession which will not be "damaging" to his reputation. A woman is not accepted as a witness in a divorce case; in other matters, two women are equal to one male witness. A woman cannot journey abroad without her husband's written consent. If the husband dies, she cannot act as the guard-ian of her children unless the grandfathers of the children are all dead. If there is a male heir in the family, women, however old, may not act as guardians. The son is the natural heir to the father.

When she is married, a woman obeys not only her husband but also his parents and his sisters who are older than she. She cooks and serves them, too, and acts as a servant for all. A mother tells her son: "Why don't you marry so that someone will put a cup of tea in front of me?" An old woman tells another old woman: "You should be proud of your bride. She is serving you as though you were a queen." All that a woman suffers in her youth, at the hands of older men and women and her husband, she avenges upon the young bride.

I remember very well: my granny used to beat my mother almost daily with a long smoking pipe we had at home. When her son, my father, came home, she would tell him all kinds of dirty stories about my mother, who would then submit to another beating from him, my father. The father is the king of the house, his mother is the queen, and the young woman is the lower stone in this watermill of human misery. Behind all this lie the economic relationships of the whole society, with its structure of monarchy, patriarchy and Masculine History.

Even in the present court of Iran, a woman is a second-class citizen. The Shah married two women, divorced them and remarried, because he demanded a male heir who would replace him upon his death. None of the women around him—his mother, the scandalous Ashraf, the beautiful Sorayya (his second wife), the other sisters, even the present queen, Farah Diba—may replace him. Who is he that no woman on earth, including the one who gave birth to him, those born along with him or she who slept in the same bed with him, may replace him upon his demise? No woman, throughout thousands of years of Iranian monarchy, has had the right to be the first personage of the country. One or two princesses have risen to a very transitory power, but they were immediately replaced by other males.

The Shah has designated Queen Farah as his regent in case he dies before his son, the younger Reza, comes of age. This means that when the Shah's first son is eighteen, he will be wiser and more sophisticated and rational than his mother, who will then be forty-three. The traveling she has done, the schools she has attended, the men and women she has met in Iran and all over the world are all of use for the type of power practiced in Iran. By all rational standards of judgment, the Queen is far better equipped to run the Iranian monarchy than the young boy.

This is not to advocate the monarchy of women—far from it. I condemn and negate monarchy, period. But one cannot help thinking about the irrationality of a regime based on the first-born male, who is sometimes the least able of his family. This policy has brought as much havoc to the country as the monarchy itself. Some of the most feeble-minded men in history have ruled simply because they were the first sons of idiotic male monarchs. They have immediately called themselves Shadows of God.

The present shah was not a Shadow of God until he was well advanced in age. It was only in retrospect that he thought about the so-called visions and dreams of prophets and saints. He found out about those early myths after the CIA put him in power.[52] Did the CIA provide him with those ideological props, too? I doubt it. He always had a few antediluvian nincompoops around to advise him on saintly apparitions.

But I wonder what will happen to his son. The boy has claimed no prophetic dreams for himself, and, though there were rumors that he was mute or stammering until he was about eight years old, there are few signs that the saints are in his pocket. Perhaps he is waiting for one of those saints to stop protecting his father and enlist in his service. Nobody knows for sure when he will be ordained as the official God's Shadow on earth. His father has said that perhaps he will resign in a decade and stand by, watching his son rule. Paul Theroux has said about the boy: "The smiling son might be one of those precocious child entertainers who tap-dance in talent shows, singing, 'I've got rhythm.' "[53] So far, the heir has given no indication of possessing an average talent even for what Theroux suggests. We think we will have either a young Caligula or a Nero. The future character of that monarchy is prefigured by its past.

One person among the women in the court who may equal the present shah in tyranny and brutality is his twin sister Ashraf. There is a rumor that she slapped him on one of those difficult days of the pre-coup era. After the coup she lined up the journalists of the country, started slapping them and shouted: "You sons of bitches, the day is gone when you used to write those dirty words about me and the royal family." Jack Anderson has said of her: ". . . a twin sister, Princess Ashraf, is a forceful, aggressive, vivacious woman quick to slap the face of anyone who displeases her. 'It's too bad she was not the boy,' the old shah used to muse."[54] Even this woman, with such exceptional accomplishments to her credit, has not been found worthy of succeeding her brother. Even in the court, with all its lofty claims of sponsoring the cause of women's liberation and which has spent millions of dollars on world organizations for women, a woman is considered to be a second-class citizen. A boy two months old, if he is the first son of a king, is the future father of the whole nation.

One other aspect of Masculine History can be seen in the

[52] See "My Images of the Shah," following this section.

[53] Paul Theroux, p. 57.

[54] Jack Anderson, "CIA Profile," *loc. cit.*

Iranian conception of male homosexuality and its relation to the position of women. An Iranian male will never admit that he has been the object of a homosexual act, but if pushed hard for an answer he will admit—sometimes even in polite circles—that he has been the subject, the doer of the act. There is a very clear-cut distinction between a gay who is passive and a gay who is active. An active gay can be proud of his action, but a passive gay is ashamed of himself. Suicides are rather frequent among young men who have been found to be the passive partner in male homosexual intercourse. The Iranian papers call this *amal-e shani'e* (an obscene act), and the common belief is that the gates of paradise are closed to those who have committed an act of sodomy, particularly those who have been the object of the action. If all active sodomists were doomed to go to hell, the kings would be the first to be sent there. Haven't they, after all, been the buyers, breeders and promoters of the best and most beautiful young slaves of the world? As we have seen, in the past they even asked their sons to get young, hairless slave-boys for them. If it were understood in the public eye that they would go to hell because of their active homosexuality, they would simply hush it up. But not only don't they suppress it, they even promote the idea that they are the possessors of the best young men on earth. Books written by them or their scribes are full of the names and adventures of these young men. There is not a single book of Iranian history in which pages have not been dedicated to the love affairs of kings with young boys. Yet there isn't even one king who is supposed to have been the object of a homosexual act. Such an act of degradation is unthinkable for the almighty.

Several versions of a fable which has been found among the writings of Obeyd-e Zakani, the famous classical satirist of Persian literature, may be of some relevance here. I quote a version which immediately comes to my mind:

It is said that a certain man came to one of the kings of Dailam and told him that his daughter was the wife of a Turkish slave of the king, and that the slave regularly came together with her through her hind orifice. The king, out of his great sense of justice, sent after the Turk slave. When the slave was brought to the presence of the king, he was asked to give his reasons for this most obscene of acts. The slave said, "Long live the king! I was first bought as a slave in Turkestan. The man who bought me came together with me through my hind orifice, and then sold me to a man from Khorassan who came together with me through my hind orifice, and brought me to Mazandaran and sold me to you; you took your turn and came together with me through my hind orifice. I felt there was nothing wrong with it, and slept with my wife the way you people kept sleeping with me."

We saw earlier what the colonel told his lieutenant to do. With the above story we can retrace this to its origins. The ultimate source of these vices lies with the possessor of power. The slave does to his wife what the kings did to him. He pretends to be the master at home while he is the slave in the bigger home, society at large. Just as he was a piece of meat for the kings and masters of the society, his wife and other people with whom he sleeps become pieces of meat for him.

This is very important in understanding the sources of Iranian history and the cannibalism of its monarchy.

A man sleeping with another man doesn't mean, in the totally oppressive and opprobriously hypocritical society run by the Iranian monarchy, that they are each other's equals and are indulging as such in a love affair. One considers himself the subject of the action and the other the object. But if someone asks the object what he was doing, he will say he was doing it to the other fellow and that he was the subject. The slave pretends that he is the master. He tries to rise above his destiny as a piece of meat in the eyes of the other fellow—and of society, for that matter—through saying that it was the other man who was the meat and not he. As for the other guy, he walks away from his victim like Achilles leaving Hector's rotten dead body. Walking away, he looks like the Shah's executioner stepping down the ladder on the top of which hangs the noose with the victim's throat caught in it.

In prison one of us cracked a joke and the occupants of the adjacent cells joined in the laughter. The guard flung open the door and asked us what was so funny. We didn't have an answer. Then he asked the men in the other cells. The same silence. The guard started swearing at all of us. He slammed the doors and walked away. A few minutes later we heard him shouting: "We will fuck the nation of Iran in the ass! All the doctors, the engineers, university students, intellectuals, writers, poets, workers, yes, everyone of them; we will fuck them in the ass."

This response cannot be interpreted in the context of any gay liberation movement. Quite the contrary. The guard's statement represents the sexual extension of the Shah's rule. The Shah has turned all his political prisoners into meat and has included in this category even the guards themselves; this guard was taking his turn as the slave had taken his turn with his wife.

The same happens in the torture chambers. The torturer pulls down the prisoner's pants and rapes him, or tells him that he will rape him tomorrow. This means that tomorrow is the day he will turn into meat and be served to the executioner—who is, after all, the Shah's representative and heir apparent in prison. This simply means that the crowned cannibal is raping us all and eating us up.

The recantation process, through which the victim is supposed to be subjected to total emasculation and intellectual impotency, also has something scatological about it. When the father is beating his son, the son cries out: "I eat shit, I won't do it again!" The recantation document has been called in colloquial Persian *goh-khordam-nameh* (the letter in which I have eaten shit). The torturer brings down the whip, shouting: "Say 'I have eaten shit'! Say 'I have eaten shit'!" This goes on until the victim faints and the torturer falls, totally fatigued, into a chair.

The homosexual act in Iran is a transaction in which there is a victim and a victor. The subject-victor emasculates the object-victim. From then on, the victim will be a second-class citizen in the eyes of other men, which means that they will consider him to be only a half-man, i.e., a woman. Such a man in Tabriz would be called by the name of his anus; even his name becomes a hole in his bottom. They say: "That boy is an asshole."

But more than that, he is banished into the female world. Whole families move from one sector to another, or even to a different city, in an attempt to cover the shame they suffer because the son was a victim of a homosexual act. The victor doesn't have to move. His power is respected. In the street, when two men—one hefty, big and older, the other younger, thin and weak—walk together, the people of Tabriz will say: "The young man is the anus of the older man!" Similar sentences may be heard in cities such as Esphahan and Qazvin.

In fact, the cities of Iran are sometimes judged by the alleged potency or impotency of their men. All the men of Ardebil are supposed to be passive homosexuals; those of Qazvin and Esphahan, active homosexuals; those of Rasht, impotent. That is why all their wives have become prostitutes and wait for the men from Teheran to drive up.

But no such jokes exist about the people of Teheran. Men living in the Shah's capital are miniature shahs and no one makes light of them.

What is significant, of course, is that everything and everyone is judged according to his power. Whoever can forcibly twist someone else's arm is considered to be powerful, that is, a man, an ideal man, the authority on everything. A man is a two-way element of emasculation: he emasculates those below him and is emasculated by those above him. But the one who really holds the absolute power, turns it into the charismatic *farreh,* rules by divine authority and becomes a walking god on earth is the Shah.

All emasculated men move in degrees toward the status of women. Women are judged by the criteria of men. They are not women; they do not have an identity of their own. They are men emasculated to the ultimate degree. Even a poor worker, who belongs to the most oppressed class of society, becomes a bourgeois as soon as he sets foot in his own house. His orders rain upon his wife and daughter in the same fashion as the orders of the factory owner had fallen upon him. Repression and oppression multiply oppressors.

One final note on women. It was an economic factor, the exploitation of women by men, that shrouded all women in the Middle East, including Iran, in the obnoxious veil. This custom originated not with Islam—a later form of patriarchy—but with tribal and, later, national monarchy, supported by patriarchal religions such as Zoroastrianism, Mithraism, Manicheanism, Judaism and Christianity, all antimatriarchal institutions. They all contributed to the relegation of women to the interiors of high-walled houses in the cities and mud cottages in the villages. But the main cause for this blind banishment in Iran was monarchy itself.

The polygamy of men, as opposed to the monogamy of women, also had an economic factor behind it. All the wives of a man in a village or small city worked, and their income was poured into the man's pockets. The arrival of the Shah's men in the city or village meant the plunder not only of a man's wealth but also of his work force, his women and children. So the father of the house built high walls around his home in the city or structured his mud cottage in the village with little holes as breathing space to keep his women from tempting the Big Father, the Shah.

Thus privacy became an excuse to protect personal belongings. The possessive power of men built those walls around women and at the same time shrouded them in veils. And through centuries of oppression the veils and the walls enclosed women's minds as well. Not only did they become second-class citizens, but they thought of themselves as such. The consciousness created by the men became imposed upon the consciousness of the subjugated women.

One reason for the failure of all attempts by the monarchy to overthrow the rule of the veil in Iran is that monarchy created the veil and perpetuated it, and all those walls and veils are part and parcel of its tyranny. Only with the downfall of the monarchy and a drastic change in the production relations of the society will women get rid of the barriers, both subjective and objective, that hold them back.

To be sure, it is quite certain that Islam made its own contribution to this pattern of exploitation. But Islam as an ideology, rather than as an institution such as the Caliphate, the Ottoman Empire and the Safavi monarchy in Iran, was far more advanced in its approach to women than the Iranian monarchy of the pre-Islamic Sassasanid period in which the King had thousands of women in his court. The Caliphate saw the adoption of regality into the framework of Islamic legality, and since the two—Islam and monarchy—were incompatible with each other, what arose from their admixture was something which was monarchial in its infrastructure and Islamic in its cultural superstructure.

After the death of Mohammad and the four men who replaced him—none of whom had courts, harems or hundreds of wives—Islam became an institution modeled on a combination of the temporarily defunct Iranian monarchy in the East and the Roman Empire in the West. Islam, which was mostly antimonarchical, became an empire of patriarchy in full swing. Women remained the slaves of the society of men.

We have seen how previous kings thought and acted in relation to women. The present Shah has shown himself to be no different from his predecessors:

> "I wouldn't be sincere if I stated I'd been influenced by a single one of them [women]. Nobody can influence me, nobody. Still less a woman. Women are important in a man's life only if they're beautiful and charming and keep their femininity. . . . This business of feminism, for instance. What do these feminists want? What do they want? You say equality. Oh! I don't want to seem rude, but . . . You're equal in the eyes of the law, but not, excuse my saying so, in ability. . . . You've never produced a Michelangelo or a Bach. You've never even produced a great chef. . . . You've produced nothing great, nothing!"[55]

Gerontocracy, Infanticide and Masculine History

We were given very little meat in prison. The diet of cold rice, with some obnoxious liquid poured on top as a sauce, gave us either constipation or diarrhea.

One day they brought a cadaverous-looking young boy into our cell. The next day he was taken out to the torture chamber. I didn't see him afterwards. Two days later one of the guards whispered into my ear: "Remember that thin boy? He died under torture!"

The following day I was in my cell with a man called Ali. When they gave us food, there were pieces of thin, colorless meat in it. Ali was surprised. He looked up from the nauseating bowl: "How come? I've been in this jail for the last two months, and there's been no meat, and suddenly there's this meat!"

Almost by instinct, another prisoner said: "Maybe this is the boy's flesh we're eating."

We could no longer eat the food.

I know that I may be quite wrong in supposing it was that young man's flesh we were fed. But such a question does haunt one's mind. Hundreds of young Iranians, at the average age of twenty-one, have been killed during the last six years alone— either in the streets, at the firing ranges or in the torture chambers.

[55] Oriana Fallaci, pp. 271–72.

Where are their bodies? The government has not returned a single one to the bereaved family. Where are they buried? The number of people killed under torture or by firing squad during these six years—more than one hundred in 1976, in this so-called "island of stability" in the Middle East—is higher than the number killed in calamity-ridden Northern Ireland in the same time period. Where are the bodies of these young men and women?

There is only one man who knows: the Shah of Iran, our crowned cannibal, because he is the one who has swallowed them up. It is the youth who revolt against the monarch; it is they who are tortured, it is they who die and disappear. In fact, one definition of the kings of Iran is that they are youth-killers. Our crowned cannibals find the flesh of young men and women more palatable. Our history is the history of infanticide. Iranian literature is imbued with such striking examples of gerontocracy, infanticide and cannibalism that we can say with certainty that the most important pattern in all the genres of Persian literature is the killing of the young for the preservation of the old. The godhead of all myth, legend and history in Iran is the aged male—the traditional devourer of the youth. No wonder the present Shah is likened to the legendary Zahhak, the Cannibal King of Iran.

King Zahhak's story appears in *The Book of Kings,* by the greatest epic poet of Iran, Ferdowsi. The King kills his father at the instigation of the devil, who later kisses his shoulders and disappears. Two snakes grow from his shoulders, and when the physicians cut them off they grow again. The devil appears in the form of a physician and tells the King that there is only one way to be safe from the snakes: feed them the brains of young men. The advice is taken and acted upon:

> Every night, two young men
> Whether of low or noble birth
> Would be taken by the cook to the Shah's castle
> As cure for the king's malady
> He would kill them, take out the brains
> And feed them to the dragons[56]

Zahhak lives a thousand years minus a day, and his snakes eat up at least 700,000 young men. Eventually, he is overthrown by

[56] Ferdowsi, *The Book of Kings* (Shah-Nameh) (Teheran, Amir-Kabir Publications, 1967), p. 29.

Prince Fereydoun and Kaveh the Smith, whose sons have been killed by the Cannibal King. The prince becomes king and rules for five hundred years, during which time he witnesses the death of three sons. They are beheaded on his orders. He mourns them at his own death, with the heads at his side: "They didn't obey me; the world became dark for all three of them."[57]

But these are not the most tragic events of this epic tale. At the center of most of the legends in *The Book of Kings* we see Rostam, Zal's son by Roodabeh, who has given birth to him by means of a magical caesarean operation. The boy is too big to be born naturally. He grows up to become the most important heroic figure of the Iranians, living to be six hundred years old while his father is still alive. The first great tragedy in *The Book of Kings* takes place when Rostam kills his own son Sohrab on the battlefield. In fact, Rostam lies to the boy when he knocks him down. He tells Sohrab that it is ungenerous to kill a hero when he is knocked down the first time. The boy gets up to give his father another chance. When Rostam knocks him down in the second sequence of the battle, he tears open the boy's body with his dagger. It is only in the last moment of his life that the boy and his father become conscious of their relationship. Rostam asks the King for the primitive antidote to bring his son back to life. The King refuses and Sohrab dies. The father laments the son's lot at the end of the narrative poem.

The second such story treats the life and death of Siyavash, son of Kavoos and stepson of the King's wife, Soodabeh, who becomes enamoured of him. When he refuses to make love to her, Soodabeh tells the King that he tried to violate her. The boy takes the oath and proves his innocence by passing through fire. Then he wanders away from the court of his father to that of his father's enemy, Afrasiyab, the King of the land of the Turans. Afrasiyab gives his daughter to him, but he also marries the daughter of Peeran, the foremost fighter of the King's court. Though he is given land on which he builds cities, he is later killed at the order of his father-in-law, the King, who is perhaps the oldest man among Iran's enemies in its legendary history. The King has been pushed into killing Siyavash through the conspiracies of Garsivaz, the King's brother. Even now, people in some of the villages and

[57] *Ibid.*, p. 47.

small cities of the old Khorassan mourn the death of this young hero.

The third story relates the life and death of Esfandiyar, the son of King Goshtasp. Esfandiyar revolts against his father, asking for the kingdom of Iran. The King refuses him, claiming that to prove himself worthy of the kingdom he must fight Rostam, the greatest hero known to the Iranians. The father is aware from talking to his prophets that the boy's life will come to an end at the hands of Rostam. In the two days of battle that follow, first Esfandiyar's sons are killed, then he himself. Having won the first day, with Rostam taking to his heels, he falls on the second when Rostam, helped by his father Zal and the legendary bird Simorgh, shoots arrows right into his eyes—the only vulnerable part of his body. But Zal, Rostam's father, knows very well that whoever kills Esfandiyar will soon die himself. Rostam falls into a well full of spears with their sharp tips sticking upward. At the last moment he realizes that it is his own brother who has laid the trap for him. Before he breathes his last, he manages to pin the brother, Shaghad, to a tree, with an arrow thrust from the depth of the well. Thus the two brothers die at the same time, but the father goes on living. Goshtasp also lives to die a natural death.

There are no stories surpassing these in the epic literature of the country, and all four of them are stories of fathers killing, or participating in the killing of, their sons and other young men. The action of death does not have the dimensions of the brutality of an Achilles toward Hector. Almost all the moral values of patriarchy are discussed in terms of a chivalry characteristic of all the heroes of *The Book of Kings*. They face each other with courage; they speak of their deeds and the memories of their ancestors with eloquence; they rarely insult the other heroes. Yet it seems that the pattern in which they have been trapped transcends mere bravery and eloquent words. They fall as the victims of a partiarchal pattern, dying so that men older than they, and less worthy, will continue to live. They bow in front of gerontocracy and the tradition of Masculine History.

A comparison with Greek tragedies will help clarify the matter. In her exceptional book *Women's Evolution—From Matriarchal Clan to Patriarchal Family*,[58] Evelyn Reed speaks of three Greek plays in

[58] *Women's Evolution* (New York, Pathfinder Press, 1975), pp. 447–64.

which the final fall of woman-oriented society occurs and patriarchy takes off in full swing. These are: *Medea* by Euripedes, *Oedipus* by Sophocles, and *Orestes* by Aeschylus.

In the first play, a woman, Medea, kills her brother and later her sons, in order to avenge herself upon the rising patriarchy in Greek legendary history. In the second play, a young man kills his father, marries his mother and, upon revelation of these deeds, blinds himself and walks away into oblivion. In the third story, a son, Orestes, kills his mother, Clytemnestra, to avenge his father, Agamemnon, who had died by her hand.

In the first of these dramas, Medea appears as the last cry of a matriarchy in decline. Her husband Jason is left sonless; his whole house is shattered and with this all his hopes for eternity. Medea defied all the laws of her world and reached an identity of her own, in a world soon to be dominated by men.

In *Oedipus* we see a son killing his father and turning his mother to a thing of pleasure, but also suffering for it. To kill the father, the head of the tribe and the family, is unthinkable in a society dominated by men. But I would like to suggest that the murder committed by Oedipus has a dramatic aspect to it. Subconsciously, he knows that the world (kingship, fatherhood, the mother and all productive forces) should belong to him and not to his father. Macbeth kills Duncan for the same reason. The fact that Lady Macbeth incites him to this action is further indication that Macbeth, in order to be a better man in the eyes of his wife, has to get rid of the father figure. The man beneath rises against the man above and strikes him down in order to find his own identity. We are still in the world of patriarchy in both of these examples, be it Sophoclean or Shakespearean. There is a struggle in the Western family between two forces embodied in the two male members of the family, with the young man as the final victor and the old man as the victim.

A parallel example in early Greek mythology is the story of the birth of Zeus. Whereas Cronus has swallowed his other sons, Zeus stays alive through the conspiracies of the mother and finally compels his father to pay for what he has done. He must vomit the other sons and be banished from the face of the earth. The class of Titans comes to an end and the dominant class of the Olympian gods is born.

Oedipus belongs to the class of Zeus. His only crime is that his story is being written by someone who has become acutely conscious of the existence of the Greek society of families, with men, women and children in them, and within a society of family orientation a young man should never violate his father's laws, the most predominant of which is the one he has laid down for the chastity of his wife. But the struggle in the family, for the possession of the father's most precious property, goes on; Oedipus is symbolic of this struggle.

Orestes is the reverse of both Medea and Oedipus. The young man avenges his father by killing his mother, thus moving toward the ultimate establishment of patriarchy. Oedipus kills his father; Orestes kills his mother, on one hand taking revenge on behalf of Jason, his sons, Medea's brother, Agamemnon and all fathers, and on the other depriving himself of a mother who gave Oedipus his children, and could have given them to Orestes, too, if he had killed only Aegisthus and not his mother as well.

Is Orestes a free man, as Sartre in his interpretation of the drama, *The Flies*, represents him to be? Orestes has dealt the final blow to matriarchy, and such a thing can only result in a patriarchy in which the man emerges as the oppressor. Can we accept this oppressor as a free man?

A comparative look at the myths of the Iranians and Greeks will reveal that the first people viewed the father as the victor and the son as the victim, while the second people held the opposite to be true. Some of the things that happened in abundance in the East occurred in the West with some scarcity, and this differential has determined the nature of the temperaments, the existence of diverse patterns of culture and different modes of living. The roots of these differences lie in the Iranians' Asiatic Mode of Production versus the early Greeks' slavery as the mode of production.

A few methodological explanations are in order here. Three major approaches come immediately to mind: Freudian, Jungian and structuralist. We cannot approach the problem through Freudian analysis of sexual desires, instincts and complexes, because sexual manifestations, whether covert or overt, make up only one part of the issue and we cannot afford to take the part for the whole. Nor can we approach it through the archetypical patterns of Jung; we cannot afford to reduce human activities and phenomena to the overpowering primitive patterns of the collective unconscious and claim that patterns of primitive genes lead us through all phases of human civilization which we can do nothing about. When we study magic, dreams, the symbolic and metaphoric structure of literature and poetry, we find Jung pleasant because his own vision of these phenomena is really a poetic contribution, almost like an additional poetic dimension. This we can appreciate, but we cannot surrender to it.

There remains the structuralist analysis. Claude Lévi-Strauss reduces all patterns of diverse human societies and histories to the mathematical abstraction of a singular formula. This formula is an excellent poem of space, an exuberant geometry of space dotted with stars and names, presented in a masterful flight of imagination. Daedalus would have coveted such an architect. But there isn't a single insect breathing in that labyrinth. All the globes are unpopulated, and the names seem to be those of mountains on the moon or Mars. The content of humanity doesn't breathe in there. Beautiful spears dart in a void. The content is nowhere to be found. The omnipresent structure is only a part of the structuralist's imagination.

We can appreciate all these methods, but we cannot surrender to them. We study structures in the process of change because of a change in their content, both material and abstract; we study types in the process of yielding their places to other types, and we study sex within the context of the specific society in which particular human beings live.

I have already discussed the significance of the Asiatic Mode of Production in the creation of the Oriental despot, and I can only say here in passing that because of the basic changes in Greek economic life, the Greek artist's whole conception of various characters in literature—and even his understanding of literary genres—became somewhat different from those of the Iranians, with whom they had been in contact for thousands of years.

The Greek epic evolved into the form of drama in a matter of a few centuries. A stable family on the stage of the society manifested itself in the form of a family of men and women on the stages of the theater. In the short span of a century, drama gave way to Plato's *Republic* and Aristotle's *Politics*. A criticism of the highest order, of life, literature, art, society and history, and the Greek philosopher's rationality were born.

Drama is the most social of literary arts. It is more than a mimesis; it is actual men and women on the stage. It is also the most objective of arts. To stage a play requires great administrative and managerial imagination. The Greeks showed their capacity for government both in their society and in the form of drama. It was quite natural for literary criticism and the social sciences to come into existence in such a society. This showed that in spite of the foundation of its economy on the exploitation of slaves, there was a certain level of dialogue among the citizens in the society. The stage was an arena for this dialogue. The use of slaves had given the society enough of a surplus in the production of material wealth to enable the Greeks to indulge in a pleasure of the highest degree, the art of poetry on the stage.

Iranian despotism, on the contrary, had no room for the social art of drama, for its give and take. The degenerate family existed and continued to vegetate within walls and veils. Only one element of the family was reflected on the social scene—the father, the old man, the gerontocrat, the son-killer and the thingifier of women. One side was so overwhelmingly strong that it crushed the other two sides of the family triangle and turned them into carrion.

Rostam on the stage would be a father who kills and a son who is killed. The fate of other sons would be even worse: death by their fathers. Even in Greek, there isn't a play on Cronus. This stage of Greek patriarchy is not material for drama. There is nothing dramatic in swallowing young men one after the other. Those who have tried to dramatize the life of Zahhak have done so only in the light of modern interpretations; they have read their own later ideologies into the legend. A one-man drama is a difficult thing; even the most modern form of drama, such as the theater of the absurd, uses groups of people. Without women and children on the stage, without a sense of societal verisimilitude, without a gathering of people for the sake of acting and interacting upon each other, without an inner meaning quintessential to an assembly of men and women and children, drama cannot exist.

The fable behind the epic in Iranian literature was too simple to afford the intricacies of a plot, a complication, a denouement, or a reversal of the Grecian type. The climax would always be the same: a father killing his son, and a son surrendering without the least dramatic conflict. But the nonexistence of drama and the dramatic elements enumerated above mirrored the monolithism of the society itself. There was only one hero in the whole society—

the king—and he was heroic mostly in relation to his own people. In more than one case in actual history we saw that this hero was determined to plunder first and foremost his own people, then the peoples of the neighboring countries, and afterwards, if possible, the peoples of distant lands.

Drama, as an official art form, was never created and established in ancient Iran. Even when a form of passion play was created and when, during the past two centuries, the house comedy, *roohozi*, came into being, these plays never developed into highly conscious and workable forms of art. Drama, in its present meaning, was introduced into Iran around the beginning of the twentieth century and established itself as a workable form only after World War II.

The Iranians of a thousand years ago, i.e., during the time when Ferdowsi was writing his great epic, had already come to know that drama existed. There was a fruitful interchange between the Islamic world and the West, Greece and Rome. An Iranian philosopher writing in Arabic, the scientific language of Islam, was sometimes called the second Aristotle or the second Plato. And we know very well that the Islamic revival of ancient Greek thinking contributed immensely to the rise of Renaissance rationalism and humanism. Thus it would have been impossible for the Arabs and the Iranians not to know about the poetic forms of the ancient Greeks. Some of the examples given for rhetorical devices in Persian books of rhetoric and prosody are the same as in Aristotle's *Poetics,* and in fact the book had been translated into Arabic—a language without which great achievements would have been impossible for a serious poet in Iran.

Yet, although drama was the highest form of art for Aristotle, these second Aristotles never encouraged drama in Iran. Out of the thousands of classical Persian books of poetry, there is not even one single dramatic work. Drama was discouraged and stifled by the atmosphere of the society itself. The people and the poets were not even consciously concerned with drama.

In the court of the Iranian kings either the poet himself or a *ravi* (narrator) read his poems; sometimes each poet had his own *ravi.* The main form of court poetry was the qasida, the panegyric ode. Its pattern was that of the Masculine History of Iran: the poet belittled himself and glorified his master—to such an extent that the glorifier faded away and the glorified appeared in all his might

The poet effaced himself from the words of the poem and made his subject—generally a king—emerge as the sole personality of the poem. Although there were formalistic considerations and sequences in the qasida, and although each poet spoke of his personal experience of nature and language, the central figure was always monotonously the same. The form was in substance a man-to-man poem, but one of the men was almost as weak as the feeble son of the patriarchal family, and the second man was as powerful as God or his Shadow.

The poet or the *ravi* read the poem, and if it was good, i.e., if the eulogy was successful, the poet's mouth would be filled with gold or he would be given lands, horses and mules. In fact, many poets grew to be the richest men of the court as a result of gifts from the King. It is said that Sultan Mahmoud had four hundred poets at his court, and most of them were rich.

Iranian epic poetry, in the form of either the narrative or the qasida, did not evolve into a social form on the order of drama. The relations between the two men, the poet and the King, while still representative of human relations in society, gradually became subjectivized in the form of Iranian mysticism and Sufism, and reduced to the ethereal, abstract relationship between man and God. The Sufi and the mystic took the place of the weak and tyrannized poet, and the objectively real king was replaced by the subjective god.

Sometimes the mystic-poet submerged himself in God to such a degree of abstraction that he could not be encouraged to come back to the reality. The story of Mansur-e Hallaj, one of the great early mystics of the Islamic world, can be studied only in the light of such an absorption into the presence of God and the emergence of the new man as God. He shouted at his dismemberment: "I am truth!" or "I am God!" But such an exalted transfiguration could not be acceptable to the dogmatic Moslems of the time, who believed that either a man believed in the God of the Caliph-Shah, the God of God's Shadow, or else should be dismembered or hanged, which was the fate of Mansur himself.

Yet the father-son relationship is ever-present in the works of the two major poets of Iran, Rumi and Hafiz. Rumi's leader, who represents God on earth, is Shams-e Tabrizi, about whose homosexual love affair with Rumi there can be little doubt. The death of Shams turns into the biggest tragedy of Rumi's life. Though he chooses other men as his leaders, he does not stop singing the glories of his beloved and the greatness of his loss. He has chosen God as his king, one who will cure him of the sickening alienation he suffers in the material world—a strange place to him, to which the poets are banished. He can do only one thing: sing of the sorrow of separation and the joy of reunion, which will take place in the future world. The poet rushes headlong in the wind toward the omnipotent beloved who is none other than the male king, idealized, subjectified and lifted on the shoulders of the poet's imagination to the roof of the uppermost layer of heaven.

Rumi is the drunken whirling dervish, the most Dionysian of all the Iranian poets. Objects, embedded in love, singing all together and rushing in ecstasy toward one another, and altogether toward the male beloved, become in actuality symbols of a humanity yearning for a world beyond the realm of the earthly kings. But the beloved one is indubitably masculine, manifesting himself through various corporeal incarnations, lending to every corpuscle the qualities of his own being. The poet lays his world, like a bouquet of flowers, at his feet.

Hafiz is not the joyful dancer but rather the weeping willow, the sad wayfarer who has Pir-e Moghan, the Old Man of the Magi, as his leader. The patriarch is now the mystical leader in a rotten world ruined in the age of Hafiz by armies, kings and tyrants. So the poet falls in love with one who is idealized to such a degree that he cannot hurt him. It is impossible to tell whether manifestations of the beloved are men or women. Persian language itself here becomes a source of confusion with its third-person singular pronoun *oo*, standing both for masculine and feminine.

Hafiz is more Apollonian than Dionysian. His symmetrical, statuesque line, excelled by none other in Persian poetry, makes his poem the most polysemous—a word with several meanings ever written. One can interpret it as he wishes. No wonder people see their fortunes reflected in his lines. If ever Chinese, Central Asian and Persian miniatures could be put into words, this is a case in point. If objects are in love with each other in Rumi's poems, here it is the words. There is no word of the poem that can be replaced by its synonym; otherwise, the symbolical constellation of the whole construction is in danger of collapse.

Living in a weird world of absolute lawlessness, a monarchy at the peak of its anarchy, Hafiz created an iron-clad law for the

Persian *beyt* (a line of two hemistiches with a central image) which excluded all possibilities of change. Here, a line is a line is a line —a vertical structure of words, made of steel and roses, speaking with the several mouths of its words, each opening into the heart of a male beloved, the abstract patriarch, inviting the poet to the cruel nest of its blood-soaked arms.

> The dark night, the fear of waves, and a whirlpool so
>   terrifying
> How can the light-burdened spectators on the shore
>   know our situation?

Or:

> If you, Hafiz, desire his presence, then don't absent
>   yourself from him
> When you find the one you desire, quit this world and
>   forget its cares . . .

The poetry of the nonmystics had the same masculine quality. They were not all homosexuals; far from it. They lived in a masculine-oriented world in which it was difficult to speak of the face and figure of one's female beloved. Thus they all spoke of a beloved who could be taken for both a young man and a woman. Saadi's poetry is the best example. The French translators have turned all his ungendered beloveds into feminines and, in so doing, have read aspects proper to Western culture into Eastern poetry.

Persian literature as a whole can be characterized in the following way:

(1) The epic is a man-to-man form of literary creation. Men address themselves to men. There are women involved, but generally it is the actions of men that count. The general rhythmical pattern used for the epic is masculine.

(2) The qasida, or the ode, is also a man-to-man form. The poet eulogizes the King or the minister, or one of the princes. There is great thematic unity in the ode, but the imagic unity is lacking. The poem is not an imagic composite whole. The external form, the rhythmical pattern and the rhymes have unity; the theme also is unified, but the internal form of the poem—the imagic and metaphorical unity—is not there. One finds harmony of imagery in each of the lines but sees no harmony among all the lines, as far as imagery is concerned.

(3) The ghazal, or the sonnet, whether mystical or lyrical, is generally the poetry of imagically independent lines (two hemistichs). As in the case of qasida, there is external unity in the rhythmical and rhyming patterns; thematic unity, however, is rather rare, and the imagic unity among all the lines is seldom present. There certainly are exceptions to this rule, but generally it is difficult to find internal or, rather, metaphorical unity among all the lines of a ghazal. The poet speaks of something in one line and of something else in the other, but he speaks of all of those things in the same rhythmical and rhyming patterns. Harmony exists only within the images of one line. This may be due to the artistic effects of repression. The poet seems to be afraid to carry the image in the first line over to the other lines—to reinforce, transform and change it through subjecting it to the structure of the other lines. Harmony in the greatest of all forms of Persian poetry, the ghazal, is unilateral and monolithic, and in the line only. When Nima Youshidj, the founder of modern Persian poetry, said that he was "the founder of modern harmony in Persian poetry," he was dealing with his revolt, in both the external and internal forms of poetry, against the unilateral and monolithic unity of the line of classical Persian poetry. His work has a triangular harmony in the whole of one poem: the external form, the internal form and the content merge together in a monolith made of all the lines and images and meanings of the piece. Another aspect of the ghazal is the difficulty in deciding whether the poet is addressing himself to a man or a woman. Generally, the beloved has all the characteristics of a beautiful male with some feminine qualities. What is explicit in Rumi, in connection to his male lover, Shams-e Tabrizi, is implicit in the poetry of Hafiz and Saadi, the other two major Iranian lyrical poets.

(4) The narrative romantic mathnavi, a kind of poetry which generally deals with the love affairs of men and women, is usually very objective when it comes to men but rather abstract in its depiction of women. Still, it is the only form of poetry in which women appear as near-equals to men. This is understandable in light of the fact that the poet writing his narrative about the court romance could hardly afford to introduce a man-to-man pattern. His audience, however, is made up of men. He writes his poetry for the ears of men, not those of women.

(5) The philosophical mathnavi deals with the visions of men;

one great example, the mathnavi of Rumi, uses women to explo
the world of men in relation to God.

(6) All books of history are books about men—by men and f
men.

(7) The picaresque novel deals with women in the same wa
as does the narrative romantic mathnavi. Yet women are less a
cessible than men, and the writer is more realistic in his descriptio
of men than of women.

(8) Stories dealing with the biographies and spiritual cond
tions of saints, mystics and prophets are about men. This does ne
mean that there are no women in these books but that, as in th
philosophical mathnavi, they women are means to the ends c
men. It is impossible to find an independent vision of women i
any of these books. Men speak about them behind their backs. I
fact, all Persian literature speaks about women in the abstract an
almost with a feeling of their absence, just as one speaks abou
someone who is not in the room.

After Hafiz, Persian poets found it impossible to excel the
predecessors. When the Constitutional Revolution took plac
Iranian literature received its first shocks from the West, throug
Russia and Turkey. Literature was politicized; the idiom of poetr
and prose changed, and for the first time Iranian women starte
writing both genres. Shams Kasmaie, an Azarbaijani woma
broke the patriarchal traditional line into the freer form of expres
sion closer in structure to blank verse; it is small wonder that th
first person to revolt against the traditional iron-clad line was
woman. Second in line was Nima Youshidj, a man from a provinc
near the Caspian Sea whose dialect had been suppressed for centu
ries; though he wrote most of his poetry in Persian, Nima generall
wrote about the objects and people of his own province, Mazanda
ran. The man who broke down all regulations of Persian prose wa
Djamalzadeh, who had been educated in Europe; he wrote the fir
collection of Persian short stories, which opened the way for a
other writers of the country. The impact of the Constitution.
Revolution was such that almost all literary forms were revolu
tionized.

The two revolutionary periods in Iran—1906–1912 and 194
1953—were each followed by their own counterrevolutionary se
quels. From 1920 to 1941, when Reza Khan gained power an
ruled as Reza Shah, is the period in which there was complet

disregard of the ideals of the Constitution. The tyranny resembles that of the old patriarchy, with a few differences: a growing middle class in the cities, a growth in industry and a concurrent growth in the number of wage workers. Yet the Oriental despot is there in the center of all the affairs of state, as if the preceding revolution against the monarchy had not taken place.

The preeminent writer of this period is Sadeq Hedayat, one of the most somber pessimists in all literature. Nourished on the culture of France in the West and India in the East, frantic about the pre-Islamic culture of Iran and detesting the influence of Islam and the Arabs, a defected aristocrat who could not be fully integrated among the ranks of the unprivileged masses, Hedayat summed up the essence of Masculine History in his short novel *The Blind Owl,* a book hailed as a masterpiece by André Breton.

The novel takes place in two short sequels: the world of dream and the world of reality. In the dream world, a woman appears from the ancient world, ethereal, celestial, beautiful, untouchable. In the world of reality, the woman appears as the protagonist's prostitute wife, who sleeps with every man except her husband. The young man appears to be impotent. He does not have the courage to touch the girl in the dream section because he is afraid that he may destroy her beauty, and he cannot sleep with the woman in the reality sequel because he is impotent.

But there is a reason for the impossibility of touching the woman, both in dream and in reality. An old man appears whenever the protagonist approaches the young woman. His eerie laughter is so emasculating that the young man simply feels dead. At the end of the story the husband kills his wife and he himself turns into the old man.

There is more than one old man in the novel: the protagonist's father, his uncle, the butcher, the driver of the hearse also appear. The lonely young man could have been happy with his wife if only these old men had not existed. It seems that he could have resolved all his personal problems if only the old men had disappeared. The young man's failure entails the old men's triumph, and this in itself means the failure of a better and freer human world, with young and free men and women, a new nation of youths, a new nation, liberated from the bondage of patriarchs and kings.

The butcher reminds us of Reza Shah, and all the previous

cannibalistic monarchs, and of all those other old men who appear and disappear—at their own whim and without the authority of any other person in the novel—remind us of all the familial and historical tyrants of Iranian history. Thus we have a triangle of the impotency of youth, the impossibility of either physical or spiritual rebirth, and the domination of a demonic alienation, both in reality and in ideality based on that reality. This condition has a dialectic of its own that can be understood only in the light of Masculine History.

The father as a positive thesis in the literature of Masculine History is so powerful that he rushes headlong toward his antithesis (the son), not to be negated by him but rather to be moved by him toward the completion of his task in the process of self-gratification. The thesis-father conspires against the poor, horrified antithesis-son, and before the antithesis can rise to full power to face the enemy, he is castrated by the sweeping authority of the despotic thesis. What results is not the rise of a progressive synthesis as the basis for a new evolution, but the reiteration of the earlier, almost primeval thesis. Dialectically speaking, the son is crushed under the weight of the father. The historical pattern is semistatic, semidynamic. It is history in embryo, an inborn dwarf, boasting of its magnificence in pitch darkness—the world of butchers and hearse drivers and gravediggers, the world of crowned cannibals. In this world there are fathers replacing fathers replacing fathers, a tedious succession of men in blood with sleeves tucked up to ravish ages of people. And the people, young men and women, these potential creators of great societies and civilizations, are massacred or, if not massacred, subjected to a spiritual degradation far worse than massacre—antitheses lying in the abyss of total degradation and subjugation, infernal antitheses.

In the following period of revolutionary upsurge, Iranian literature responded with a move conforming to the feelings of the whole era. Parties came into existence; democracy was reborn; the nationalities spoke out and formed their own autonomous governments. Hedayat responded to this great revolutionary wave with his satirical piece *Hadji Agha,* tearing to pieces one of the dominant patriarchs of the preceding period with his pungent colloquial style.

But the rebirth was short-lived, and Hedayat's own days were counted. He left the country in the aftermath of the fall of the two republics of Azarbaijan and Kurdestan at the hands of the Shah's army, and within a few years he killed himself in Paris.[59]

In that period of uplifted hopes, Nima Youshidj wrote a long poem, calling it *The Amen-saying Bird.* One of the most beautiful pieces of poetry in modern Persian poetry, it is made up of the three characters of Masculine History: the world devourer, the people and the Bird, the symbolic embodiment of all the aspirations of people for a rebirth. The triangle is exactly the same as that in *The Blind Owl,* only here an open dialogue takes place between the people and the Bird, and there is unrestrained discussion about the King, the world devourer. The people speak of their aspirations in the form of a chorus which brings to mind both ancient Greek plays and Iran's indigenous passion plays. The Bird calls out "Amen" to all these aspirations, the voices of free human beings resemble a river rising out of its bed, and finally "The night runs away/The day arrives."[60]

The reverse of the aspirations of the Bird—the symbol of rebirth, almost a kind of feminine hope for birth and rebirth—coincides with the CIA coup in 1953 and the reestablishment of Masculine History in Iran on a neocolonial pattern, this time made in America. Years of total blackout in culture and literature follow.

Now not only the fate of Iranian society but also the forms of its poetry are determined in the State Department, the Pentagon and the CIA. All poets publish elegies, and even lyrical poetry is burdened with the elegiac theme. Almost a decade after the coup Forough Farrokhzad, the greatest poetess of all Iranian poetry and the first to address herself to men and then both sexes, would write in her very lucid, laconic and feminine style:

> No one thought of love any longer
> No one thought of triumph any longer
> No one
> Thought of anything any longer
>
> In the caves of loneliness
> Futility was born

[59] *The Blind Owl*, trans. by J. P. Costello (London, Calder; New York, Grove Press, 1957).

[60] *Nomoonehaie az Ash'ar-e Nima Youshidj* (Examples from Nima Youshidj's Poetry) (Teheran, Pocket Books, Franklin Publications, 1973), pp. 40–50.

Blood reeked of bang and opium
Pregnant women
Bore headless children
And the cradles, shamed,
Took refuge in the graves
. . . .

In the eyes of the mirrors
The movements, colors and images
Were reflected upside down
And above the heads of base clowns
And the faces of insolent whores
A bright, sacred halo
Burned like an enflamed umbrella
. . . .

Sometimes a spark, a petty spark
Set off this silent, dead society
Suddenly from within
They would assault each other
Men would slit each other's throats with knives
And would copulate with child-girls
In a bed full of blood
. . . .

The sun was dead
And nobody knew
That the name of that sorrowful dove
That had flown away from the hearts
Was faith[61]

The roots of this immense faithlessness and sense of futility
were portrayed in 1961 by Jalal Al-Ahmad in a treatise called
Westomania. This article brought a whole generation of Iranian
writers and intellectuals under its magnetic influence. The author
wrote:

I use the term "Westomania" (West-beaten) in the same
way you would use "cholera-ridden" or, if this is distasteful
say, in the same sense as "cold, heat, or weather-beaten." . .
This "Westomania" has two sides to it. On the one side

[61] *Tavallodi Digar* (A New Birth) (Teheran, Morvarid Publications, 1963), pp. 99–
105.

there is the West, and on the other, we who are West-beaten —we, that is to say, a small corner of the East. Let us posit two poles to represent these sides, or, if you prefer, two extremities, since we are talking here about the two ends of a measured scale. On the Western side let us put all the developed or industrialized countries, or all those countries which are able, with the use of their machinery, to exploit their raw materials more efficiently and to bring their goods to market in a similar fashion. These raw materials are not simply iron ore, viscera, cotton or gum tragacanth. They are also myths and legends, basic principles of belief, music and spiritual manifestations. On our side—we who are a small fraction of the other pole—let us put Asia and Africa, or all the underdeveloped nations, or the nonindustrial nations, or that group of nations which consume products manufactured in the West —products whose raw materials are derived from this very portion of the globe. By way of illustration we may cite oil from the Persian Gulf, jute and spices from India, jazz from Africa, silk and opium from China, studies of anthropology and sociology from the islands of the Oceanic archipelago and from the indigenous tribal inhabitants of Africa. Yes, each item is derived from its own proper habitat. And we are right in the middle of this whole situation. We have more common interests with the second group of nations than differences. . . .

It is not a question of denying or renouncing the machine —never! The universalization of the machine is a historical necessity. The question is our attitude toward the machine and technology and that we are not the makers of the machine, but rather, because of economic and political necessity, we have to be submissive consumers of Western manufacturers. At most, we have to be easily contented, submissive, low-waged repairers of what comes from the West, since this in turn necessitates our identification with the machine; not only ourselves, but our government, our culture, and our daily life. Our whole existence has to be tailored to the height and size of the machine. If the person who has made the machine is now rebelling against it and feeling its oppressive force, we who have become the servants thereof do not even show signs of complaint. We even put on airs. And this is what I mean by "Westomania." My main contention is that we have not been able to preserve our own original cultural identity in the face of invasion by the machine, but have in fact given way to it completely.[62]

This rather rough formulation led, a decade later, to my formulation of Double Alienation in my book *Masculine History*.

Alienation in the West is the outcome of deteriorating processes in the production system of the whole society. Everything in the West has been created through the assistance of a central element, the machine. The machine's invasion is total, and it has created the present consciousness of the Western man. A combination of bureaucracy, exploitation of the majority by the minority and a systematized anarchy in the form of government have contributed to the alienation of the Western man. In sum: the Western man has become alienated from his vision of natural action through the machine. This is a one-layered form of alienation. The Western man created the machine, which carries with it all the vestiges of his historical evolution. He is the servant of the machine he himself made, as he has gradually grown to be the slave of the governments he created to serve him. Now neither the government nor the machine serves him. This creates the Western man's alienation.

But the Western man's alienation looks like the machine he created. The man who first made the rifle is also the rifle. Now the West has a machine moving inside the machine. The machine-man is facing the machine-machine. This is a giant step in alienation—and certainly of the greatest significance—but it is only one layer of alienation.

The situation in the East is quite different. We are alienated not once but twice. We did not create this technology, this advanced capitalist system and the administrations and the bureaucracies involved, but they make use of us as their raw materials, subjecting us to a process of reification from afar. A universal myth of general progress is being imposed upon us, something in whose creation and evolution we were used only as raw materials. Our human consciousness and the consciousness of our culture

---

[62] Jalal Al-Ahmad, *Gharbzadegi* (Westomania) (Teheran, published in part by Kay-han-e Mah, in full by an underground publisher, 1961), pp. 5–8. The translation, in manuscript, has been done by Prof. William G. Millward and Reza Baraheni.

did not develop along the lines of the development of this machine which now makes use of us. This is one layer of our alienation: a system grafted on us from above and through our Masculine History, which sucks our blood for the benefit of other species of things somewhere else, is as blind to us as we are alienated from it. The West estranges us from itself by coming like a rapist in a masquerade—a rapist who devours, ravishes and departs. The West is another planet with a very advanced structure of things; its emissaries contact the peak of our pyramid, the Shah, submit their proposals, have their contracts signed and fly back to their home planet. It was difficult enough for us to make contact with the palace of the King in the first place and find out what was going on; now it becomes more difficult for us to make contact with a total stranger, the Westerner.

On the upper floor of our indigenous home, the second floor of our society, our Masculine History has been built. As in the famous Parable by Kafka, the imperial messenger from the palace hasn't yet left the first walls of the inner castle and the peasant is sitting thousands of miles away, waiting in his dream for the messenger to arrive. On the roof of this floor of our Masculine History the West has descended in the form of another upper floor and taken control without our knowledge or consent. But the pressure is on the foundations, on us who live on the first floor. This is the first layer of our alienation.

In the process of our mystification and stupefaction, we suddenly find another layer of alienation. So many values—and styles of values—have been imposed on us, so many objects and structures of objects are forced on us, that we cannot be sure of any kind of indigenous roots or identities. Wherever we look we find objects, faces and values from other places, and we ask: Where are our own objects, our own values and faces? Where are our identities? Where are we as human beings?

First, we are alienated from the West because the colonial calamities bred by the Western world have been thrust upon us without we ourselves being or having become Westerners; second, the West plunders and destroys all our languages, literature, folklore, the identity of all our positive visions, poetic and artistic rhythms without replacing them with something that can originally be called Eastern.

Hence our double alienation. We are aliens both to the West

and to the East. Our indigenous Masculine History finally turned into a pimp, a comprador pimp, and pandered us all to the West.

A young man who died in battle with the Iranian army wrote:

> The consumer society every day accepts more of the culture and values of the colonial West, and destroys its bonds with the people of Iran. This society cannot see the deprivation of the other society but looks down from its lofty throne at the deprived community without recognizing it. The technocratic values of the West, with the old bureaucratic values, are the criteria and support of this society's existence. Profiteering, opportunism, isolation, individualism, and self-worship are the rule of life.[63]

The fable of Power in Iran goes like this:

Kavoos, the legendary king of the ancient world, wanted to reach the moon. He made a double-decker flying bed. Four eagles were tied to the bed, one to each corner. On the second deck fresh pieces of meat hung from the tips of spears. When the eagles became hungry, they flew up to reach the meat and consequently lifted Kavoos and the bed on their wings. They flew as long as there was meat on the spears. Kavoos wandered pridefully in the air. But the meat was ultimately consumed, and there was an energy crisis in space. The King, the bed and the eagles tumbled down from the sky and fell into the forest. In the myth the King was saved.[64]

But will the Shah survive a different kind of energy crisis, this time generated by the masses of human beings he has wronged? When the people rise to resist the devouring crowned cannibals, subjecting them to a permanent starvation, will the Shah survive? Will he?

[63] Frances FitzGerald, "Giving the Shah All He Wants," *Harper's* magazine (November, 1974). Also see Mohammad-Bagher Falsafi, "Propaganda in Iran," *Harper's* magazine (January, 1975).

[64] Ferdowsi, p. 99.

MY IMAGES
OF THE SHAH

Listen
Do you hear darkness blowing[1]

I first saw the Shah in my hometown, Tabriz. I was twelve years old, I had never set my eyes on a Shah before and I decided I was not going to miss this chance. My older brother agreed with me. We should see the Shah at all costs.

We were lined up one day by the school principal in the large, dust-covered courtyard under the volleyball net. Very carefully, the principal examined our faces and hands, our clothes and shoes. He even raised the collars of our jackets and looked for the lice that might have nestled in the tears and the threads. Finally, my brother and I, along with a dozen other kids, were pulled out of the line. We were told to get the hell out of the school and never come back until the Shah had visited the city and left. Our tattered uniforms, our worn-out shoes with bald heels showing obscenely from their backs, our demonic, hungry eyes and anemic complexions were no fit sight for His Majesty's eyes.

On the way home, my brother and I started such a roguish brawl with each other that we were both crying, cursing, limping, and bleeding miserably from our noses and mouths by the time we got there; the armpits of my jacket and the knees of my brother's pants were torn, and I had lost one of my shoes. Father opened up

[1] Forough Farrokhzad, *A New Birth* (Teheran, Morvarid Publications, 1963), p. 30.

his thick leather belt and beat both of us to a pulp. The next day, in order to make up for this undeserved beating, he took us out to see the Shah.

Father was a huge, hefty man, and his muscularity had already won for him a small reputation in the neighborhood. So when he walked past the marketplace at about ten in the morning the paupers and the porters, the servants of the rich and the small shopkeepers got up and followed him. He had a firm grip on the hands of his sons. People said: "Taqi is taking Reza and Naqi to see the Shah." When we reached the large square, there were more than two hundred men and children behind us. We went and stood in the front row, our eyes fixed on the newly washed and swept road along which the Shah was to travel.

He arrived about four hours after the scheduled time. The crowd burst in every direction, running, shouting and trampling each other. Army units and police officers rushed into the midst of this sudden hullabaloo, creating yet another cause for commotion. The huge black car turned several times around the small pool in the middle of the square, and when it was about to take off in the opposite direction, Father moved forward and stood in its way. He was still grasping our hands. Then the door opened, and a smallish, somewhat dark young man emerged, with a nose too big for his face and thrust out shamelessly as an erected phallus upon a polite gathering.

The Shah's small figure stood in front of Father's huge figure. Father smiled magnanimously, his blue eyes rimmed with blood on the lids. The Shah smiled back, his head moving up and down slowly but rhythmically, and the protruding phallic nose clumsily accompanied the rhythm. The whole crowd had been lulled to silence, as if they knew that the ritualistic mime between the Shah and Father had to be conducted in silence.

Father himself could stand the silence no longer. Almost uncontrollably, he blurted out in his simple and harsh working-class colloquial Azarbaijani Turkish:

"Kefoon Yakhjidi? [Are you all right?]"

The Shah continued to smile and move his head up and down. We had seen pictures of him standing with Stalin, Churchill and Roosevelt, but in those pictures he resembled a newly graduated corporal from the army, waiting to be ordained by a general. Standing in front of us, he was different. The head went up and down. Unacquainted with the fashions of royalty and undaunted by the Shah's head, Father repeated his question, smiling with his bloodshot eyes.

"Kefoon Yakhjidi?"

The Shah didn't even blink. He looked at my father as at an animal, appreciating it but not knowing whether to buy it or forget about it. Father was impatient. He didn't care for the young face, the perfumed figure, the phallic nose and the nodding. He simply wanted an answer. It was impolite not to answer a question as simple as Father's. The people who had followed him to the square wanted an answer, too. But the answer didn't come. Father turned around, squeezing our hands in his perspiring palms. We walked away, and the crowd from the neighborhood followed. Father spoke in his typical manner:

"Bu Shahdan bir pokh chikhmaz. Gada adam dili dooshoonmir. [No shit will come out of this Shah. The fellow doesn't understand the language of human beings.]"

The Shah didn't know Father's language. Father didn't know the Shah's language, and since Father was a citizen of the Shah's kingship in every way except linguistically, he belonged to the world of beasts and birds, and not of human beings. Father's language was that of unnamed beasts, and he himself was the epitome of an infernal, bestial world. He didn't know that the Shah also knew nothing about the language that he himself had spoken for years. Father had implicitly declared a war against the rich Shah through his poverty, through his alleged bestiality, through his having turned into a mere thing in the Shah's eyes. And now he felt that he had no language whatsoever, and he was doomed to absolute tonguelessness for the rest of his life. He was only an inarticulate animal, and his language was made up of a bunch of meaningless sounds and syllables.

His tonguelessness followed him to his death and, in fact, became the most outstanding feature of his death. He died in Teheran, an alien to the Persian-speaking majority. And he died of a cancer in his mouth which made it impossible for him to say anything in any language during the last three months of his life. His inner muteness found its ultimate physical manifestation in this opprobrious manner. Nature assisted the Shah to mute a man who had declared twenty years earlier that the Shah didn't understand the language of human beings.

We buried Father in the religious city of Qom, on the northern shoulder of the desert that covers almost one-fourth of the entire country. First, we had the body washed and shrouded. I bought a grave for fifteen tomans (two dollars) in a graveyard that stretches for several leagues into the desert. Qom is Iran's burial place, and with the dust blowing from the desert and covering the buildings and the people and the graves, it has a very deadly look. My brother and I lowered the body into the deep pit, each of us holding it from one end. We covered the body with the dirt newly dug out of the ground. We walked away.

As we left the graveyard, my brother said that maybe we should order a tombstone for Father. I walked up to the man who was cutting the stones and engraving names, prayers and verses on them.

"I want one of these stones of yours," I said. "How much?"

"It depends on the size and labor," he said in a professional manner, betraying with his dialect that he came from the same part of the country as my family and I did.

I spoke Azarbaijani Turkish with him, and he answered back in the same language. I chose a stone and brought it to the man and put it beside him. He handed me a piece of paper:

"Write and tell me what I should put on it."

There was a poem that Father loved to recite when he was in Teheran and not yet incapacitated by cancer. There was something in it both of Chekhov's plays and of the Japanese haiku:

> When I came here some time ago
> The pomegranate trees were blooming
> My life rotted in exile

I handed the poem to the man. He looked at it, bedazzled by the strength of the poem in his own mother tongue. When he raised his head, there was a look of nostalgia in his eyes. He handed the poem back to me:

"I cannot put this on the stone!"

"Why? What's wrong?" I asked.

"Government orders," he said. "We've been ordered not to use Turkish on the graves."

Thus there is only a small number on the grave. Father is now a number on the sandy shoulders of the desert. His identity is buried deep down in the bowels of the earth. Cancer was in the roots of his tongue when he was born. Cancer has been in the roots of all the subject Iranian nationalities at birth. By the decree of the Shah's father, and the execution of the same decree by the son, we were christened to become Aryans.

In 1946, a year before the Shah came to our city, at the end of the cold month of December when the Democratic government of Azarbaijan was overthrown by the Shah, our music teacher at school was brutally beaten because he had taught us songs in our language. Our composition teacher, who had corrected my early childish poems in Turkish, was arrested and tried for treason to the Motherland because he had refused to teach composition in any language other than his own mother tongue, which was also the language of the whole city and the whole state. In the same month we were ordered to take our schoolbooks to the square and set fire to them. The Shah's agents and gendarmes warmed their hands by the flames. Then we were given books which we could hardly understand.

Anytime I walked out of the house on those last days of December, I would see three or four of the Shah's goons knocking at the doors of those whom they suspected of being sympathetic to the overthrown Democratic government. They would ask the man of the family to step out for a minute, then order him to walk ahead of them and be sure not to look back. The man could actually read the minds of the goons. He would walk with his eyes wide open, as if they could jump out or expand cubically to the back of his head. "Four-eyed men" was the phrase coined by the people for such men. The execution would take place there and then. I saw so many men killed in this manner in those days that even now I have the habit of looking behind me wherever I go.

For several months after these events we were bemused by the news that "scoundrels and traitors" were to be hanged in the square. Before we read the morning prayers at school, we rushed to the square and there they were, a whole lot of them, the frozen figures of our own neighbors dangling clumsily from the gallows, eyes bulging and tongues spread out on the beard or chin. How could our neighbors be scoundrels and traitors? We had seen so many kind things from them, so many brave things. They were our courageous men, those utterly familiar, utterly deformed faces. We blew the warm steam from our mouths into our hands

and watched those hanging nightmares for hours until they pene-
trated our dreams and never departed. Gallows seen in childhood
are the gallows of eternity.

We move from the gallows of 1946 to the gallows and firing
squads of 1953 in the aftermath of the CIA coup in Iran. We pass
through the streets of Teheran in 1952 where blood is sifting
through the bodies of popular demonstrators. Police and army
raids on the innocent, peaceful demonstrators add another dark
page to the history of the Shah's atrocities. Then we walk into the
room of General Teimour Bakhtiar, the military governor of the
capital. The general stands in front of us, not as a memory from
Hitler's time, but as a piece of solid steel, six feet two and forty
years old. He moves to his desk, opens the drawer, takes out his
pistol and shoots point-blank into the face of a trembling intellectual standing in front of him. The intellectual dies instantly.

We are not in a movie called *The Night of the Generals.* We are
living through the night of the generals. Bakhtiar himself has shot
so many people that if we are to shoot him for every man he has
killed, we must put a thousand bullets into his body. Later, he
himself turns against the regime and is shot by members of
SAVAK, the police organization he had helped create through the
assistance of the CIA and the FBI.

But our appalling night of the generals is endless. We take a
walk westward to the office of the Prime Minister of Iran in the
latter part of 1953. There we see General Fazlullah Zahedi, a man
trained by the Nazis before the war to take over the affairs of the
country in case Reza Shah fails to comply with the wishes of
the German dictator. Reza Shah abdicates under pressure from the
British and the Soviets. The general is trapped by the British
before he is able to make a move. When he is arrested, the following items are found in his hiding place: "a collection of German
automatic weapons, silk underwear, some opium, letters from
German parachutists operating in the hills, and an illustrated register of Teheran's most exquisite prostitutes."[2]

Zahedi is later picked by the CIA to oust Prime Minister
Mossadeq. Immediately, he arms all the pimps and the goons, and
agitates all the prostitutes and pickpockets from the red-light dis-

[2] David Wise and Thomas B. Ross, *The Invisible Government* (New York, Vintage,
1974), p. 111.

trict in Teheran, to march against Mossadeq under the leadership of Sha'ban the Brainless, one of the formidable goons of the city. From that moment on, Iran will be the realm of the night, filled with spies, goons, informants, pimps and prostitutes, the night of the Shah, the Supreme Commander. As the apex of a pyramid of corruption and treason, the Supreme Commander deserves our observation from every angle.

A friend of mine tells me there is going to be a masquerade in the palace of Princess Shams, the Shah's older sister. The Princess lives with her husband, Mehrdad Pahlbod, the Minister of Culture and Art, outside the city of Karaj, in Mehrdasht (Lovefield), thirty miles to the west of Teheran.

"How do you know about it?" I ask.

"My girl friend who works in the oil company is invited."

"Are you going too?" I ask.

"She wants to take me along as her fiancé."

I begin to wonder. I have always wanted to know what happens at one of those royal parties, but I have never had the chance.

"Can I come with you?" I ask.

"That's impossible. They'll know immediately who you are, and we'll all get into trouble."

"I thought you said it was a masquerade."

"So what?"

"I could take a mask."

"No, you cannot. Two men accompanying one woman will arouse the suspicion of the guards."

"Don't be clever," I say. "The guards are used to even a hundred men accompanying a woman."

We discuss it further and decide that we shouldn't take risks. A few days later I receive a call from my friend:

"Listen, it seems that I won't be able to go to the party. I shouldn't let you miss the best chance of your life. I'm sick. Come to my place, take my car and the girl, and go to the party."

He couldn't be more generous. When I start to thank him, he stops me:

"But find a mask. I don't have one!"

And he hangs up.

The girl doesn't have the slightest idea why I want to accompany her to the palace. She thinks I am being kind to her. She has studied in most of the famous boarding schools in France and England, and in her speech everything but the word "order," which betrays her Persian background, is either French or English. I find it easier to speak English with her. She feels happier that way.

The parkway leads directly to the Princess's palace. We drive through factories to our right and left until we reach the green, flat land, with tall trees silhouetting the crimson sunset on the horizon. As we rush toward the palace the girl tells me about her daddy living in France, and her mummy living in Britain, each with a new partner and in their separate villas. She points to a row of trees in the distance to my left and tells me that it is called *Shahdasht* (Shah's Field) and is where the Queen Mother lives. I tell her I have seen the Queen Mother on TV, but I don't say I think she has the ugliest and the most hypocritical face I have ever seen. The girl tells me that all the lands in the area belong to the Queen Mother or the Princess, but they are selling them piecemeal— mostly to army officers, SAVAK agents and other government officials.

She speaks so innocently of SAVAK that it would seem the agency is just another internationally known orchestra, there to perform in the presence of the Shah and the Queen at Rudaki Hall and depart the next day. I pretend that I appreciate everything she tells me, particularly the feeling of health and light and music she conveys despite my black feelings toward everything and everyone. We arrive at the gate of Mehrdasht. She gives her name to the guard and identifies me as her fiancé. We drive in, put on our masks in the car and get out. I am the royal clown, she is the Chinese dragon. We walk into the building.

> In the palace, all flashed like a clock-dial,
> precipitate laughter in gloves, a moment
> spanning the passageways, meeting
> the newly killed voices and the buried blue mouths.
>   Out of sight,
> lament was perpetual and fell, like a plant and its
>   pollen,
> forcing a lightless increase in the blinded, big leaves.[3]

[3] Pablo Neruda, *Five Decades: A Selection*, transl. by Ben Belitt (New York, Grove Press, 1974), p. 89.

It is a zoo in a glass tower. There are no kings, queens, princes, princesses, generals, ministers or secret agents here. There are beasts instead. Nobody speaks the language of human beings here. The gory shadows of these animals are reflected on the walls and the mirrors. The beasts hop up and down on the tiles and silk rugs, howling, bleating, roaring, mewing, grinding their teeth and breathing savagely through their palpitating nostrils. It is like being in a public bath with lepers. The tails, the muzzles, the claws and paws rise in the air, scratching at each other, touching and twisting each other, cornering, buggering each other, and sinking in an infernal, abysmal pleasure. Are these mules, jackasses, apes, leopards, dragons, sharks and gorillas the chosen members of our society? Is this zoo the ruling class of Iran?

A mask externalizes what is inside. Here the masks are projections of the mind. They conceal the faces so that what is hidden will strip itself naked of all that is shame and fear, and rise to the level and dimension of exteriority. Masks are interiorities objectified. Otherwise, there would be no reason why I myself should use the mask of the clown. The poet is certainly a clown at this moment in history—or maybe at all moments in history. The absurdity of the situation is so overpowering and crushing that to comment on its *Weltanschauung* I consider simply getting up and reciting to my beastly audience Lucky's soliloquy from *Waiting for Godot:*

> Given the existence as uttered forth in the public works of Puncher and Wattmann of a personal God quaquaquaqua with white beard quaquaquaqua outside time without expansion who from the heights of divine apathia divine athambia divine aphasia[4]

But my mind is interrupted by something. I have a feeling that something is about to happen in the hall of beasts. The animals look extremely subdued, almost deflated, with ears and muzzles dilapidated, and sides diluted and shrunk. I look around to find my dragonet of boarding schools and seek her innocent advice. She is nowhere to be found. I can hear only the barking of a dog. Nothing more. It seems that others are also listening, with their heads obediently turned in the direction of the door and the windows

[4] *I can't go on, I'll go on: A Selection from Samuel Beckett's Work,* Richard W. Seaver, ed. (New York, Grove Press, 1976), p. 413.

from which the sound is heard. I listen more carefully.

There is a sudden cough, then another, and a third, each punctuated with an equal interval of silence. Then a yelping that extends to half a dozen coughs, then silence, and then another yelping of equal length. The interval between the coughs disappears, and I hear the howl of a dog in pain, or with rabies, or being chased by a pack of wolves. The howl breaks into a whine and whimper, and fades away. There is a moment of silence during which this whole congregation of bestiality waits in obeisance. Then the silence is torn to shreds by the sudden outburst of a dozen volleys of turbulent barks, and a huge dog jumps into the hall from one of the windows and assails the other animals, biting their ankles, ears and buttocks. The animals snuggle to it, letting it do whatever it pleases. They even embrace its bites. These lions, gorillas, panthers and vultures are the dog's inferiors. Then someone behind me breaks into my dream: "His Imperial Majesty, the Shah of Shahs, the Light of the Aryans!" I am dumfounded. I withdraw behind the other animals and hide. A king turned into a dog may tear a clown to pieces.

We are all jammed into a smaller hall, where we sit and watch an adult movie. It is a cheap film, a mediocre sexist extravaganza in which men trample on women and girl-children, and in several cases rape them. This must have the utmost appeal for the zoo dwellers; after all, they are the professional rapists of a whole nation. The so-called liberator of the Iranian women, and his sisters who participate in all organizations for women's liberation in the world, amuse themselves with the sexist films of the underground world. But why should I be surprised? Women have always been, for the ruling class men in Iran, a collection of things with holes in them. As for the princesses, haven't they always thought of the men around them as thingified stags and depersonalized male organs?

The most nauseating scene takes place afterwards, when the animals are already at each other's crotches. Then they move out into the field around the building. The smell from the newly mown grass reaches their nostrils. Soon the fresh grass will be trampled under their naked bodies. Beasts copulating in the open! I walk to the car and sit down with the mask on my face.

The next evening I see in the paper the names of five men who have been executed by firing squad. Their pictures have been published, too. The paper says they are all smugglers. Are they? When I was tortured and shaven three years later, and my picture was taken with a number on my chest, I resembled exactly one of those smugglers. The Shah kills the opposition not only as the opposition, but also on trumped-up charges such as smuggling.

In that very paper I see the dead face of a man sunk in dementia and so badly deformed that it would be impossible for anyone to recognize it. The Justice Department of the City of Karaj has published the picture in the paper, asking for people's help in identifying the man. The man has been killed and his body thrown among the trees between Karaj and Mehrdasht. Who is he? Nobody knows. But other pictures are published later in the same place in the paper. Other demented faces. Who do they belong to? I am told in 1973 by two prisoners in two separate instances that all those faces are of victims of the SAVAK and other intelligence agencies of the government. There are living witnesses to this, but one example achieved even world publicity: that of Hedayatollah Matin-Daftari. Mr. David Carliner, attorney for the case of Khosrow Kalantari, a student in danger of being deported to Iran in 1968 by the U.S. Immigration and Naturalization Service, interviewed Mr. Matin-Daftari when he was in Teheran:

> Mr. Daftari confirmed the information that he had in fact been taken into custody by persons who identified themselves as the police intelligence members, but who were not officers of the SAVAK, at approximately 7 P.M. on April 3rd, 1968, as he was leaving his office to go to his home; that he was blindfolded and taken to a room in a building which he sensed to be in the city of Teheran; that he was beaten by his captors; that thereafter he was driven a number of miles outside of the city and removed from the car; that his blindfold was then removed, and that he was shoved down a hill, while his captors drove away. Mr. Daftari stated that my information that he was beaten to a loss of consciousness was incorrect and that he was conscious at all times. His captors gave no explanation for their conduct. Mr. Daftari did not offer any explanation.[5]

[5] *Documents on the Pahlavi Reign of Terror in Iran: Eyewitness Reports and Newspaper Articles,* a portfolio presented by (Iran Report) The Documentation Center of Confederation of Iranian Students—National Union (Postfach 16247, 6 Frankfurt/M, German Federal Republic, n.d.), pp. 154–55.

When observers say that people simply disappear in Teheran, they are not wrong. If Mr. Daftari had died under torture, no one would have known anything about his identity. Fortunately, he was able to get up, walk away and find shelter in the house of an Iranian writer who would, under no circumstances, betray him to the police.

The situation had changed in 1973, when I came out of prison. When there was a rumor that they were going to rearrest me, I took all my correspondence and a few manuscripts out of my apartment to the houses of a dozen friends and asked them to keep them for me. They all rejected my request. I left them in the house of a distant relative, without telling him that they might be sensitive to SAVAK. All the papers were lost after a few months due to the carelessness of people who felt no obligation to protect literary documents.

A woman in her early forties walks into the office of *Ferdowsi* magazine in 1971. She is extremely elegant and beautiful. She has written a short story, and she wants me to read it and give her my opinion. She doesn't look like a professional short-story writer. The piece is only a few pages long, and I read it as she is sitting beside me, watching my face.

The story is called "Revenge." I tell her I don't see any signs of revenge in the story. The plot involves a highly placed minister who divorces his wife; the wife is solicited by a very important pimp whose identity is very confusing. She is taken to the bedroom of a far more significant personage whose identity is even more puzzling. She becomes his mistress. Then one day she is told not to come to him any more.

I speak very politely: "I don't think we can publish this story very successfully."

"I don't want to publish it. I want to know whether it means anything to you."

"Well, it doesn't mean anything to me."

She gets up and goes away. A few days later I receive a telephone call from her. We meet. She speaks of the document behind the story. I really don't know why she trusts me. I don't believe that I could easily include her among my readers. But she finally convinces me that her story is true: the minister is her former husband; the woman is she herself; the pimp is the most famous court pimp, A.M.; the man into whose bedroom she is taken is the Shah, and the bedroom is located in the palace.

I tell her I am not interested in gossip, and she tells me that we people should open our eyes and look at the reality behind gossip.

"Ninety percent of what you hear in the court is about who slept with whom, and the court bedrooms determine the fate of your people. All appointments are made through the decree of the bedroom."

Then she goes on describing her own affair. She draws such a vivid picture of everyone and everything that I tell her if she wrote the way she spoke, she would produce one of the best stories in the world.

"On the way up to the palace, A.M. says that if I let anyone know about what's going to happen to me, that'll be the end of me. A.M. puts his hand on his throat and makes the signal of cutting it with his hand, as if his hand were a knife. I promise him that I won't tell anyone. He says I've been given an honor that very few people get to have in their lives . . . Then I'm led into a room in which a large bed draped with silk stands in the corner.

"Suddenly the Shah appears through another door and walks toward me. This is the first time I've seen him without his glasses. He tries to impress me with his eyes. He looks exactly like the times when he gets a bouquet of flowers from a young schoolgirl. This is the first time I notice his very bushy eyebrows. He goes back and puts a record on the gramophone. He has a red-striped shirt and a pair of comfortable pants on. I don't know how I'm performing. I didn't know that I was being taken to him. He smiles. He says a few kind words. In the middle of the dance we slowly move to the bed.

"Every Monday, for a period of six months, we sleep with each other in the same room. Later, I find that there are others who go to the same room, mostly people like myself, and he sleeps with them. Then we are all simply handed to the other dignitaries in the court."

"But why did you call the story 'Revenge'?"

"Six months ago my son from my first husband—not the minister, but an ordinary man who was forced by the minister to divorce me—was arrested, tortured and tried, and now nobody knows where he is. People disappear every day and night. By telling my life story, I'm trying to take my revenge."

This whole thing sounds like a story from the Middle Ages, but isn't Iran living its dark ages at this moment in history? The Iranian court thinks of everyone, man and woman, as courtesans. An opposition paper in 1945 warned the people of the religious city of Mashad to hide their daughters and wives because one of the princes was coming to visit the city. The members of the Shah's harem live in the houses of the Iranian ministers, prime ministers, generals and similar "respected authorities" of the government. The collective consciousness of the people of Iran is made up of the names and affairs of men and women who have had something to do with the bedrooms of the Shah and the Royal Family. The myth is of the most ancient quality, with its ever-fresh reflections in present history. Behind the myth we see the ugly face of corruption unfolding its wrinkled reality.

A story is told of one of the Qajar kings (the dynasty preceding the present Pahlavi dynasty) who exhausted all his sources of income, had his son recircumcised so that he would collect the *Shabash* (gifts) which rich courtiers had to present as a traditional gratuity at the celebrations, sold the gifts to these very courtiers and went on a tour of Europe. After a few months he came back very depressed because he had fallen in love with a woman he met in Europe and had to leave her behind for religious reasons. When he got extremely nostalgic for the woman, he had the son recircumsized once more and took off with the money to see her. None of the hundred and fifty wives and concubines could satisfy him and keep him in the country. On his return he again felt very dejected and ordered another circumcision. By this time the son was eighteen. When the order for circumcision came, he opened up his fly and shouted: "Look at it, Your Majesty, there is hardly anything left for additional surgery. I already look like one of your castrated slaves!" The King had to reconsider his fund-raising methods.

The same Qajar king was shot down by a revolutionary in a shrine fifteen miles to the south of the capital. The courtiers were afraid that if the populace knew what had happened, there would be an uprising. His carriage was brought to the gate of the shrine, and his corpse was seated, with all its medals and ribbons, on the lap of one of the King's goons. The prime minister sat by the corpse in the carriage, smiling discreetly and pretending that he was simply giving a report to the King. The goon underneath hoisted up one of the dead arms to wave to the people gathered along the way. The carriage was driven for fifteen miles through the streets of the capital. The prime minister kept on smiling and reporting, the dead King was waving his hand and the miserable goon was choking underneath the dead body. The people shouted: "Hail to the Shah! Long live the Shah!"

A few years ago, when the present Shah was opening the joint session of the assembly and the senate, one of the senators fainted because of exhaustion. In the ceremony everyone had to stand as the Shah read the inauguration address. The old senator raised himself to his feet but in a moment fell down again, only to lift himself up again and collapse in another fall. No one had the courage to help him. He died on the spot. The Shah went on reading the inauguration address. Such is the significance of ritual and ceremony for the Shah and his ruling class.

Of all the ceremonies during the last thirty-five years of his reign, two sets of festivities are of the greatest significance and most worthy of our appraisal.

The Shah's coronation takes place on October 28, 1967. The preparation for the ceremony goes on for more than two years. The King, the Queen and the courtiers have had to watch the film of Queen Elizabeth's coronation a dozen times to produce an exact duplication. They practice day and night. Professor Lotf'ali Surat-gar, the court poet, tells his colleagues in the University of Teheran that everything is ready: the King, the Queen, the Crown Prince, the ministers and generals have practiced everything more than twenty times. The poet is going to recite the coronation ode.

The ceremony is a parade of tens of five-pound pearls and thousands of diamonds, emeralds and brilliants; Dior patterns, gold-studded mantles, peacock feathers; a peacock throne, three feet wide, three feet deep, seven feet high, inlaid with 27,773 precious stones; an Imperial Carriage of ebony made in Vienna; belts of gold mail with sapphires and emeralds, a gold scepter, white cashmere, blue trousers with red stripes, thousands of medals and ribbons; and a million Iranian flags ordered from abroad to decorate hundreds of arches erected in honor of the coronation. The buildings carry flags in every nook. The Shah crowns himself, his queen and his crown prince in the Hall of Mirrors in Golestan Palace. The carriage takes the royal triangle to the Marble Palace.

The Shah's biggest hit comes in October, 1971, when he celebrates the two thousand five hundredth anniversary of the Iranian Empire. A few months before the actual celebrations start, he has more than ten thousand suspects arrested and tortured so that when the guests arrive they will see no opposition to the throne. A student of mine tells me later: "There was no room in the prison cells. We slept in the corridors and the rest rooms, and even in the torture chambers." The press comes under the tight grip of SAVAK. Most of the famous writers of the country are thrown out of the press and the publishing houses. For months we are ordered to withhold any writing because SAVAK is afraid we might make allusions to the millions of dollars being spent for the festivities. When the celebrities arrive, people are told not even to appear in the streets because if someone shoots at random it may result in the death of at least a couple of world leaders. This may tarnish the image the Shah has created in the eyes of the world of Iran as the great "Island of Stability" in the Middle East.

Among the celebrities there are sixteen presidents, nine kings, five queens, two dozen princes and princesses, a dozen sheiks and emirs representing the oil, gold and copper industries and most of the ruling classes and governments of the world. Emperor Haile Selassie of Ethiopia, short, bearded, catlike, stands with clean-shaven, funny-looking, tall Spiro Agnew. What a concatenation of Beckettian absurdity. The King of Denmark, who was in fact arrested by one of the SAVAK agents for having sauntered away from his imperial tent without the permission of the "authorities," stands like the ghost of Hamlet's father beside a row of turbaned fat cats from the Persian Gulf. The sheiks are pissed off because they have not been allocated royal tents like the rest of the kings present, with bathtubs, mirrors and all the fauna and flora.

We watch the event on television. The Shah is the master of ceremonies. He walks to Passargade where the tomb of King Cyrus is located. The celebrities follow him at some distance. We hear the Shah's weak and childish voice: "Cyrus! You rest in peace, I am awake!" When the Shah speaks in this ludicrous manner, Agnew touches his nose and the King of Denmark squints his eyes as if to say: "Adieu, adieu; remember me, I've sworn't." Dust rises from the wind in the desert, disturbing the eyes of the rulers of the world. Several delicate princesses cough into their handkerchiefs. A storm may rise and cleanse the surface of the earth from all these rulers who have shown they are the representatives of the thieves of the world or will be so later. I can easily imagine the wind lifting the frail Haile Selassie on its wings, his black chihuahua chasing him, Spiro Agnew trailing behind. The masters and mistresses of the world leave this part of the desert for the slopes of Persepolis and an encampment of luxurious tents—all made in Europe and flown along with a thousand other items via Teheran and Shiraz to Persepolis.

The ceremony starts right away. Hundreds of royal guards and SAVAK agents have grown beards in order to resemble more closely the armies of all the dynasties of Iranian kings throughout history. The beards have been trimmed and shaped to the size and pattern of beards in archaeological monuments and museum paintings. First come the armies of the Achamenians, saluting Haile Selassie and the rest, then the Seleucidae and the Sassanides—pre-Islamic armies, one saluting with the hand stretched out to the left, the other with the hand stretched out to the front in the Nazi manner and the third using the French style. Now it is the turn of the Islamic period, so many dynasties that it proves impossible to find enough convenient patterns of military salutes. The armies of one dynasty blow their noses en masse, it seems, to show their military respect to the leaders of the world; those of another dynasty appear to be scratching their ears. The whole scene is a clumsy admixture of *Ben-Hur*, *El Cid* and *The Ten Commandments*—with only Charlton Heston lacking—played up to such heights of cinematic absurdity that one feels fairly certain the Shah himself must be laughing at his bearded phonies. Fortunately, the dust from the desert and from the stamping of feet is so thick and high that sometimes one is totally lost in a maze of confusions. The kings, the queens, the princesses, the princes and all the rest of the leaders of the world have tucked their handkerchiefs in their mouths and noses, and are wiping the sweat from their faces with their sleeves. If only one could wrap up all the spectators, guards and the imperial director of this black comedy in a collective winding sheet and pack them all off to hell! The world would certainly be a better place.

This proves to be impossible. The leaders of the world wash up, have their siesta and return to the banquet, drowned in gold, diamonds, brilliants, sapphires and silk. The food is as various and colorful as the jewels and the more than thirty genuine crowns: "quail eggs stuffed with caviar (the only Iranian food at the dinner, Farah complained), lobster Mousse with Sauce Nantua, flaming lambs with arak, a traditional dish of peacock with foie gras, platters of cheese, a salad of cheese with raspberries, champagne sherbet, and to mark Farah's thirty-third birthday, a seventy-pound cake. Maxim's was in charge of catering and provided 165 chefs, wine stewards and waiters—not to mention 25,000 bottles of wine."[6]

Twenty-five thousand years of poverty are honored by the richest men on earth. Thirty-four million people have been excluded from the banquet, from all the banquets of the world. Jets carry the world leaders back to their home countries. Not one fat cat has asked a question about the Shah's political prisoners. The representatives from China and the Soviet Union are as silent as those of the West.

The Shah's mania for ceremonies has no end. When he came back a few years ago from a long vacation in Europe, another great performance was staged. Its directors were conscious of the fact that the Shah's long absence might represent to the populace his indifference to their plight. They immediately called it the "Oil Victory," pretending that OPEC talks for higher oil prices were initiated by the Shah and that the victory for the Middle East would not have been won had the King of Kings, the Light of the Aryans, refused to take the necessary measures.

He landed at the airport to the cheers of thousands of people rushed to the area in army buses and trucks. There was a rumor that one out of every four persons was a SAVAK agent. The Shah drove into the city in an open car, giving the agents and guards the fright of their lives. They ran after him and in front of him, their hands on their hilts, watching with wild eyes the innocent populace and awaiting all the while the bomb or the bullet that might put an end to the life of their hero.

The procession came to a halt only once, in front of a long line of religious leaders who bent as low as they could when the Shah prepared to step down from the car. One of the leaders thanked the Shah for what he had done to wrest the rights of the Iranian

[6] Gerard de Villiers, *The Imperial Shah* (Little, Brown, Boston, Toronto, 1976), p. 284.

people from the clutches of the Western usurpers. The Shah nodded and smiled, smiled and nodded. Another of the religious leaders handed him a volume of the Koran, the religious book of the Moslems. He kissed it and turned it over to one of his minions. Then he was driven away to the frantic cheers of the crowd.

I watched the ceremony on television. There was something cynical in the Shah's eyes as he stood facing the priests. Who were these men? You might get a few corrupt religious leaders to pay their respects to him in public, but not this many. The riddle was solved for me by a friend who had heard something about them at a gathering. One of the Shah's adjutants had said that a whole company of the Iranian army had been ordered to grow beards for a period of two months. The poor sergeants and soldiers feared they were scheduled to be dispatched to Dzofar in Oman, where the Shah's army was helping King Qabus defeat a revolutionary movement, and were relieved upon finally being told of their mission. They were given turbans, robes and rosaries, and were strung along the royal route. Later they shaved off the camouflage.

Our hero's hypocrisy can be seen everywhere. When he was shown on Iranian television a few years ago praying in the mosque along with another Moslem king, he bent whenever he was supposed to get up, and got up whenever he was supposed to bend. In fact, he watched through the corners of his eyes to follow the other king, whose movements proved too fast to follow. In desperation, he turned around to his minions, something which a Moslem is not supposed to do at such times. The minions were as helpless as the Shah, and he gave up praying.

The mask of hypocrisy is the most outstanding feature of his reign. The shrine of Imam Reza, one of the sacred places of the Shi'ite sect of Islam, is swept and washed clean because the Shah is going to pay his respects to the Imam in Mashad. He stands there in his typically pensive and melancholy mood, beribboned in military uniform, touching the fence with his lips and hands, while the television film makers videotape him for the populace. Then he takes off to gamble in St. Moritz, or to ski, or to sell oil and buy arms in the capitals of Europe and Washington.

What is behind the mask? Who is he? What is he made of?

The Shah of Shahs, who claims 2,500 years of royal ancestry for himself in the annals of modern history, was born in Shahr-e

Now, the red-light district of Teheran.[7] His mother was the daughter of a Caucasian sergeant, a very superstitious woman who taught her son blind belief in hobgoblins, apparitions and the ghosts of imams. After Reza Khan's coronation in 1925, this woman was given the title Tadj-al-molook, which literally means the Crown of Kings. Nothing else is known beyond this about the Shah's mother.

His father was the famous Reza Khan, who rose from absolute obscurity to absolute dictatorship. He was so illiterate that the journalists of the country would play all kinds of tricks on him through simple literary devices. He would honestly believe that he was being praised by the press until he was informed by those around him of the intentions behind the metaphors; then he would become angry enough to sign orders for a few more shootings and throttlings in prison. He was so illiterate that he found it difficult to pronounce the names of his ministers who came with all kinds of historical titles. He was cruel, not only to the people, but also to the members of his family. I heard from Mrs. Sh—an old woman of about eighty who had been a close friend of Tadj-al-molook during the Reza Shah period—that anytime the King summoned his son, the present shah, the boy would come back in wet pants and for a few days would be totally confused. The Shah himself has told us in his official and unofficial biographies that he and his sisters and brothers and their numerous mothers and stepmothers were terrified of the brutal man. If this was the case with the whole family, the condition of the nation was no better. Bozorg Alavi, a famous Iranian novelist of the post–Reza Shah era who now lives in exile, tells us that out of rage and nervousness in prison he had pulled out his beard with his own hands,[8] and I remember a prisoner with the initials F.R. in my cell who would pluck his beard from his chin in utter helplessness and fear. Nineteen seventy-three was the mirror of 1937.

The chronic illiteracy was acutely felt when it came to the education of the Crown Prince. Reza Shah put his son in a school which he had built for him and the sons and daughters of the dignitaries in the palace. The boy proved to be a very bad student. The King packed him off to Le Rosey, the famous Swiss school for

---

[7] Ibid., p. 24.

[8] Bozorg Alavi, *Panjah-o-seh Nafar (The Fifty-Three)*, p. 45. For reasons of persecution by the security agents of Iran, this book has no publishing data.

the offspring of European aristocracy, where he learned French and English but never succeeded in getting a diploma. The super-rich students in this school detested everyone except their own clan, and the boy felt very deeply the hatred to which he was subjected. In the eyes of his peers, he came from a country of things and not of human beings, and after all he was the son of an illiterate colonel while their families had been brought up gen-eration after generation in the grand palaces of Europe. It was here that the present shah was first instilled with the hatred of the people of his own country.

At first, the Shah wanted the students at Le Rosey to respect him as his father's servants did. This proved to be impossible, because the kids thought of this "corporal's son" from the Middle East as their inferior. They were negligent of the fact that another corporal who had risen to power in the heart of Europe had founded a racist cult stronger than the cult of their doomed aristo-cratic values and was even then gnawing into the heart of all the democracies of the world. The Iranian corporal had already shown allegiance to the Aryan cult of the German corporal by recruiting as many spies as the Fuehrer could afford to give him and begun the purge of the Iranian "communists" as well as the expulsion of Semitic words from the Persian vocabulary. He believed more strongly than before that at the origin of everything lies the arro-gance of power. When in 1936 he called the boy back, he simply lifted him on one hand above his head and showed him that what he had learned at Le Rosey should be washed down with this single exhibition of power, that his education should not count for much.

But the boy already had a language barrier separating him from his own people. If only he could communicate with them in French and English! Everything would be so easy. He had detested his peers at school, yet he had gained enough knowledge of their ways to know that they all considered the peoples of Asia, Africa and the Middle East as subhuman species. The young man became their equal simply by hating what they hated and loving what they loved. They hated the people of the colonies, and although Iran was not an official colony of a European nation, there was no difference between the people who had actually been colonized and those of Iran who lived under the iron-clad fist of Reza Khan and the unofficial hegemony of the British. They also loved the blond princesses of their own palaces in Europe. Later, the Shah imported blond women from Europe by the dozen to satisfy his taste for a whiter flesh, and when he married Farah, his third wife, so much facial surgery had to be done that she came to look like a mummified movie star from Hollywood.

There is not a single note or allusion to prove that the young boy read anything interesting when he was in Europe. He lived in the happy cell of his ignorant youth. What were the major intellectual influences on his character when he was living at the center of all the intellectual and sociohistorical events of the world? Which one of the great personalities of his time was the subject of his study and appreciation? None. A blinding wall had fallen over his mind. He learned only one thing: to look upon the people of his own country as subhumans, just as the European princes looked upon the peoples of the colonies.

He gradually became the colonialist in his home country. Whenever he was in Europe or, later, the United States, he would open up and socialize, but at home he was a god—a frowning, dark-glassed, savage god—who had come from a better world and was superior to the rest of the population. He was E. M. Forster's Rony in *A Passage to India*, stricken with the schizophrenia of a young man who has nothing wrong with him when he is in London, but who turns into a god when he sets foot in Chandrapour and hates to mix with the earthly insects of the world. He became a missionary, and later he even had a book written and published under the title *Mission for My Country*; its main thrust was that as a missionary sent both by God and the West, he was doing superbly. In Iran he gradually replaced the colonialist colonel, the Christian missionary, the politician, the representative of the company and the professional henchman of imperialism.

The reason he brought in so many missionaries from the Western countries, particularly the United States, was that he wanted to build a larger Le Rosey in Iran. These advisers did to Iran what the official colonialist had done to India, Southeast Asia, China and the whole of Africa—and is doing to Latin America. They bought the raw materials at low prices, turned them into manufactured commodities and sold them to the hundreds of millions of peoples who had no industry at their disposal. What the Dutch merchant, the Belgian mining companies and the British settler had done to Africa and India, what the white man had done and keeps doing to South Africa, the Shah and his adviser friends, in the grand Le Rosey they created on the slopes of Ablurz mountains, did to the people of Iran.

The CIA coup in 1953, the so-called land reform via White Revolution which began in 1963 and, according to the New York *Times* "is a joke,"[9] the massacre of thousands of men and women in the country and the imprisonment of several hundred thousand others during the last thirty-five years of his reign of terror amount to only one thing: the consistent plunder of Iran's wealth through the perpetuation of imperialist rule in this country. The Shah is the stooge of the multinational corporations, but the country's wealth is so great, and the percentages and the bribes are so immense, that the Shah can claim to be an independent stooge. In fact, this position is so acutely a part of his consciousness that in a recent interview with Mike Wallace of the CBS television network he brought it up himself without there having been previous allusions to it by the correspondent: "So you would like me to be your stooge?"[10] Selling the oil would not by itself give him this status, but selling it the way he does and desperately buying arms in such quantities—arms for which nobody can claim any use except through a direct U.S. involvement in the area—would certainly turn him into one of the basest stooges of imperialism in the world.

But the Shah accepts his position in the way that a duped missionary undertakes a spiritual obligation. Over and over again, he has told the press it is not an honor to be the ruler of a poor and miserable nation Over and over again, he has said that his people are not yet ready for democracy. And recently he has reiterated that Western democracy was not made for the Iranians, and that Iran has its own traditions at the heart of which stands his crown. And he has told the press a hundred times that he is serving his country by divine right, and that all the attempts on his life through the long and turbulent years of his reign have failed because divine authority has stayed the hand of the mur-

---

[9] Alden Whitman, New York *Times* (September 18, 1976). He says: "But Iran is an authoritarian military state; its land reform is a joke; its politics are corrupt and feudal; and its reigning head, armed to the teeth by the Pentagon, poses a very real danger to peace and stability in the Middle East."

[10] New York *Times* (October 22, 1976).

derer before he could aim and shoot into the heart and mind of Iran's history.

As soon as Reza Shah abdicated in 1941, his son became the father of the nation in the same way his father was the figurehead of the family. He expected everybody to wet his pants when he appeared. But perhaps the greatest characteristic of the new king was his hatred of those intellectuals who had a better understanding of both the West and Iran. His total alienation from both the East and West resulted in two tragic catastrophes for Iranian culture: first, all fresh voices were nipped in the bud or brutally suppressed, and a traditional culture of the most degenerate nature was revived and presented as the only identity Iranians could possess; second, all that was stupid, mediocre and meaningless in the West was introduced into Iran. This only contributed to the uprooting of the healthy elements of the traditional culture and prevented the emergence of young, dynamic cultural forces of a modern type.

These two catastrophes took place in the name of Iranism and of the national Aryan spirit of Iran, which the Iranians were led to think of as quite distinct elements in the Middle East. Walls were built between Iran and the rest of the Middle East. We knew what was happening in the artistic circles of France, England and the United States, but we knew hardly anything about the names and works of the Arab writers, the Turks, the Pakistanis, the Indians or even the Afghanis, with whom the Persians in the country shared a culture and language. The Shah's alienation from both the East and the West became the dominant pattern of the culture of his reign. If there is something called colonial culture in Iran, it is the Shah who is responsible for it.

Jalal Al-Ahmad, one of the foremost intellectuals of recent years, wrote in 1961 in his great manifesto *Westomania:* "Our country is the country of barren deserts and high walls; mud walls in the villages, and brick walls in the cities. And this is not only in the outside world; walls have been erected in the internal world of everyone."[11] Walls were built in every work of art and in every symbol and metaphor. A withering, dying national culture came into existence at the expense of all that could have been beautiful, lively and permanent.

[11] Jalal Al-Ahmad, *Garbzadegi* (Westomania) (Teheran, 1961), p. 48, published in part by Kayhan-e Mah, in full by an underground publisher.

On the other hand, a culture of resistance was born which Franz Fanon has called in other places "a culture condemned to secrecy."[12] Several hermetic schools of literature were introduced, each more difficult and esoteric than the other, and each school and its devices and symbology were subjected to the examination of the Shah's censorship. The Shah was as brutal to the creators of these metaphors as he was to those who hurled hand grenades at the iron walls of his thuggery.

The last concrete image I have of the Shah belongs to my prison days. Dr. Rezvan, my interrogator, asked me what I meant by "the horrendous prehistoric beast of tradition." I didn't know how he wanted me to respond to this question; I didn't answer. He asked me a second time. I didn't want him to get angry; his anger could easily mean the torture chamber. I qualified his question with a new question:

"Who was it that ordered my arrest and torture? Who was it?"

> And bludgeon by bludgeon, on the terrible waters,
> scale over scale in the bog,
> the snout filled with silence and slime
> and vendetta was born.[13]

[12] Franz Fanon, *The Wretched of the Earth* (New York, Grove Press, 1968), p. 237.
[13] Pablo Neruda, p. 89.

THE STRANGULATION OF IRANIAN WRITERS

There is no doubt in my mind that two factors were immediately responsible for my imprisonment and torture by the Shah's government: my involvement in all the antirepression activities of the Iranian writers and intellectuals, and my personal activities and writings against the oppression of the nationalities of Iran by the Shah's regime. I will speak of these two factors in some detail.

My literary career coincides roughly with the post-coup era, from 1953 to the present. I wrote generally of my personal experiences in the context of the broader scope of experiences of the underpriviledged masses of the society. I introduced these experiences in each form I used, be it poetry or fiction or literary and social criticism.

The whole fabric of my writing is composed of two elements. The first involves the experiences of a family belonging on my mother's side to Iran's landless peasantry since time immemorial and, on my father's side, to Iran's pauperized, traditional working class of meager skills. My individual experiences fit right into the pattern of the experience of the majority of my people in Azarbaijan and the majority of the people in Iran. I went with my mother to the village of Ravasan on the south of Tabriz, worked in the fields, helped my father load and unload bricks from the surrounding factories in Tabriz, worked in the stocking factory, the tea packaging plant and public bathhouses, and cleaned people's houses and the mosques in the neighborhood; as a youth I worked at all those jobs considered by everyone everywhere to be the hardest, least pleasant and lowest paid. This was the case until I was eighteen. The second involves my inner feelings about my repressed nationality as an Azarbaijani Turk whose language was taken away from him by the Pahlavi regime, particularly after 1946, and never given back to him.

I learned Persian at great cost to my identity as an Azarbaijani Turk, and only after I had mastered this language and was on the point of becoming thoroughly Persianized was I reminded of my roots by those who were directing polemics against me in the Persian press. Whenever I wrote something good about an originally Persian author, I was hailed as a man who had finally left behind his subhuman Turkish background and should be considered as great as the Persians; whenever I said something derogatory about a writer's work, the response was always that I was an Azarbaijani, and, given that according to Persian proverb all Azarbaijanis are *Turk-e-Khar* (Turk donkeys), whatever I had written could be of no significance at all; since what of value could a Turkish donkey have to say in regard to Persian gods? When I succeeded in establishing myself in their literary *Who's Who*, in their own language and on their own terms, they came up with the sorry notion that there was not even a single drop of Azarbaijani blood in my veins.

When the jackass finally learned to bray just like all the Persians, and the Persians were liking it, he decided for himself that he did not like it at all. He decided that if anything was wrong, it was with their brand of braying, not his. The notion of rebellion crept in. The Persians and the Persian-oriented government had taken away from me a language, an identity, a culture and a rhythm. There was something of reality, of harshness in that culture and identity. At this point in its evolution, what the Persian language and literature lacked was an adequate reflection of that reality and harshness, and I tried to breathe that spirit into them.

This sense of reality, of harshness, belonged to the most downtrodden layers of the people of the country, those who were experiencing or had experienced pauperization at the hands of the Persian or Persianized ruling classes and had been deprived or were being deprived of their own languages as well.

But I found myself in a great dilemma. I was so immersed in Persian style, form and rhythm that it would have been difficult to go back and acquire comparable skills in Turkish; moreover, nobody in the country was allowed to read and write in Turkish. There remained only one alternative: to weave that harsh reality into the fabric of the Persian language and turn that language into the medium of revolt against the upper-class Persian and Persianized rulers. That harsh reality forms the substance of my revolt, and this revolt is the essence of my writing.

It took me a long time to extricate myself from this problem. I did it in the following fashion. First, I wrote descriptions of my hometown in the form of prose, which later became a solid backdrop for the imagery of my poetry. I saw all around me alien and tongueless men and women walking in the streets of Teheran, trying to communicate but failing the minute they opened their mouths. The hostility of races toward each other, the background of suspicion on one side and the resulting insolence on the other, the nauseating arrogance of the oppressors and the deep deposits of humiliated and repressed feelings accumulated in the minds and hearts of those oppressed, plus the historical impasse created by a racist regime fashioned on Aryanomania, all contributed to my disillusionment with the dominant culture of the Persians—not only of the ruling class but also of some of my literary colleagues. These circumstances helped to fashion the language of most of my poetry, fiction and literary criticism. Its social impact was felt most deeply by my contemporaries in the field of literary criticism, because here was the area of close confrontation with and comparison, evaluation and open assault of the strongholds of hypocrisy, the ruling class and racist mentality and morality, and the pools of sentimental bile and tears. Thus criticism, in order to be effective, had, at first, to be destructive, especially in a culture with no viable literary critical tradition, so that it might later become creative to the full capacity. The language, the terminology, the rhythm and the capacity for dialogue of criticism had to be developed in all dimensions—theoretically, aesthetically, analytically—and in a short span of time.

I wrote day and night, covering page after page with literary criticism, and these writings contributed to the mainstream of dialogue among the intellectuals of the country during the sixties and early seventies. I know that many people thought I was being brutal to some of their idols as persons and as concepts. Yet if Persian literature was to raise its head above its provincial shoulders to observe a larger world of values, if the gloomy, romantic character was to cast away the dark complexion of his thoughts and examine the world of objects and ideas with fresh, healthy eyes, and if the sentimental critic was to give up his language, his foppery, his techniques of *ta'arof* and decorum, replacing them with rationality, then all my attacks were justified. Looking back on those years, I feel no compunctions about my work.

The nationality question appeared first in the form of allusions scattered in my writings. But there is a passage in my long poem "The Forest and the City" (1963) which played a significant role in my own evolution as a poet and helped me return more consciously to my roots. Poetry has sometimes a contradictory sort of magic in it. It catches you unaware. You speak about something or a pattern without knowing anything about its origins, and then suddenly, one day when you are reading it in a crowd somewhere, you find the source of your inspiration for the poem (or someone else discovers it for you). In 1965, before I began a poetry reading for the students of the University of Teheran, the person who was supposed to introduce me simply recited the following poem and sat down. Here is the passage of which I speak:

> My father was one of an old king's clowns
> My mother was of the Turkish gypsies
> All my sisters stand
> and dream of that sterile prince
> dream of the arms of powerful mountain men
> And my brothers, yes, my brothers,
> are eunuchs serving the brides of a new king
>
> I was the first son
> My eyes went dry in the city
> an alley woman stole my tambourine
>
> My father was one of an old king's clowns
> My mother was of the Turkish gypsies
> One day my father aged
> no longer made the old king laugh
> They tore out his tongue and threw it to the crows
> They carried this gift to my mother's garden
> her face like a dark rainy sky
> her hands like dead birds hanging in the air

her eyes shining wax in deep dark night
her legs stumbling doves
her shoulders made of paper
her breasts lighter than bags full of straw

My mother sang in the streets so long
her voice went blind
My mother was of the Turkish gypsies
at the end of her life no one understood her speech

My father was one of an old king's clowns
My mother was of the Turkish gypsies . . .[1]

The poem was the song of an old man singing in the streets of Teheran. I was not conscious of my Turkish roots when I wrote that song, but they were there, and later they declared themselves —throughout the bulk of my work during the next decade, as a matter of fact. The declaration of these roots was one of the major factors behind my imprisonment and torture. The potential in me was fulfilled, the subconsciously active and engaged became rationally, consciously active and engaged. I came to feel that I had been cheated out of the most valuable aspect of my identity. I came to recognize my enemy, the present establishment in Iran. I raised my voice, trying to strike back at the enemy who had done all he could to paralyze the language of my entire consciousness. I could not hit back in the language of which I had been deprived through an historical necessity devised by the enemy. I took the sword of the enemy in my hands. The enemy, by imposing his conditions on me, had given me training useful in the combat. The enemy's strongest weapon was his language, his culture, and these I had learned as much as any of the sons and daughters of the enemy. I tried to be the tongue of my oppressed nationality in the language of the oppressor. Linguistically speaking, the deep structure of my revolt against the establishment was in the language of my own nationality, but under the given historical conditions the deep structure had transformed itself into the surface structure of the Persian language. I tried to sing in the words of the master against the dominion of that very master. Now the falcon could not hear the falconer, the center could hold no longer. I was free.

Such was the dialectic of my liberation. Fanon had written

[1] The translation is by Prof. Harris Lenowitz and Reza Baraheni.

about the French torturer and his psychology in the language of the very torturer himself. Let the master as well as the slave see what the first had done to the second. And this was what happened to me.

I wrote *Masculine History* in the language of those who were responsible for the creation of that history. I asked for linguistic autonomy for the Turks and Kurds and other oppressed peoples in Iran in the language of those who had deprived those nationalities of their languages. Whenever I was asked for biographical data by a paper or an anthologist, the first thing I mentioned was that history had made me a linguistic orphan and that the oppressed nationalities should have their self-determination. The faces and events of my people filled long pages of my writing.

At the end of the summer of 1973 the establishment found the situation intolerable. I was kidnapped. But my emerging consciousness of nationality was not the sole factor responsible for my arrest and imprisonment. The other factor, equally important, was my sustained participation in activities against repression and censorship in Iran.

The censorship in Iran had always been both brutal and stupid. These two adjectives are applicable even now, despite the co-optation of many former intellectuals into the ranks of government censors. In the old times, if a poet composed anything against the established ruler of the city, the society or the country, he would be forced to lick the ink off the pages of his poem. But this was a very minor punishment. Sometimes the King would order his men to fill the poet's mouth with gold or silver till the poet, unaware of his impending fate, finally suffocated. Poets were also drowned on the orders of kings, and there are dozens of recorded instances in which they were thrown into the most horrible dungeons in the land.

During the twentieth century the writers of the country have suffered as cruelly as in the past. The poet Bahar lived a very precarious life both during the Constitutional Revolution and afterwards. Mohammad Ali Shah had the two writers and orators Malekol-Motakallemin and Sur-e-Esrafil hanged in the Bagh-e-Shah Garrison, while he himself sat on the balcony facing the gallows and ate an entire plateful of rice and kebab as he watched. Reza Shah killed Mirzadeh Eshghi, the great revolutionary poet and journalist, and had the mouth of Farrokhi-ye Yazdi, another outstanding poet, sewed with needle and thread so that he could not recite his poetry. Farrokhi stayed in prison for years, and later his bones were found at the site of a hospital which had been rented by Reza Shah's police to eliminate Iranian dissidents without a trace. Taghi Arani, a foremost political theoretician of the opposition, was eliminated while in prison.

During the present shah's reign dozens of writers have been liquidated: the journalist Mohammad Mas'oud, was allegedly killed by Princess Ashraf's goons; the journalist Karimpour-e-Shirazi died by the same hands; Morteza Kayvan, a poet, was shot right after the 1953 coup. In terms of the last few years, many names come to mind: Samad Behrangi, a short-story writer, folklorist and linguist was drowned in the river Arras on the Iran-Soviet border; his friend and colleague, Behrouz Dehghani, was tortured to death in prison while his sister, the brave Ashraf Dehghani, was being tortured and raped in the neighboring cell (though she finally escaped); Jalal Al-Ahmad, one of the most formidable writers of oppositionist literature in Iran, was mysteriously killed on the coast of the Caspian Sea; the poet Khosrow Golesorkhi was placed before a firing squad. The names of those writers and intellectuals who have suffered incarceration and/or torture during the last twenty-four years make up a very long list. Some of the outstanding names will suffice: the poets Ahmad Shamlu (Bamedad), Mehdi Akhavan-e-Sales (Omid), Nima Youshidj, Houshang Ebtehadj (Sayeh), Yadollah Ro'yai, Fereydoun Tavallali, Mohammad-Ali Sepanlou, Saeed Soltanpour, Ne'mat Mirzadeh (Azarm), Ja'far Kooshabadi; the novelists Ali-Mohammad Afghani, Ahmad Mahmoud, Mahmoud E'temadzadeh (Behazin), Fereydoun Tonokaboni, Gholamhossein Sa'edi, Mahmoud Dowlatabadi; the translators Nadjaf Daryabandari, Ebrahim Yoonesi, Djahangir Afkari, Manouchehr Hezar-khani; the Islamicists Mahdi Bazargan, Mohammad Taleghani, Ali Shareeati; the social critics Khalil Maleki, Mohammad-Reza Zamani and Vida Hadjebi Tabrizi; the theater directors Nasser Rahmaninezhad and Mohsen Yalfani; and many, many other intellectuals from other fields. If similar occasions had arisen in the United States, the blacklist of those affected would have to include all post–World War II poets, novelists, playwrights, critics, translators and theater and film directors. It is no wonder that the whole of contemporary Iranian fiction, poetry and criticism revolves around the one central theme: repression.

This theme has acquired so crucial a significance in the life of Iranian literature and the lives of its creators that a writer's authenticity and integrity are, more often than not, veritably measured by the degree to which he has suffered under torture, repression and censorship.

In order to reveal something of the inanity of the established censorship in the country, I would like to recount an incident which took place some fifty-three years ago. The historian Hossein Makki speaks of an article which was published when the present shah's father was pushing everybody around in his ultimately successful attempt to dethrone the dynasty preceding his so that he might become President of Iran. During the period between the reigns of the two dynasties there was much talk about a change of the regime from a monarchy to a republic, and Reza Khan had decided that he would first become President and later turn himself into the King. People who knew about this were afraid to talk openly about their apprehensions, so they resorted to using all kinds of literary devices to apprise their readers of Reza Khan's evil intentions.

An article was published in the press praising Reza Khan in very bombastic rhetorical language. At first glance, the article appears to be one of those mercenary pieces paid for with bribes to the press. But the writers had used a rhetorical device called *Movash-shah,* in which only the first words of each line and the whole of the last line contained the essential meaning of the piece. Separated from the rest of the article, which was pure drivel, and arranged in order, these words read:

> How could the illiterate Reza Khan, who was not even capable of introducing his Cabinet to the Parliament, be worthy of becoming the President of Iran? The security forces do not allow us to write our opinions freely. We publish, therefore, this "Movash-shah" about our opinions, and of these scoundrels we say, let the reactionaries excommunicate us![2]

Reza Khan was pleased with the piece until he was apprised of the *Movash-shah* and its intent, where upon he ordered the writers to be savagely punished.

Such devices have likewise been used to spite the censorship

[2] Hossein Makki, *Tarikh-e Bist-Saleh-ye Iran* (Twenty Years of Iranian History) (Teheran, Elmi Publications, 1944) p. 19.

in the country during the reign of the present shah. I once published a poem called "Triumphal," which dealt with the Shah's walk in front of his generals and agents and their wives. The poem eluded the notice of the Shah's censorship and was quoted in several newspapers, including some which published nothing that was anti-Shah. Only years later was I told in prison by one of the officers that he knew that I had likened the Shah to a clown and his agents to dogs. In "Fiction in the Age of Night," i.e., the age of the Shah, I wrote a whole section on the situation of repression in the country and simply signed it Bertolt Brecht. The piece is still in my book *Writing Fiction*. I even invented a reference for poor Brecht, who would have chuckled at the device.

The novelist Fereydoun Tonokaboni used a very ingenious method to get permission from the government censor for his book *Notes of a City in Chaos*. He wrote something derogatory about a revolution but didn't say which one. He only put an asterisk above the word and a short footnote on the page, reading, "See the Notes at the end of the book." These notes were not there when he submitted the book to the censors, and they gave it their approval. The book, however, was finally published with the notes at the end. One of them dealt with the revolution. The author had made allusions to the Shah's "White Revolution" and land reform. The censors came to know of this later, and Tonokaboni was arrested.

All Iranian writers have used tricks of this kind to get around the censors. In fact, Iranian poetry is full of double-and-triple-tongued metaphors. One meaning opens the secrets of repression to the people; the other conceals them from the curious eyes of the censors. Thus the new school of Iranian poetry is written on one hand from the viewpoint of the people and on the other from that of the police.

When I was in prison, parts of my interrogation dealt with some of the images and symbols I had used in my poetry. My interrogator, Dr. Rezvan, who couldn't understand a word of poetry, would dig out a line from one of my poems and write it down for me, saying, "Give me the exact meaning of this line." When I gave him the meaning he wasn't looking for, he would become enraged and shout, "Don't philosophize! Give me the meaning you are hiding!" I would swear on the head of the Shah that I was not hiding anything, that there could be no other meaning for the poem, since, if there were, surely he would have discovered it for himself.

In 1966 the government sent a directive to all the print shops ordering them to submit copies of every book they printed to the Writing Bureau of the Ministry of Arts and Culture; this was to be done before any of the books were actually published. A group of Iranian writers, including Al-Ahmad, Sa'edi and myself, went to the Prime Minister's office to protest against the directive. It was aimed at closing all the small publishing houses that put out the works of the oppositionists and, as a consequence, helping the big publishers who were on the side of the government. But its main purpose was to throttle the oppositionists and control everything they wrote. In fact, later on, when the government was arresting the writers of the opposition, many small publishers were also incarcerated and tortured.

Sa'edi wrote a report of this meeting with the Prime Minister for publication in *Jahan-e-No (The New World)*, which I edited in those days. The report, which gives a very objective picture of censorship in Iran, is offered here for the very first time in translation:

> The censorship of books, the way it has been practiced during the last several months, has no precedent in contemporary history. In the twenty-year period [when Reza Shah was in power] the fate of writers of this country was determined by the two seals, "lawful" or "unlawful." In those days censorship was an open, official arrangement. Nothing could be done about it. There were no detailed official ceremonies for it. Everybody knew what was and what was not permissible for publication. Nobody discussed the issue whether censorship was anticonstitutional or against the Declaration of Human Rights or such-and-such an article of the law. Now that the Constitution, the Declaration of Human Rights and all kinds of claims of liberty are being talked about, the censorship of books starts to acquire a very manifest meaning. The censorship has taken place through only one letter, a directive from a ministry. Afraid of being closed down by the authorities, the printing shops are not ready to accept anything for printing that is of a questionable nature.
>
> The aims of censorship are too evident to be discussed in this short note. But it is of the same caliber that the Ministry of Arts and Culture is trying to implement for the

theater. A play is sifted through in such a fashion that it doesn't hurt or touch anyone. (Literature, religion, traditions, underprivileged classes of the society are not to be discussed.) Now the publication of books is being subjected to the same rule.

In a literary work, the discussion of politics, family relationships, traditions and religion, eroticism, folklore—particularly when the work in question ignores the rules of bourgeois decorum—are all forbidden. Of course, the censors criticize the composition, spelling and orthography of the literary work, too, lest the "sweet Persian language" be dirtied by the author, because the Ministry of Arts and Culture has undertaken the job of policing the art and culture of the country. Two or three agents have been charged with the administering of all these duties, thinking that they should determine the destiny of the literature and thought of a whole nation; everything is to be tailored to the obsolete, stereotyped measures of the style, taste and thought of these excellencies of the censorship, who distort everything and turn literary works into a filtered squeezed mixture of bland-tasting juices. These people do not know that the virtue of every pen lies in its ability to overthrow past values and create new ones. The end result of this censorship will be the destruction of small publishers who are among the intellectuals but who have limited capital to spend for the publication of books. This leads to the creation of large publishing houses and "colonies" of big publications who move in the direction of each and every wind blowing from the ruling power. Thus the hands of the contemporary writer are tied; it is quite clear that whatever happens to the art and literature of this country, it is not the big publishers or the censors who care, because they are not the ones who carry the burden of the creation of anything. They feel no responsibility. Whatever commitment there may be, belongs to the writers of the country who still resist and do not want to give up.

It was this very commitment that led a group of the poets[3] and writers of the country to visit with the Prime Minister,

[3] Sa'edi footnoted this as follows: "These writers decided together: Jalal Al-Ahmad, Ahmad Shamlu, Darvish, Baraheni, Tahbaz, Ro'yai, Sa'edi; also present was Davood Ramzi."

protesting the existence of censorship and telling him that there was no legal basis whatsoever for this kind of censorship.[4] Al-Ahmad spoke as the representative of the writers present in this meeting and said that the "executive branch" is thinking of enslaving the "World of Logos" (the writers of the country), but it does not know that censorship and pretexts of similar nature will not be able to maintain their obstacles against the flow of the culture of a nation. Mr. Hoveyda (the Prime Minister) said that he knew nothing about censorship. The documents which had been brought along were shown to him; he admitted that there was censorship and said that something should be done about it and that perhaps the writers present at the meeting should take charge of the censorship of books. Al-Ahmad told him, "We are here to protest against censorship, not to provide assistance to it."

Then Mr. Hoveyda asked us what suggestions we might have as a solution to the problem. We responded that we wanted the publication of books to return to the previous situation, and that the censorship bureaus at the Ministry of Information and the Ministry of Arts and Culture stop harassing the writers of the country. Mr. Hoveyda asked his assistant to give him a report on censorship as soon as possible, and to create a commission to check into the activities of the censorship in the country and solve some of the problems involved.

Two months have passed since that meeting, and the censorship of books is still in the same condition. In the first issue of the "Bulletin of the Union of Printing Shops" it was announced that several printing shops had been closed. The Union had asked the government for help. The second issue of the Bulletin has announced that even those printing shops which had been open earlier are only partially in operation and the majority of the workers have been laid off. The Union had asked the Ministry to do something about the printing shops and their workers. They had even suggested solutions,

Sa'edi's footnote: "Article 13 of the Fundamental Law, Article 20 of the Supplementary Fundamental Law, Article 19 of the Declaration of Human Rights (and the general legal principle: No law or directive may be contrary to the Fundamental Law). The censorship has used Article 13 of *Regulations for Printing Houses* as the basis for its action."

among which was that the Ministry multiply the number of censors so that the printing shops can resume their work as before.[5]

When we came out of the Prime Minister's office, we realized what the situation was. The Prime Minister, who is supposed to be the constitutional head of the executive branch of the government, could do nothing about censorship. The government even prevented the publication of Sa'edi's report in the magazine I edited. We had to find other means of enforcing our will.

The Iranian branch of the International PEN (an organization of poets, essayists, playwrights and novelists) was as corrupt as the Iranian monarchy. Two of the Shah's lackeys, Dr. Manouchehr Eqbal, director of the Board of the National Iranian Oil Company, and Zaynolabedin Rahnema, a man who had been instrumental in the accession of Reza Shah to the throne fifty years earlier, shared the presidency of PEN. The membership of the Iranian PEN was drawn generally from among the traditionalist pro-Shah academics.

We could not turn to this quarter for help. After months of negotiations among ourselves, we decided that we needed our own independent organization to fight for our rights as writers and poets. The Writers' Association of Iran, the first of its kind in the entire history of the country, was born as a result of our mutual efforts to fight censorship. The charter of the Association read in part:

The Writers' Association of Iran, composed of all authors, including poets, novelists, critics, playwrights, scriptwriters, scholars and translators, is hereby created, and it commences its activities on the basis of the two following principles:

1—The defense of the freedom of expression according to the Fundamental Laws of Iran—Articles 20 and 21 of the Supplementary Fundamental Laws: and the universal Declaration of Human Rights—Articles 18 and 19.

Freedom of expression includes all forms of expression, written, verbal or through the assistance of pictures; i.e., printed material, lectures, films and radio and television. Ev-

The report comes from my personal archives on censorship. Also printed in Reza Baraheni, *Zell-ullah (God's Shadow)* (New York, Abjad Publications, 1975), pp. 22–25.

eryone in the society is entitled to create, print, and distribute his works and thoughts in any form he wishes.

The authority from whom this right is being demanded is the three branches of the nation's powers; and all those authors who try to gain and preserve this right may, by accepting the contents of this charter, register in the Association and participate in its activities.

2—The defense of the professional interests of the nation's authors according to the law or laws which at present or in the future will determine and arrange, on the basis of justice, the relations between authors and publishers and those between the government agencies and the publishers.[6]

At the end of this charter, all the writers of the country were invited to join the Association and harmonize their activities within its framework. But there were troubles right from the start, for the government was not willing to register the organization. There were about thirty founding members, and an additional fifty writers joined our ranks in a matter of months. This was the largest gathering of intellectuals and artists of the country under the banner of a campaign against censorship in the entire history of Iran. In less than two years it became the most viable organization for writers in the country, embracing men and women from all political tendencies and all forms of art and research. It set up speeches on the writers of the country; it initiated gatherings to discuss themes of vital interest to its members and the public, and it tried to establish independent publications for itself. Almost all the major writers and poets and critics of the country were among its members.

[6] Article 20: All publications, except heretical books and matters hurtful to the perspicuous religion of Islam are free, and are exempt from censorship. If, however, anything should be discovered in them contrary to the Press Law, the publisher or writer is liable to punishment according to that law. If the writer is known and be resident in Iran, then the publisher, printer and distributor shall not be liable to persecution.

Article 21: Societies and associations which are not productive of mischief to Religion or the State and are not injurious to good order are free throughout the whole country, but members of such associations must not carry arms and must obey the regulations laid down by the Law on these matters. Assemblies in the public thoroughfares and open spaces must likewise obey the public regulations.

The charter comes from my personal archives. Also printed in *Zell-ullah,* pp. 25–27.

The authorities chased us out of all the places we tried to rent for our meetings. All our efforts to become registered failed. Then the government persecution engaged in horrendous measures. Jallal Al-Ahmad, the towering figure of the Association, was mysteriously killed in his small cottage on the Caspian Sea; before him, Samad Behrangi, one of the solidest of the sympathizers of the organization, had been drowned in the river. Then the incarceration and torture of the members of the Association started and continued; it goes on even now. Fereydoun Tonokaboni, the treasurer of the organization, Mohammad-Ali Sepanlou, an alternate member of the Executive Board, Manouchehr Hezarkhani, a sympathizer of the Association, and Behazin, cne of the important figures of the Association as well as a member of the Executive Board, were detained in prison for months. The books of most of the members of the Association were removed from the bookstores, and the publishers were told not to publish their books; some of the most significant members of the Association were blacklisted, thrown out of the press and laid off from their jobs.

I was among the writers who went to see the Prime Minister to protest against censorship, one of the Founding Members of the Association, an alternate member of the Executive Board in the second year of its life, and the head of its Committee for the Campaign against Censorship in Iran. This was the most sensitive area with which any Association committee dealt, as far as its relation to the dictatorship was concerned. I collected the names of authors whose books had been suppressed; I went around and talked to the publishers who had given books to the Bureau of Censorship of the Ministry of Arts and Culture and interviewed writers in regard to the works which they had submitted to the Ministry. Out of these activities there grew up a whole mass of material which itself could be the subject of a book.

There are more than five hundred titles written by some one hundred Iranian or foreign authors which are permanently on SAVAK's blacklist. Each writer has his own stories about his relations with SAVAK and other departments of censorship in the Department of the Police, the Ministry of Information (mostly for the press) and the Ministry of Arts and Culture, headed by the Shah's brother-in-law, Mehrdad Pahlbod. Most major newspapers have a censorship bureau attached to the office of their editorial board. During the years when I worked for *Ferdowsi* magazine,

I saw that all the articles were sent to the head of the Bureau of Censorship, Ata-ollah Tadayyon, and were printed only after his approval. This man, an acknowledged member of SAVAK who has read almost everything that the Iranian opposition has written, has refused to give his approval to over half of the writings submitted to him. The number of acceptable manuscripts by Iranian writers that remain unpublished is much greater than the number of published works from these writers.

Censorship in Iran during the last twenty-four years has passed through three distinct phases: (1) the period from 1953 to 1963, i.e., the interval between the coup and the spring massacre of 1963, during which there were still organized political activities against the Shah's dictatorship in the form of demonstrations and rival parties; (2) the period from 1963 to 1971, during which the Shah's regime, backed by the U.S. government, belied any allegations of shakiness and established itself openly as a nonconstitutional dictatorship in the eyes of the world; (3) the period from 1971 to the present, during which the guerrilla movement started in Siyahkal on the Caspian coast and spread, in spite of SAVAK's concentrated efforts to stop it, to the other parts of the country in the form of clandestine urban detachments.

The two major adherents of the guerrilla movement were Cherikha-ye Fadai-ye Khalq (the Guerrilla Organization of the People's Devotees) and Mojahedin-e-Khalq (the Organization of the People's Crusaders), one with Marxist tendencies and the other with Islamic inclinations. In spite of heavy losses suffered by these two organizations at the hands of the Shah's army and SAVAK, they continue to fight in their own clandestine manner, and there have been very few commentators who have doubted their courage and devotion.

The Shah's terrorism can hardly discourage these young men and women, whose average age does not exceed twenty-two and who are generally university students from all over the country. They have chosen the Revolutionary Path of the Intelligentsia, and their movement resembles the kind of student movement that appeared in Russia from 1860 to 1885 (which subsided only when Plekhanov and Lenin appeared on the political scene). But their losses have been far greater than those of their Russian counterparts and their successes fewer. They have yet to prove that they can assassinate the counterpart of the Czar in Iran; it is not even clear at this point whether such a deed could radically alter the political situation in Iran, in whose history, which is not completely devoid of regicide, no great radical changes ever came about as a result of assassination. It is quite clear that there will be no radical changes until the economic structure of the country is altered. The foundation for such a revolution is the under-privileged majority of society, not the intellectuals. This I say with all due respect to the heroic and costly attempts of these young men and women.

During the first period under the present regime, Iranian writers suffered the worst degradation of their lives: a coup triggered by a foreign country and carried out by fascists, spies and thugs. For several years they sank into utter despondency, sneaking into their homes, crying after their mothers and lovers and burying their dead in the rhythmical images of their poetry. The last years of the fifties saw the revival of the intellectual spirit of resistance in the figure of Al-Ahmad. Censorship was openly fought. The Shah's heavy-handedness in the massacre of 1963 brought this period to a close. During its short life, the first-rate writers of the country not only failed to eulogize the king and the regime, but, on the contrary, wrote against it in their stories, plays and poetry. Of course, nothing critical was allowed to be written against the Shah or his court.

During the second period, there ensued a battle between the censorship bureaus of the government and the writers of the country, as has been delineated above in the account of our meeting with the Prime Minister and the creation of the Writers' Association. Our works were sent to the censorship bureaus, and although some of them were not published, the government could not yet conceive of the writers of the country as people who should be forced to write in the terms of the establishment. This period saw the publication of some of the best prose, poetry and criticism available in contemporary Persian literature.

During the third period, some of the members of the guerrilla movement had been among the students or friends of some of the famous writers of the country. The government began to think of writers as "terrorists" and of "terrorists" as writers. Thus came about one of the darkest periods in the history of Iranian censorship, in which the government's black-and-white-with-no-shades-in-between policy dominated absolutely. One was either a "terrorist," i.e., a guerrilla, in which case he could be treated as an enemy of the government, or he was not a guerrilla, in which case he was obliged to openly declare his allegiance to the Shah and his regime.

This was the age of the government of Iran dictating to writers what and how they should write. A great part of this period was dominated by the presence of the former director of the CIA, Richard Nixon's appointee to the ambassadorship of the United States in Iran, Richard Helms. The guerrillas had succeeded in killing a few Iranian generals but had failed in the attempted kidnapping of the then U.S. Ambassador Douglas MacArthur; they had also assassinated several American officers and civilians working for the intelligence network of the Shah and the CIA. Hatred of Americans and of the American presence reached its height. The 26,000 Americans resident in Iran lived in utter fear, and thousands of SAVAK officials were required just to see to their well-being.

The escalation of torture, repression and censorship has been attributed in part to the presence of Richard Helms and the large number of Americans working and living in the country, in part to the impatient building up and acceleration of activities by the armed opposition to oust the Shah and his clan by forcible assault. But there is another reason behind it. In the past it has proved very difficult to bring all the writers of the country to their knees and coerce them to write the way the Shah wants them to write. As in Hitler's Germany and Stalin's Russia, total indoctrination has proven impossible. Great confusion arose in the minds of intellectuals as to the correct path to take under the given circumstances. They had no doubt as to the totalitarian nature of the Shah's regime. To be sure, several Iranian writers were co-opted by the regime as spokesmen, but there was no doubt in anyone's mind that these were the third-rate writers who had already been nibbling at the possibility of being co-opted during the second phase of the Shah's censorship. These co-opted writers created all kinds of problems for the genuine writers of the country. Having lost the favor of the whole nation, they were loath to see around them writers who were becoming favorites of the people. They worked hand in glove with SAVAK to disgrace these "good guys" either through the dissemination of rumors and scandals or through encouraging the authorities to imprison them and force their recantation under torture.

Moreover, the "good guys" had become divided among themselves into two factions: those who had not recanted and considered themselves to be heroes, and those who had recanted and either considered themselves to be victims of torture and repression or had simply become demoralized. Thus the tactics of the government had divided the writers, among whom polemical scuffles and suspicion and bitter cynicism were rife.

In my own case, I should say that between the cup and the lip there was the slip.

It was rather difficult to publish anything in 1971–1972. I started speaking on university campuses. I still managed to get a few things into the press but not the strong, solid material that I wanted to see published. The campus speeches were given due to the paucity of publication.

In the winter of 1972, government agents were circulating a petition—to be signed by religious leaders, social scientists and prominent figures—that I was *mahdoroddam,* which simply meant that if somebody killed me he would not be answerable to the authorities. At the end of 1973, when I was in prison, I found out that the same kind of petition had been circulated in regard to the famous Islamicist professor Ali Shariati. A friend of mine who was a prominent social scientist and had refused to sign the petition told me that quotations from my works had been assembled out of context on two separate pages: one proving that I had gone mad and was doing things against Islam, the other purporting to prove that I was a communist along Chinese lines and was therefore extremely dangerous to Islam, not to mention Islamic society.[7]

I started receiving threatening letters with whole lists of signatures, letters from cities all over the country. Many of the letters stated that the undersigned would soon be in Teheran and would put me to death. My social scientist friend sent someone to tell me that the petitioners had approached him a second time and that once again he had refused to sign. Then the threats turned into mud-slinging and slander campaigns in the press, and during my public speeches *agents provocateurs* would get up in the middle and ask me why I was alive while my friends Al-Ahmad and Behrangi

[7] The ironic thing is that a group of Iranian Maoists at Berkeley recently published a pamphlet called "Confucius and Baraheni—Reactionary Traitors!!" Meanwhile, the Queen of Iran and Princess Ashraf never ceased paying visits to Chairman Mao and Chou En-Lai when they were both still alive, and Chinese authorities continued to praise the Shah's "anti-imperialist struggle."

were dead. Other agents would pick up the theme somewhere else and attack me on the kind of jacket, shirt or shoes I happened to be wearing. In a gathering of a couple of thousand people, even with the agents occupying the auditorium, such questions would fall on deaf ears. But the message was clear. They didn't want me to go on speaking to the students of universities.

When I spoke in the Faculty of Accounting at the University of Teheran, to an audience of about five hundred, I was told by the Dean of the Faculty that I had to leave at once—and I really had to leave, much to the consternation of the listeners, who had heard only half a poem and sat waiting for the rest.

Eventually, speaking became impossible. I decided to leave the country, at least for a short time. Even my best friends told me I should. I accepted invitations from the University of Texas in Austin and the University of Utah in Salt Lake City and came to the United States in the summer of 1972, carrying with me the printed but unpublished version of a long novel (which remains unpublished to this day), versions of four books lying at that time in the Censorship Bureau of the Shah's brother-in-law, and copies of poems which I had not been able to publish.

During my absence, the shortened, moderated version of my *Masculine History* came out and in a matter of six months went through six printings. The daily newspaper *Ettela'at* called it a best-seller. While in the United States I made contact with many of the prominent poets and writers of the country, requesting them to make serious efforts to secure the release of political prisoners in Iran, particularly their own counterparts and colleagues.

When I returned to Iran in the summer of 1973, the first article I published was "The Culture of the Oppressor and the Culture of the Oppressed," which dealt with the problem of nationalities, the impossibility of a cultural revolution from above, the existence of our Masculine History and our plight as doubly alienated creatures of the twentieth century. I published two other articles dealing with two other dissidents, one from the classical period of Persian literature and the other from recent times.

I was kidnapped from the middle of the street on September 11, 1973, taken to my home where everything was ransacked and torn to pieces in a matter of an hour, then hustled downstairs and placed in a car with two men in the front seat and two on either side of me. We drove for almost half an hour to the center of the city. I could tell this because we were going downhill. Yes, I had been blindfolded. I was taken to the prison, which I later recognized to be the Komité, one of SAVAK's several torture stations in Teheran.

The story of my arrest and torture on the first day appeared as an introduction to *God's Shadow*, a collection of prison poems. The reader can also consult the "Index on Censorship" (Spring, 1976). The present memoirs deal with the remainder of the days I spent in prison.

PRISON MEMOIRS

THE HEAD INTERROGATOR

The man who interrogates me the first night is very handsome: hazel eyes, fair complexion, rather tall and extremely well-dressed. His hair and mustache are light brown. He has an icy, indifferent tone and laughs only when he turns to the tall, darkish wrestler-type fellow on his right. This darkish fellow asks me:

"Did they get you at the paper, Doctor?"

"No, on the way home," I say.

He gets up and walks over to a thin young man sitting on the floor. I follow him with my eyes. Where have I seen him? Is he a soccer player or wrestler or someone whose face is seen regularly on television? I don't know. I will never know. So many questions are left unanswered in the jigsaw puzzle of the prison world that it is preferable to speak of questions rather than answers. The answers are hard to find.

The wrestler leans on the thin man, puts his hand under his chin and lifts his head. A deathly, suffering, dehumanized face looks up at him.

"Are you going to write down the answer, or do you want me to crush your toes with my boots?"

He doesn't wait for a response. He puts his boot on the young man's toes and presses as hard as he can, as if he wants the toes to disappear completely. Blood spurts from beneath his boot. The boy hugs the man's legs, asking for pity while he screams at the top of his lungs from the pain. His toenails have already been plucked out. His words and his screaming attest to this. I am already sick in my mind and heart.

The handsome interrogator is calling to me. The question-and-answer process begins:

"Name?"

"Reza."

"Family name?"

"Baraheni."

"Are you married?"

"Yes."

"Your wife's name?"

"Sanaz."

"Her maiden name?"

"Sehhati."

"Her name is familiar. Does she have a political file?"

"No, I don't think so."

"Your age?"

"Thirty-seven."

"Do you have any children?"

"Yes, a daughter."

"Her name and age?"

"Aleca. She is thirteen years old."

"Any brothers and sisters?"

"Two brothers and one sister."

"The names of the brothers and their professions."

"The older one is Mohammad-Naghi Baraheni. He is an assistant professor of psychology at the University of Teheran. The younger is Rassoul. He is a schoolteacher in Tabriz."

"The name of the sister?"

"Ashraf. She is a student of social sciences at the University of Teheran."

"Your travels during the last twenty years?"

"Turkey, Egypt, France, Britain, Greece and the United States."

"We have been told that you have cooperated with the Confederation of Iranian Students Abroad. We charge you with this crime."

"I never cooperated with this organization, and I deny the charges of the crime, any crime."

"Sign here."

I sign a paper.

He calls the guard and tells him to take me back to my cell.

"May I ask what your name is?" I ask.

"We don't answer questions here. Fuck off!"

"What is the name of this place?" I ask.

"None of your business, you son of a bitch!" he shouts. "Here the questions come from us, not from traitors like you!"

Later, I will learn his name. He is the head interrogator, Dr. Mostafavi. All the interrogators and torturers call themselves doctors, or sometimes engineers. They, too, are professional technicians. We will meet many of them in the following pages.

A PROFESSOR

The next day I am given my first dose of torture. I am beaten by the head torturer, Hosseinzadeh. My beard is pulled out with a pair of surgical scissors. I am taken to the *Otaq-e-Tamshiyat*, which is only another name in the prison lexicon for torture chamber, meaning literally "the place where they make you walk." I am given seventy-five blows on the soles of my feet with a plaited wire whip; one of my fingers is broken; I am threatened with the rape of my wife and daughter; then a pistol is held to my head at the temple by another torturer, Dr. Azudi, and, in fact, I hear it fired. I faint. When I open my eyes, I am being carried downstairs on the back of the soldier who tied my feet to the iron bed in the torture chamber and was introduced to me as the potential rapist of my wife and daughter. It must be a great honor to be carried on the back of a potential rapist.

As soon as the guard sets me down, one of the four civilians who were whipping me in the torture chamber appears and orders me to get up and stamp my feet on the ground.

"Pa bezan!" he shouts.

I get up but fall down. There is blood all over my feet, and they are already as thick as two heavy mud bricks. The man wields his long wire whip in a circle around my head.

"Get up, you son of a bitch, and stamp your feet on the floor!"

I get up and start stamping my miserable feet on the floor. I look like a huge circus bear dancing heavily with a bleeding hemorrhoid. Dr. Hosseini, the whipper, moves around me like a circus animal trainer. Then he tells me to sit down on the chair. He himself sits behind a desk.

I cannot put my feet on the floor. I try to reexamine my position, but my mind is fuzzy. The torture chamber is a nightmare from which I will never wake up. Who are these people? Why are they doing this to us? There are screams all over the place. Are they real or artificial? Are they genuine or recordings from past events?

Then in walks one of the funniest and stupidest men I have ever seen. Tall and thin, with black, indifferent eyes, pursed lips, thick hair and rather big ears, a taller Goebbels, addicted to the best opium to be found in the land of the Aryans. The face, in fact, is the color of opium; you can put it on the pipe and smoke it off in one round of inhaling.

He asks Dr. Hosseini who I am. Dr. Hosseini responds in an ironic tone, "The most important literary figure in the history of mankind, Professor of Persian, English and many other things besides these, Dr. Reza Baraheni, and we just fucked him upstairs!"

The man surprises me at first with the story of a book he has written on the Arab-Israeli conflict; he surprises me further with the book he carries in his hand: the second volume of Sholokhov's *And Quiet Flows the Don* in the Persian translation by Behazin, a writer who was in prison only a few years back.

"Who is greater, Rumi or Victor Hugo?" he suddenly asks.

I am flabbergasted. He is staring right into my eyes and waiting for an answer.

"Why do you ask, sir?" I inquire.

"My name is Ostad [Professor]," he says. "You may call me by that title."

"Why do you ask, Professor?"

"Because I thirst for knowledge, you damned fool. Now tell me!"

"Rumi," I reply.

"You must be mad! Who the hell is Rumi? Victor Hugo is the most famous writer in the world. Tell me, was Rumi translated into Tibetan?"

"I don't know," I tell this SAVAK agent suddenly turned Hugo freak. "Ask the Tibetans or Rumi."

"No, you have to tell me what you think. Why do you think Rumi is greater than Hugo? He is not so famous."

"He is not, but certainly he is a better poet than Hugo. There are as many Rumi freaks in the West as there are Hugo freaks in Iran."

In the heat of this dialogue I have forgotten about the pain in my feet and ribs and the broken finger. I hadn't know that the theater of the absurd could have such a relaxing effect.

The agent prompts the whole conversation to a climax:

"Who is greater, Rumi or Hugo or you?"

I have never thought that I belonged to the rank of such immortals, but I cannot disappoint this SAVAK professor with an anticlimax in the competition. I say:

"Of the three of us, Hugo had the longest beard."

"But did you have a beard?"

"Yes, I did, but someone pulled it out in the morning."

He opens the Sholokhov novel, takes out a xeroxed copy of my article and shows it to me.

"Is this you?"

"Yes, the one in the middle."

"It is impossible. This is Rasputin."

"In the morning someone told me I looked like both Imam Ali and Che Guevara. Now you tell me I look like Rasputin."

"No, you look like Rasputin."

"And you, Professor, look like—" I want to say Goebbels, but I stop short, fearing for my life.

"Like what?" he insists.

"Like yourself, Professor. Only I don't look like myself."

The dialogue changes as abruptly as it began. I simply don't know what to say.

"The cosine of one plus the sine of one becomes what? Tell me."

"Tell you what?"

"The result of trigonometry."

"As you know, I am only a poet."

"We don't need poets, we need people who can tell me what the cosine of one plus the sine of one becomes."

"I can hardly be the right person to answer that."

"Do you think that by memorizing and reciting thousands of lines of poetry you can prove that you are a human being?"

"But you see I don't even have a good memory."

"You do and you will pay for it." He answers as coolly as if he were simply telling me, "Wash your hands and come back here."

"What were you doing in the United States?"

"Teaching."

"What?"

"Literature."

"What kind of literature?"

"English literature."

"What! What!" he shouts, almost driven from his senses.

"English literature." It is my turn now to be cool.

"You mean you were teaching Americans English literature?"

"Yes, Professor," I answer, as cool as before.

"Liar! You are a damn fool liar."

"I taught English literature, and that is the plain truth."

He turns to Dr. Hosseini, who sits behind his desk almost as lifeless as a tree trunk in freezing winter weather.

"Dr. Hosseini, do you want me to speak English to him? Do you want me to, so that you can see he doesn't even know English?"

"I don't know, Professor. I cannot be the judge of that. I don't know the language of *az ma behtaran* [those who are better than we], but"—and here he points to the cable whip hanging from the nail on the wall—"if you want, I can make him sing like a nightingale, crow like a raven, howl like a dog. You tell me, and I'll make him speak the language of all men and beasts."

The Professor turns around and walks out of the room. Three huge men come in who look exactly like pirates from an Errol Flynn movie. They start poking me in the ribs and ears and man-handling me, occasionally slapping me hard on the face. Then a blindfolded man is brought in. A guard is holding him by the hand. A black curtain on the right side of the room is pulled aside. The man is told to raise his feet one by one and go through the door. The three pirates give up on me and go into the torture chamber. Then someone is screaming at the top of his voice and saying words that are utterly inhuman and incomprehensible. What is happening to him now happened to me a few hours ago. I know that in the torture chamber people forget humanity's most precious gift—language—and turn into beasts.

I see the Professor several more times while I am in prison. Once in cell number 17 of the ward 1 the door is opened. I get up as I always get up when someone opens the door of the cell, and the Professor, standing in the same dark suit and starched shirt and tie with white dots, says, "Who are you?" as if this were the first time he had ever seen me.

I introduce myself, making allusions to the first meeting we had together. He stretches out his hand toward my face and grabs my beard, which has already grown back, and pulls my face toward him and holds it there in front of him and in front of the man whom all the prisoners say is a captain and in charge of prison discipline but who is now dressed in an awkward civilian suit. The two of them examine my face as if I were a piece of rug or clothing and they wanted to see if they could afford the price. I prove to be not worth the trouble. The Professor lets go of my face and all of a sudden asks:

"Can you define culture?"

I know the Professor's habit. He has somehow strayed into the real world out of some Ionesco play. And I have to deliver my lesson to him. I start out like an elementary school kid, reciting as fast as I can an encyclopedic definition of culture. He stops me here and there, and then he asks me to add a few words on the great philosophers of Iran. I do this, like an obedient student, and when I finish he closes the door without saying a word. What a character!

One evening the door of my cell is opened, and I am told by a man with a blindfold draped over his shoulder to dress and put on my shoes. I obey, and he follows me out of the cell. He puts the blindfold over my eyes from behind as we walk. We leave the ward and go through the courtyard to the room where the Captain of the Guards sits like some tribal king. I know the whole scene by heart. I have seen it once without the blindfold, and its image is branded on my consciousness for good. The Captain tells the guard to handcuff himself to me and then commands: "Take him to the General!"

We pass through the same curving alleyways around the Komité prison and walk into the large courtyard of the Central Department of Police. It is getting cold. We turn to the right and go up a flight of stairs. I am pulled by my handcuffed wrist through several doors and windows, and finally the blindfold is removed and I see the Professor sitting at a desk across the front of which is written BRIGADIER GENERAL REZA ZANDIPOUR. So, the Professor is a general. He gets up and comes away from the desk and sits down on a sofa in the middle of the room. He tells me to sit down. I do so on the opposite sofa.

"I've read the interrogation, and I've come up with a final decision. You know what that decision is?"

"No, Professor, how can I possibly know? It is your decision."

"The decision is that you are a fool, and you should be shot, not because you are a traitor but because you are a fool."

"If you were to shoot fools, Professor, you ought to be shooting more than one."

"And that's exactly what we are doing. We are shooting more than one."

"Why do you shoot the fools, Professor? Let them say whatever they want to say. Wise people won't listen to them. Since you are wise, they will listen to you, and fools like us will be eliminated automatically."

"No, this society is full of fools who will listen to fools like you, and the Russians will come in and piss all over the nation of Iran."

"If the Russians come in here, Professor, they will shoot me before they shoot you, because I am one of those fools who could live neither under a monarchist nor under a Stalinist bureaucracy. These two systems will never shoot you. They will shoot me."

"But others might shoot."

How could I know at that time that this man, in spite of his stupidity, was foretelling his own death? Iranian guerrillas would stop his car in the spring of 1975 and shoot him down.

"If they shoot you, it means that they think you are irreplaceable. Someone else from your rank and file could be promoted to become a general or a professor, and he will do exactly what you are doing."

"What would you do with me, if you had the power?" he asks.

"First of all, I will neither have power nor bow to those who do have it. But let me think of myself in a hypothetical situation and tell you what I would do with you if I had power over you. I would give you a thousand sharp pencils and thousands of pages of blank paper and let you write your version of the story of this prison, the prisoners and the torture chambers, and I would publish it in millions of copies so that everyone would know what our nation passed through when you had the power."

"And then you would shoot me."

"There would be no need for that. Your testimony would be your catharsis, and that catharsis would be the end of your days as the head of the torturers in this prison. You would be a free man, even in your own eyes."

Until now he has found no opportunity to make a racist attack on me. He shifts rather uncomfortably in the sofa and all of a sudden blurts out:

"You really are a *Turk-e-Khar* [Turk donkey]!"

He rings the bell; the guard comes in. I am taken out, blindfolded and handcuffed to the guard, and we go back to the prison and into my cell. But something very strange happens on that night. The key to the handcuffs is lost. We go back to the room of the Captain of the Guards, the blindfold still over my eyes. We move around, looking for the key. Wherever the guard goes, I go, too. The Captain gets angry, grabs a knife, and tries to cut the metal. But he doesn't succeed. Then someone suggests that they should shoot off the handcuffs. We raise our two hands in the air, but the Captain says that it is impossible. They try to get hold of the General/Professor, but they cannot find him. They try Dr. Hosseinzadeh, the head torturer, Dr. Azudi and all the rest of the torturers; they are nowhere to be found. The Captain gets even angrier. I am about to suggest that they call up the palace and ask the Shah what to do. The guard and I are locked to each other like dogs in an inseparable state of copulation. My blindfold is removed, and I see the Captain's pink, sweating, angry face in front of me.

"If you fucking intellectuals didn't exist, we would have no prisons, and this young man who is tied to you would be happily tilling the land on his farm, and I wouldn't be hurting my hand by slapping you on your mouth!"

And he actually slaps me several times on the mouth, hurting his hand. He tells the guard to hit me with his free hand, and my double turns and starts beating me in the stomach. Then we are told to sit down on two adjacent chairs. One of the other guards gets some food for my double. He eats with his free hand. I watch him eat. When he finishes, he gets up. I get up, too. He puts the blindfold over my eyes. The Captain tells him that he has to sleep in my cell until tomorrow. We go back to my cell. On the way, he takes me to the toilet. We piss together. We come back and lie down and sleep, only to be awakened by the sudden opening of the door. We both jump to our feet. I see Dr. Azudi, who administered the torture that first day. He doesn't even look at the guard.

"Remember what I told you in the torture chamber. If you talk like that to the General once more, I'll have the guards fuck your wife and daughter in front of you. Remember!"

He slams the door. The handcuffs are removed the next day by someone from the army.

MY INTERROGATOR

How can I forget him, my inquisitor, the red-eyed, importunate solicitor, the information-devouring vulture who gave me a hundred nights and days of sleeplessness, combined with exhaustion, spiritual torture and mad imaginings?

I meet this man after I am brought down from the torture chamber on the third floor, and after I have met the General/Professor for the first time. He comes in half an hour after the General has left. He has a file in his hand and a guard with a blindfold over his shoulder behind him. He tells me to get up. I obey. He tells the guard to put the blindfold over my eyes. The guard obeys. Then he asks Dr. Hosseini, the whipper, whether my mouth "has been opened," which means, as I later come to learn, have I confessed or not. Dr. Hosseini says no, and we go downstairs with the guard leading me by the hand and the man following behind. We enter a room. The blindfold is removed. The guard leaves. The man sits down behind the only desk in the room. He tells me to pull up a chair and sit down. I obey. I look around the room. The walls are bare—no pictures, no mirrors, no nails, bare like the walls of a public bathhouse. It is strange. I don't see any pictures of the Shah on the walls in this room or any other room in the prison. They are afraid, I later learn, that some of the prisoners might decide to insult the Shah in their presence, and they would be at a loss as to what to do with them. This doesn't really sound plausible as a reason, because, as I have seen, they always know what to do with a prisoner. They are afraid that they won't know what to do with themselves upon the commission in their presence of a verbal affront to the Shah.

"I am your interrogator," he says, like someone talking to himself. He has on a reddish tie; his hands are extremely fleshy, his cheeks clean-shaven and pouchy . . . and the eyes? I can swear by the Shah's crown that this man will suddenly die one day, right here in this room or up there in the torture chambers when he is interrogating a prisoner or using the electric baton on a prisoner's genitals. Each eye is a clenched fist of blood, and the eyelids rise and fall reluctantly with nothing of a natural human rhythm.

"Could you tell me why I am here and why I have been tortured?" I ask.

"You are here because of the article you published in *Ettela'at*, the one dealing with the nationalities and the role of intellectuals."

"Why have I been tortured?" I ask.

He doesn't answer. He leaves the room and doesn't come back until an hour later. A barber is with him. The barber shaves my head and clicks his clipper over my face to remove the tufts of my beard that still remain from when they plucked it out. I am taken out into the sun. The man puts a number around my neck and takes three pictures, one full-face and two profiles. I go back to the room, half-limping, half-crawling, hardly able to touch my feet to the ground because of the pain.

There are two men in the room this time: my interrogator and another huge fellow, who immediately asks the interrogator who I am. As soon as I am introduced, he asks me whether I use my right hand for writing. The question seems an odd one, but I answer it in the affirmative.

"Well then, let me see your left hand, and I'll read your fortune," he says.

"I don't believe in telling fortunes," I say.

"Oh, but you should, you should," he says. "Now, open your fucking hand!"

I open my hand; I still have swollen hands from the whips in the morning. Out of nowhere, the fortuneteller produces a thick-wire whip—he has been hiding it behind him—and brings it down on my hand. It burns like red-hot coal. I try to conceal my hand when he raises the whip for another blow, but he screams as loudly as he can, telling me to open it or otherwise he will "wear the whip out on my head and face." I open my hand, screaming. Suddenly, there is Persian music coming from a radio somewhere behind the desk; they have done this apparently to smother the sound of my shrieking. The man shouts, "Keep your hand open!" He is extremely angry. My interrogator gets up and tries to control him, actually pleading with him and promising him that I will answer his questions from now on. My interrogator addresses him as Dr. Shadi. The whipper tells my interrogator that it is for his sake that he is stopping and that he should let him know any time I ask strange questions and don't answer the questions he puts to me. My interrogator assures him that I will answer all questions from now on. They are clearly making some kind of deal over me between themselves. Dr. Shadi goes away, and I am told to sit down.

"Do you have any further questions?" my interrogator asks, with a bitterly sarcastic tone to his voice.

I understand, but I answer neither yes nor no. The interrogation begins right away.

The pattern of the interrogation is along the following lines: (1) written questions and written answers, all of a very formal nature; (2) the oral accompaniment of the interrogator to the written questions, which consists of explanations of and commentaries upon the questions, the answers, you; the oral portion of the interrogation is not of a formal nature, but is rather a matter of the interrogator feeling free to employ the foulest of language. Notice how the same question can be put in two different ways:

> *Oral:* "You son of a bitch, you wrote in your article that you will fuck the ruling class in Iran if you get to be some big fucking shit somewhere else in the world!"
> *Written:* "Your excellency says in the article that he doesn't believe that culture can be transformed from above. Would you please explain and elaborate on just what it is you would do if you had the power?"

One does not need the Swiss linguist Ferdinand de Saussure to tell him the difference between *la parole*, language in flux and as spoken, and *la langue*, language in repose and as a system. The Iranian interrogator-torturer knows the difference as well as President Richard M. Nixon did.

In fact, the comparison is apt. Those who have read the White House transcripts, with all those "expletive deleted," "inaudible" and "unintelligible" insertions in brackets, will understand what I am talking about. The President told the nation in an address on April 29, 1974, "We live in a time of great challenge and great opportunity for America . . . I intend to go ahead with the work that you elected me to do." But in the actual transcripts, he says, "I do not want to be in a position where the damned public clamor makes, as it did with Eisenhower, with Adams, makes it necessary or calls . . . to have Bob come in one day and say, 'Well, Mr. President, the public—blah, blah, blah—I'm going to leave.' Now, that's the real problem of this damned thing, and I don't think that kicking Dean out of here is going to do it. Understand, I am not ruling out kicking him out. But I think you got to figure what the hell does Dean know."[1]

Between *la parole* and *la langue* of lying politicians and interrogating torturers lie reality and its distortion. More than ten times during my imprisonment, Dr. Azudi, one of the horrendous names in the torture industry of Iran, tells me, "I'll have your wife and daughter fucked before your eyes!" But in the written documents, the torturers speak of the institution of the family in such a way that they would appear ready to kill anyone who touched a person's wife or daughter. They rape the young students in prison, but if someone rapes a young boy outside of prison they call him a *monharef* (pervert). They never admit in *la langue* to being perverts themselves. That would be a breach of their moral code. Between *la parole* and *la langue* we find a whole system of listening, wiretapping, harassing, bribing, blackmailing, torture, and a whole structure erected on hypocrisy, deception, lies.

If you read the files of Iranian political prisoners, you will see that the interrogator is even more polite than the person who is being interrogated. That politeness is a cover-up. Behind it stand the ugly face of the torturer and his filthy language, which originates in his bowels rather than in his brain and defiles every word and every sentence. The interrogator has two mouths—his real mouth, right there under his nose, and his nether mouth, his anal orifice. With the upper mouth he lies to the world; with the lower one he excretes reality, *la parole* of reality. He tells the real truth about himself through his nether mouth.

"Your name?" my interrogator asks. And then the whole process I went through the night before begins in tedious repetition. But here the questions are longer, and the interrogator, whose real name I later learn is Dr. Rezvan (and from now on we will call him by that name), writes every question down in his bad handwriting

[1] The White House Transcripts, edited by the New York *Times* staff (London, Macmillan, 1974), pp. 21–22, 624.

on a legal pad, puts the paper in front of me and tells me to answer the question.

When he writes the question, your mind becomes a rabid dog looking for water, the leg of a victim, a source of carnal consolation. You look at his face, all screwed up with concentration on the question he is formulating, and you move in a maze of words, faces, objects, houses, and you hear from everything inhabiting your memory a sickly sound of barking. There is only one way you can define this situation, and that is through the distortion of the meaning of words. You don't have to be a surrealist poet to do this. Words bark out all around you in prison. I talked to several prisoners who had little poetic faculty, and they told me that my definition of the situation and of the use of words in prison is what they had tried to formulate in their own minds. The prison turns everybody into a poet of hell.

What is Joyce's "steady monoloquy of interiors" compared with what is happening in the mind of the prisoner when he sits in front of Dr. Rezvan or lies on the bed waiting for Dr. Azudi's next question or hangs upside down from the ceiling in the torture chamber waiting for Dr. Rassouli or Dr. Ardalan to commence questioning him from behind with their phalluses? Words fly like furies from the pores of his body. Aquinas and Vico, Nietzsche and Freud, the aesthetics of stasis and kinesis, beauty and rhythm, all whirling in circling pools of bile and excrement, suck him in and suffocate him and he curses the father who begat him and the mother who gave him birth.

You don't know what he is going to ask you. It might be a question about your father's second wife or your aunt's working class son, or about some image from a poem or the characters of a novel. Once he asked me why I had written a poem which started with the words "My god is dead." At first I didn't even remember the poem. I had forgotten all about it. How could I have known when I was seventeen and writing the line that twenty years later a torturer was going to ask me why I had written it?

And once he asked me about *The Infernal Days of Agha ye-Ayyaz*, a novel of mine which had been printed in Iran but never released or distributed.

"We have received a report that you have written a novel called *The History of Ayyaz*, in which you have insulted the State. How, tell me, have you insulted the State in this novel of yours?"

I started in quibbling with him and told him all sorts of little half-lies on the style, the character and the plot of *Ayyaz,* but I was stuck and he knew it. Then Dr. Shadi, his best friend among the torturers, walked in and suggested they stop early that day because they had to go after someone else. Dr. Rezvan told me to get up and go to my cell but to think about the question he had just asked, for he would want to hear the answer the next day.

It was another week or so before he called me for interrogation. This was one of the darkest weeks of my life, a kind of "recherche du temps perdu" in hell. The lightning had struck, and I had to rebuild an entire city on the basis of what little I had seen during the flash. The characters of the novel arose from the abyss of the written pages and stood before me asking my pardon. I was interrogating the creatures of my own imagination. Events which I had digested years ago rose up in the form of new morsels of hard, stinking, unpalatable food, and I wished they had never existed. I felt that every character was a betrayal, an informer for SAVAK, determined to expose me to the tyranny of my torturers in the torture chamber. Every word in the novel became a time bomb, its sinister ticking a warning of impending ultimate disaster. I tried to see what there could be of an "anti-State" nature in the actions of a man and a woman who had slept with each other quite innocently somewhere in my imagination on a rainy night. But I was sure that Dr. Rezvan's illegible handwriting had engraved itself upon the walls of the couple's bedroom; his bloodshot eyes descended into the bedroom like a pair of scales, each pan brimming with reeking poison declaiming the ethos of justice and tyranny. To be frank, I thought I felt that I was serving as a panderer for those poor creatures of my imagination, delivering them up to the violation of Dr. Rezvan's scrutinizing glare, and I hated myself. And not only the characters of the novel but the events, the conflicts, the plot—I hated them all equally. Why hadn't I suppressed the whole novel so that now I would not have to stand responsible for the actions of those imaginary figures? I should have turned it into an "expletive deleted" from my literary career, so as not to have to face up to the scandal and censure it would surely bring upon me.

As human beings turn into beasts in prison, so do their values change. The metamorphosis takes place on all levels. The novelist becomes a criminal; his characters, symbols of his crime. Every imaginary figure, large or small, major or minor, must be summoned to stand trial. True, the novelist could claim the artist's privilege and speak of artistic distantiation, saying that a novel is constructed in terms of its own credo of form, that you cannot punish the author for what his characters do and say. There are a number of first-rate critics, of course, who would hold the author accountable, and Dr. Rezvan, who rewrites everything others have written before in his scribbled questions, would no doubt side with them. In his eyes the novelist is the accomplice of his characters, and this complicity should be used against him.

Ironically, when I was called for interrogation after a week, prepared in my mind to speak about the novel and argue for its and my own absolution in the eyes of this archcritic, Dr. Rezvan simply forgot to ask me about it, as if the novel did not exist at all, and I realized that I had suffered in vain over this issue.

When I came out of prison, I asked my publisher about the fate of the novel. He told me that he gave a copy to a friend of his who worked in SAVAK, telling him that it had been written and printed abroad and that he wanted to see whether SAVAK would give him permission to distribute it. The man from SAVAK took it home and read it very carefully and made notes on pages which should be omitted to make it distributable in Iran. My publisher gave that copy to me. The novel was 424 pages long. The man from SAVAK had written the word "omit" on some 412 pages, thus turning a long novel into a very short story. Such ingenious mastery of the art of précis is unparalleled in other societies. A literary editor in the West could hardly aspire to become a disciple to a discerningly critical agent of SAVAK.

Let us go back to Dr. Rezvan and the initial interrogation.

The routine questions are finished in almost half an hour. Then the "recherche du temps perdu" begins.

"What were you doing in 1953?"

Well, I was digesting food most of the day and night. I was learning the rules of Persian prosody and trying to master the 240 rhythmical patterns used by the classical Iranian poets. I was flirting with a girl, who would put her *chador* (face and body veil) over both our heads, and we would stay that way together for hours without any of the passers-by knowing that there were two of us under there. I was also beginning to teach the children of the rich their elementary English. And there were a million other things I did in 1953, but I had no idea which of these things it was that Dr. Rezvan wanted to know.

"I was studying."

"Politically! What were you doing politically, you jackass?" This would be *la parole*, the written semiology being: "What was your excellency doing politically in 1953?"

"Jackass" and "excellency" correspond, it would seem.

"I was too young to do anything political in 1953, and besides, even in my later years I have done nothing political."

He gets up, goes to the window, shouts into the courtyard, "Dr. Hosseini, Parviz Khan!" and comes back and sits down. He is very angry, but I hope not at me. I interrogate myself: "Have I done anything to hurt this man sitting before me?" The answer is most definitely no. He opens a small tin box, takes a pill, swallows it, takes the glass of water, drinks it, takes out a cigarette, puts it to his lips, lights it with a lighter, inhales the smoke, blows some of it out. I, the chain-smoker, haven't smoked for twenty-eight hours; I try to inhale the smoke on the sly. Never did I imagine that someone else's exhaled refuse might be a source of pleasure.

"Outside you act as political heroes, but here you claim that you have nothing to do with politics. Those millions of young people who were shouting 'Mossadeq! Mossadeq!' in the streets before the day of the National Uprising on August 19, 1953 [the CIA coup], I suppose they were imported from abroad? You, you bastard, were you not among them?"

"No, sir, I was not."

"When did you go to Turkey?"

"1958."

"And what were you doing between 1953 and 1958?"

Shall I tell him I was trying to put images together? Shall I speak of the poetry of Pound and Eliot, the early works of Jean Genet and Sartre in English translations, of Faulkner and Stein; of my learning English the hard way, learning it as a carpenter does, starting from scratch and working his way up to a table or a chair, learning it, learning it, until the learning of it becomes an obsession and I even dream in English? Shall I tell him all of that? No, I can't disclose my literary sources to him; he'll make something out of that, too.

"What were you doing? And who were your friends during those years?"

The idea of "friends" triggers the appearance of the faces of so many young men and women in my mind that if I reveal the identity of all of them, he will become so confused that he will swallow all his pills at once and drink up all the water from the courtyard pool.

"You see, I was working and studying at the same time, and it was extremely difficult for me to form any lasting friendships. At the University of Tabriz I could not attend classes regularly, and—well, you know—it is almost twenty years ago. People go away, die, migrate. I really don't remember any particular names. There was an army captain and also a fortyish man from the Department of Finance, and a young woman who died later in an accident. This is as much as I can possibly remember from my college days in Tabriz."

How do I know what happened to some of those men and women after they left school? To mention their names would be to get into their files, if they have any, and I don't want to have anything to do with other people's files. Some of them may even have become agents of SAVAK by now.

"Who were your best friends in Turkey? Where were you staying?"

"My friends were among the Turkish writers. There were no Iranians studying English literature in Turkey, so I had no Iranian friends, and later even the Turks dropped me because I married a Greek woman."

Dr. Rezvan suddenly jumps up and grabs the collar of my jacket and tries to lift me up off the chair.

"The biggest file in SAVAK belongs to you. Your political activities in Turkey among the students in those days are recorded right here in our files. I only want to hear about them from your own lips. I already know everything."

He throws me back into my chair, picks up the receiver and dials a number. "His excellency, Dr. Hosseinzadeh, please . . . Yes, your excellency, the project, the one from the University of Teheran, he doesn't say much . . . Yes, whatever your instructions, we will carry them out . . . So, you are sending over Dr. Azudi? Dr. Shadi was here a few hours ago. I don't think he is coming back today. I will send the project to his cell until Dr. Azudi arrives . . . No, sir, I have to go after the other project. Any more instructions, sir? . . . Goodbye."

I am "the project" of which he spoke, but he says nothing to me. He gets up, goes to the window and calls for a guard. A guard comes in with a blindfold in his hand.

"Take this to its cell!"

In a matter of thirty hours I have become a "this." The blindfold covers my eyes. Limping and crawling, I am led to my cell.

DR. AZUDI AND I IN CELL 14

One has to see Dr. Azudi to believe him. The worst thing that could possibly happen to the title "Doctor" is its being used by Azudi. The huge face, the yellowing teeth, the smiling mouth studded with gold caps, the heavy, conceited walk, the strong fists, the virile complexion, the animal eyes—in short, the physiognomy of what in Persian we call *jahel* (moron)—bely the title he bears. He walks forward by lurching to the right with his right foot and to the left with his left, thus occupying, in motion, more space than people normally do. He was in charge of my torture in the morning, assigned by Dr. Hosseinzadeh, who is the head of all the torturers in SAVAK and is answerable to Parviz Sabeti, the second most important man in the intelligence network of the Iranian government. The four-star General Ne'matollah Nassiri, one of the Shah's most trusted friends, is the commander of SAVAK; his name has become in recent years synonymous with torture.

I am lying on the tiles of the floor with my bowl of food beside me. It is rice, with some kind of ugly-looking juice in it. I have so many pains, I don't know which one to think about first. I look at my feet. I can hardly recognize them. They are red and blue, and swollen, and they look very awkward with their stupid, obscene, protruding obesity. Later, when I call the guard and tell him I want to go and wash my feet, he tells me, "Don't wash them; they'll contract, and you'll have even more problems tomorrow when they whip you again." I don't know about these things. I figure he must be right.

Lying there on the floor, I know that I am alone and that I am the only person who can defend myself in this hell. The world outside is dead and buried; I have to do everything myself in this four-by-eight-foot hole. Everyone in the other cells is moaning, and I can hear the crying of men and women all the way up and down the corridor.

The little vent in the iron door opens, and someone puts his mouth to the hole and says, "Eat!" The vent is slammed shut. I obey: cold rice, tasting like a mixture of soap and filth. Before I finish, the door is flung open and the guard tells me that it is my turn to go to the toilet.

"Take your bowl with you and wash it."

He puts the blindfold over my eyes. He doesn't want me to see the corridor. He leads me to the toilet. He closes the door behind me and tells me to remove the blindfold myself. I remove it. The holes in the floor are overflowing with piles of excrement, little pools of urine all around them. There are no mirrors. I empty the rest of my food in the trash can, wash first the bowl and then my face, and knock on the door. The guard comes and opens the door. He covers my eyes with the blindfold. Half crawling, half limping, I go back to my cell. The door is slammed shut, and I lie down.

Are they really going to do what they told me they would do to my wife and daughter? Their lives don't belong to me. They haven't done anything against anyone. Why should they suffer? My daughter is away seeing her mother in Greece. My first wife was Greek; we separated years ago. My present wife comes from my hometown in Azarbaijan. We were planning to have a child as soon as we arrived back in Iran from the United States. She went to the hospital on the very day I was arrested. But I know nothing about the results.

I wish there was a way I could tell my daughter not to come back to Iran. She will be coming in a few days to go to school. The school opens on September 23. Today is September 12. If my wife is arrested now, my daughter will be arrested upon her arrival at the airport.

The iron door of the ward opens, closes, opens and closes again. Thingified men and women crawl in the corridor. What time is it? How am I going to tell them that I believe in certain things for myself and that I don't have to believe in exactly the same things they believe in? The nationalities, the classes of people, the poor, their relations to the rich, all the words I have said and written about them come to mind. I was trying to bring together a group of scholars who would devote part of their time to the revival of Azarbaijani culture. Has any one of them betrayed me? This is impossible. One has written single-handedly a dictionary of Azarbaijani Turkish. He is our Dr. Johnson. Was Dr. Johnson a member of SAVAK? The other one writes songs in Turkish and plays them on his setar. A third tells me he will get all the data I need in Azarbaijani folklore. They are the most dedicated men I have ever seen. They may be betrayed by others, but they would never themselves betray anyone.

My mind moves to my contacts in the press. I have read my article on the nationalities to a half-blind man on the phone. He has been in prison several times. I have talked to several writers. I trust most of them. I move to the University of Teheran. I trust two or three people there and no more. The university has been a hell for me. I have seen my students beaten in the corridors of the faculty and on campus. The Shah's special forces, supported by SAVAK, have marched onto the university campus more than a hundred times during my academic career. With their long truncheons, shields, pistols and clean uniforms. I have seen the gates of the university barred by police and army trucks, so that the students escaping from the network of the special forces and SAVAK on campus might be trapped by them there and loaded into the trucks. I have seen some of my colleagues beaten by the police. I know that the old faculty members are emasculated and the new ones are afraid. I know that the university is a beehive of agents, and I haven't kept my mouth shut. Press reports and reports from the university and abroad, from the University of Texas and the University of Utah, where I taught, and from the universities in which I have lectured or read my poetry . . . yes, reports from these places will be used against me. In all these places I have spoken of the problem of nationalities and repression and censorship in Iran. The United States is a beehive for SAVAK agents. I knew it then, and I came to know even more about it in prison.

Suddenly I wake up. Was I really asleep and dreaming all these things? The door is open. How could they have opened it so quietly? Squatting at the door is Dr. Azudi. He must have been looking at me for a long time. The guard is standing behind him. He is looking at me. All the other cells are silent. It must be midnight.

"Why you—a university professor, a well-known poet and a prominent journalist—should do something so that we will be forced to deal with you like some kind of criminal."

"But I haven't done anything."

He gets up and comes in, telling the guard to close the door and go away. Squatting again, he faces me.

"You have done something. Otherwise you wouldn't be here."

"There has been a misunderstanding. I haven't done anything!"

"There is no misunderstanding. Everyone in this country, from the simple private in the army to the First Person of the Nation [the Shah] knows that you are a traitor."

"Traitor to whom?"

"To the Shah and the country." He raises his hand and touches my cheeks, looking into my eyes. "You are a traitor. We have all the documents."

He slaps me on the face as hard as he can. I fall on the floor, and he kicks me and punches me with his fists. I start screaming. I know from the torture chamber that whenever I scream I feel some relief. The other prisoners are startled from their sleep and start screaming themselves. He goes on beating me and cursing me.

"I've fucked more than twenty poets in this cell. You know what I mean? Fucked them in the ass. The same thing will happen to you if you don't confess. You know what I mean?"

I keep screaming.

He opens the door and shouts at the other prisoners, "You go to sleep, you bastards!"

They seem to know his voice. They fall silent. I crouch in a corner of the cell.

The opening of the cells at night and the beating of prisoners to a pulp: during the one hundred and two days that I will spend in prison, this will occur a number of times.

THE MAN IN CELL 17

On the fourth day of my imprisonment I am removed from dungeon cell number 14 and taken to number 17. Number 14 is totally dark, night or day. Located in the worst part of the Komité prison, it is generally used to hold the prison's more "dangerous elements." There are six cell 14's, two on each floor, one in each ward, but the one in ward 1 on the first floor is the worst of all, wet and pitch-dark, facing the open toilets from which a nauseating odor permeates the entire ward. The little vent on the iron door is kept shut because the guards don't want anyone to see who is going to the toilets. They want to prevent the prisoners from being able to identify one another. But there are other reasons. They love to observe the naked bodies of their victims, particularly if these victims are in the awkward posture of taking a shit. They don't want anybody watching them watch their victim-objects.

Life in cell 17 is more tolerable, for two reasons. First, because I meet M. A. Sh., who is a pillar of human resistance; second, because the sun, passing in its ordinary direction in the world outside, generously sheds some light onto the opposite wall, across from the little hole located on the top of the high wall. Later on I will raise myself on tiptoe to allow this meager light to touch my face. This is to be my sole connection with the free world. I will woo the sun to take me out through the little hole in the wall, feed me to birds and beasts, and help me to escape from rotting away in the hands of these human executioners.

M.A. tries to get up and shake hands, but he cannot. He is a short and sturdy man, with heavily swollen hands and feet. The problem with him is that no matter how badly he is flogged with the braided wire, he cannot bleed. His swollen hands and feet give him a primitive look, as if the rest of his body has grown into full humanity by a miraculous accident, leaving the hands and feet in the primeval forest. His eyes shine like two spoonfuls of blood. He appears to suffer from severe diarrhea, but he tells me later that he hurts from the great pain in his testicles and penis, and he pisses blood, because he has been given shocks with the electric prod in his genitals. He is afraid he has become permanently impotent, but a few nights later, when he has a wet dream, he is happy. He undergoes torture twenty hours a day, every day. This will go on for ten days until finally he is removed from cell 17 and I am again left alone.

M.A. crawls into the cell in the middle of the night. He says, "I haven't told them yet." His torturer was Dr. Rassouli, one of the most brutal sadists in SAVAK, who tortures leftists. M.A.'s crime is that he kept a copy of *The Communist Manifesto* in his room for one night. He tells me that he hasn't read it, and in conversations we have together he demonstrates that he has not. But since Dr. Rassouli hasn't read it either, they cannot prove to each other that one or the other of them or both has or has not read it. In the meantime, M.A. undergoes all forms of torture.

He is thrown into the courtyard pool of the prison. The pool is small and shallow. Four or five torturers beat him from outside the pool with sticks and maces and batons. They spray water on him from a powerful hose, and when he doesn't know which way to turn they beat him from where they stand outside the pool. Then they strip him naked and seize the braided wire whip and flog him while he is wet. His mutilated body is taken to Dr. Rassouli and set before him. The question is the same as always: "Who gave you the *Manifesto?*" The answer, too, is the same as always: "I don't know."

M.A. would not betray anyone. When he finally tells them, it is because the very individual who gave him the book is confronted with him and admits to giving it to him. M.A. cannot now deny it, and he is sentenced to eight years in prison merely for having *seen* the book and for "Communist activity" based upon the sole fact of his having laid eyes on it.

A DESCRIPTION OF PRISON

The interrogation goes on every day and sometimes at night. The interrogator is the same person, Dr. Rezvan, with assistance from his colleagues coming generally in the form of physical torture. Dr. Azudi, Dr. Rassouli, Dr. Shadi, Dr. Mostafavi (who was a torturer as well as the head interrogator), Dr. Manouchehri, Dr. Hosseini —all those weird potentates of horror pay me their visits, sometimes at the recommendation of my interrogator, other times on their own initiative, almost whimsically. Some of these happenstance bouts of beatings take place on the way to or from my cell. I don't know whether my interrogator tells them to beat me or whether they do it on their own. They simply stop me, take the blindfold away and slap and kick me, squeeze my stomach or sides in their hands, bring down their fists upon my shoulders and chest or poke me in the sides.

Each of these men has his own reasons. Dr. Shadi tells me, "Your head and the heads of the likes of you should be cut off with an ax! Some people lay hands on a rifle and run out and shoot a policeman. That is only getting rid of one man. But you try to turn all of the people of Iran against us. We should never be merciful to you or take pity on you."

Dr. Rassouli says, "I have heard you speak, you son of a bitch, in Ferdowsi Hall at the University of Teheran! I know how you agitate the people against the government. If you had the power, you would have all of us shot. But we will shoot you before that happens."

Dr. Azudi is the ever-threatening man: "Remember what I told you in the torture chamber! Your wife and daughter . . ."

Some of them know about my cryptic style of quibbling, and they even know the way I have responded to difficult questions. "Your innocence brings tears to my eyes," one of them says: And the other echoes the same theme: "As guileless as an Imam, as smooth as an egg, as pure as a newborn baby. Wait and see how we will fuck you into confessing." There is one man, Dr. Houshang Tehrani, who tells me all kinds of odd things about me and my family, claims that he knows me very well, is a good friend of mine, and that if I tell him about my accomplices in the writing of the article, he will talk to Dr. Hosseinzadeh and I will be set free. When I tell him what I have told the others, that I write my articles myself and not with outside help, he starts beating me up, too.

Dr. Rezvan has his desk on the second floor, right by the torture chamber, and with him sits Dr. Parsa—whose real name is apparently Captain Qatri, since I have heard him introduce himself as such on the telephone. This "Doctor" is in charge of the electric shock machine. One of his victims—H.A.—has told me about it.

Captain Qatri tells me that he used to paint when he was in the United States, but now he writes poetry. He even shows me some of his poems. Not bad at all, for a torturer. Why not publish them under the title *Love Poems of the Shah's Torturer?* I don't say that to him, of course. But thoughts float freely in one's mind, even at the threshold of the torture chamber and even under torture. If one couldn't at least imagine things here, he would die. It was imagination that kept the primitive man alive, and now it is imagination that keeps me alive in this primeval hell, so that I can think about the torturer and hate him and laugh at him even as he sits there before me.

One early morning the Captain calls me up to his desk. But he is not my interrogator! What is the matter? Is the red-eyed inquisitor dead?

"Your wife has got in touch with Miss F.S., who has got in touch with my wife, and I have told my wife to tell Miss F.S. to tell your wife that you are all right, and that if there is a problem I will try to solve it."

"Thank you, sir, thank you," I say, and wait to see what he is going to ask me to do for him. He is handsome, tall and presentable in any company. He could easily pass for some romantic duke who also happened to write poetry and read it to his numerous mistresses.

"If there is something wrong with your cell, tell me and I'll send you to a better one."

"No, sir, thank you, my cell is all right." I have just gotten used to a student from the University of Teheran, and I am not going to move to another cell.

"I wanted to ask you a favor," he says, giving me the shock of my life. "I . . . well, my wife is a student in the College of Translation. She is about to graduate. She needs a short paper. Her teacher has told her that she can write a research paper on any important figure from the East, and she has chosen the life of the Buddha. I asked Dr. Ali Shariati to write an article on the Buddha; he did, but it is in Persian. I wanted to ask you to translate it into English."

There are many surprises in his words. I have heard from other inmates that Ali Shariati, the famous Iranian theologian, is in prison, but I am not sure. And now the torturer is telling me himself that Ali is here.

"Ali was brought here a few days after you were arrested. He told me that he would finish the article tomorrow. Can you translate it in one day?"

"Sure I can. It'll be good to translate something on the life of the Buddha. I'll be more than happy to do it."

"I'll send after you tomorrow," he says, and I am taken back to my cell.

When I was drafted into the army in 1960, one of my jobs was to write the B.A. theses of the wives and daughters of generals, colonels and captains. I taught the company commander a few of Shakespeare's sonnets, Wordsworth's "Prelude" and Shelley's odes so that he could take his test in the English Department of the university, which I later joined as an English professor. And now I was going to participate in the writing of the thesis of a torturer's wife. Two professors in prison would cooperate without meeting—or even seeing one another, of course—to write the thesis of the wife of one of our torturers. When I finally saw Ali Shariati in one of the cells toward the end of my stay in prison, he said Captain Qatri had told him the article was being translated by me.

After I finish the translation the next day, I tell the Captain that I should explain parts of it to him so he will know what's going on. He can pass on my remarks to his wife. Ali compared Buddhist thought with Western thought, contrasting the spiritual thinking of the Buddha with the thinking of Hegel and Marx. While I am explaining all of this, particularly the passages dealing with Marx, he suddenly turns to me.

"Wait a minute! I hope you're not pulling my leg. I hope you aren't trying to indoctrinate me. These things on Marx, they'll certainly get my wife thrown into prison!"

"It's nothing but a comparison, and it shouldn't bother anyone."

"But it may. Who knows what you sons of bitches have up your sleeves? One hardly knows whether you're talking for something or against it. Let us eliminate these passages; just cross them out."

We cross out the references; in fact, we cross so many out that the article could be about practically anything but the Buddha. When I tell the Captain that this is what happens to our articles in the censorship bureaus of the government, he gets so angry that he himself puts the blindfold over my eyes, calls the guard and sends me back to my cell.

But my stay for one whole day in his room, especially with him and Dr. Rezvan absent and my eyes without the blindfold, gives me a good opportunity to find out how the prison looks. When I hear no footsteps on the balcony, I get up, go to the window and look out. The courtyard is more or less round. There are three floors with a half a story added on the top. The round building, seen from the inside, seems to taper at the top.

When the prisoner is brought in, he first passes through narrow lanes with high walls on either side. He is brought in through an iron door to the room of the Captain of the Guards. There his belongings are taken away from him: his money, the contents of his pockets, his belt, socks, shoelaces. The books confiscated from his office or his home are listed, and he is forced to sign a letter saying that these "dangerous books" belong to him. Most of these books are by Iranian writers, with several foreign authors among them: Brecht, Gorky, Jack London and several others. They don't confiscate books in foreign languages. The men who came to inspect my apartment could have passed over the works of the great

Western revolutionaries without even recognizing them; they were looking for an anthology of poetry published after the famous Iranian wrestler Gholamreza Takhti was killed by SAVAK. This anthology was much more dangerous in their eyes than the three-volume English edition of Marx on capitalism.

The prisoner is then led blindfolded through a second iron door, which opens into the courtyard. If he could see, opposite him he would find a flight of stairs and, to their right, rooms with open windows on the first floor. To the left of the stairs, there is a corridor that leads to the showers, way back at the end of the corridor; looking up, the prisoner would see the two top floors and the half-story on top, then the round patch of sky. Each of these two top floors has a balcony attached to it, looking over the courtyard and the pool. The part of the building directly opposite contains the torture chambers of the "Joint Committee against Terrorism in Iran," or "Joint Counterinsurgency Committee of Iran." SAVAK and the gendarmerie and the Iranian army and the Department of Police have coordinated their activities and centralized them in this Joint Committee, briefly known in the world and in Iran as the "Komité."

All around those balconies and floors are the interrogation rooms and torture chambers. If the prisoner were given a chance, he would be able to examine the place in less than half an hour. But his mind and imagination can speculate in fear and horror about the things that go on inside the simple, iron-clad building. He is never going to examine it in freedom and with eyes wide open. Many prisoners have blindfolds over their eyes even in the torture chambers. They know about everything through what others tell them.

One of the guards who was gradually becoming friendly to me asked me which floor I had been taken to for torture. I told him the third floor. He said, "You should be thankful you weren't taken to the second floor. Even I am afraid when I walk in there." I didn't tell him that I had been there, not to be tortured but out of mere curiosity. A description of the chamber there appears elsewhere in this book, but I will add a few things here. The iron bed in this chamber is different from the other beds. It is taller, reaching almost to the waist of a man of middle height. When he lies on it, the prisoner feels a soft slope from his head to his waist and from then on a leveling off. At one end of the bed there is a helmet, resembling that of a motorcyclist. The head of the victim is placed in it, generally through the left side, so that when he screams he will hear his own voice but his torturers will be spared. The diapasonal quality of the helmet is such that the prisoner hears the sound of hundreds of people screaming at the same time. The prisoner's hands and feet are placed inside vises on the sides and the lower part of the bed. He can no longer move. I have heard this from many prisoners inside the Komité. The underground pamphlets published inside the country and sent abroad have similar descriptions.

If the prisoner standing by the gate looks to his right, he will see other offices. If he turns left, he will see the entrance to the wards, through stairs and the balcony. If he were free to move around, say, like a tourist, he would see the iron door to each ward by the stairs. There are six wards on three floors: wards 1, 3 and 5 are on one side; wards 2, 4 and 6, on the other. Wards 1 and 2, located on the first floor, are the worst parts of the Komité. Here are the solitary confinement cells, with nothing but a blanket on the floor. I believe there are twenty-three cells in wards 1–4, but the cells on the third floor in wards 5 and 6 are larger. On the two lower floors, there are eleven cells on the right and twelve on the left, with the twenty-third cell being larger than the others. Cell number 1 is on the right as you enter the ward, then come cells 2–11, after which is the toilet with two or three holes in the floor. Across from cell 11 is cell 12. The cells continue along the left side of the corridor back toward the ward door until one reaches cell 23.

In this, the last cell of one of the two worst wards of the Komité, I saw the two brothers of the poet Manouchehr Ateshi one night when I was mopping and washing the floor of the ward. The door of the cell was open. One of the brothers had been a student of mine. I started with half the hemistich of a poem by his brother, "The wild white horse," and one of the brothers answered from memory with the second part of the line, "stands proudly at the manger." Then he rushed out and seized the bucket and the mop from my hands to help me clean the floor.

It was in ward 6 that I finally came across the theologian Ali Shariati, who, finding out that I hadn't slept on a mattress for ninety-seven days, gave me his own, after which we talked more than twenty hours in front of a man who had been sent to Ali's cell to keep an eye on him. I had never seen Ali before, and I never saw him again.

The cells used to be smaller in number, and all as large as number 23, when the prison was used years ago for ordinary criminals. They have cut them in half and built up walls in front of the doors of the cells, so that you cannot see the doors of the opposite cells from your cell. Thus communication among prisoners is limited mainly to speaking with those who share your cell and to using codes, tapping on the wall of an adjacent cell. You divide the Persian alphabet into four horizontal and eight vertical lines, with eight letters for each of the four horizontal columns. You knock on the wall several times with your fist. The other person knocks back, signaling that he or she is ready. You use your fist for the horizontal and your knuckles for the vertical. You encode; the other person decodes and sends a response.

Once, when I was alone in cell 16 of ward 3, I heard a woman crying in the next cell. I encoded my name to her; she sent a message back with her name and telling me she was an English student in the university. We heard footsteps outside and stopped. At midnight she encoded something which was very strange for an Iranian prison. The first word was "Pablo"; the second, "Neruda." I waited. Why Pablo Neruda's name in an Iranian prison? She sent in the third word: "dead." She knew, because she had just come from the outside. In prison the outside world is totally hidden.

The prison stinks, especially on the first floor. The cells stink even worse than the corridor. You don't realize this when you stay inside, but after you come back to your cell from interrogation, you are aware of being immersed in a receptacle of foul odor. There are two places for the air to get in, one way above the iron door, with the dim light burning beneath it, and the other high up on the wall facing the door. This hole used to be a window in the old days. Now they have blinded the window almost to the ceiling, leaving only a small open space at the top. The ceiling is very high. Even the tallest prisoner cannot reach it with his hand, jumping as high as he can. The cells on the first floor get very little sun. The prisoners and guards often refer to this floor as "the basement." The guards hate the first floor, and their hatred of the place makes them hard on the prisoners. They swear at them and beat them and force them repeatedly to clean the toilets. In cell 14, where I spent my early days in prison, I would stretch my neck up as far as I could, just to try to see if there was any sun outside. I could never tell. In cell 16 on the second floor, B.E. and I would take turns standing in the light of the sun which fell on the wall for only about a half-hour each day. We held our faces to the sun until it faded. This cell at least smelled better.

The prisoner Mos. Sh., who had been in Qizil-qaleh prison in 1970–1971, told me that he had seen scorpions in his cell and that sometimes snakes were thrown into his cell to frighten him. He showed me the scars of several burns made on his hand, made by Dr. Hosseinzadeh's cigarettes. The famous Iranian guerrilla Ashraf Dehaqani, who made her heroic escape from Qasr prison several years ago, speaks in her memoirs of torture by snakes. They let several snakes crawl around your body, pretending that they themselves are too afraid to touch them.

The man who administers this kind of torture is apparently this same Hosseinzadeh. I saw him one day in the interrogation room. I had not seen him since the day of my first torture. He walked in with a cigarette in his hand. There were several prisoners writing the answers to their questions.

"This looks like the entrance examination of the University of Teheran," he said. "I think we should put Reza Baraheni in charge of the examination." He came to me and took my beard in his hand. "Who told you to let it grow? Who told you?"

"I don't know. It's just that, well, nobody has come to shave me."

"Shave it tomorrow."

"I don't have a razor!"

"I know that, you son of a bitch. I know that if I gave you a razor, you would cut your throat the minute you were alone with it. I'll send the barber to your cell tomorrow. Tell him I have ordered you to look like an egg."

He moved to a woman who was busy writing with her back to him. He put his hand on her hair and started running it through her curls. The woman shook off his hand. He put it back on her head and recited like a Shakespearean actor:

"It shines today, it won't shine tomorrow."

The woman got up and stood in a corner. Hosseinzadeh no longer paid any attention to her.

He moved to a young man sitting by one of the interrogators.

His left hand held the paper; with his right hand he was writing. The torturer put one hand on the young man's shoulder, then brought his cigarette down very coolly and pressed it to the young man's left hand. The young man tried to rise, but the torturer's strong hand held him in place until he finally threw the cigarette away and walked out of the room. After a few minutes Dr. Rezvan went to the door and looked out. Even he was afraid of the arch-torturer. The young man was suffering in silence. We were sent back to our cells a bit early that night.

Lice are most common in the Komité. H.A. got them all over him. He was in cell 18 of ward 1; I was in cell 17 of the same ward with three other men: S.A.J., a poet from Mazandaran; A.A.Y., a member of the Shah's Literacy Corps whose left arm had been paralyzed by weight cuffs; and M.R., who pissed blood for several days. They took M.R. out every night, blindfolded him and drove him somewhere downtown, where they kept him at a window, at gunpoint, so that he would betray the identity of one of the Sepehri brothers who was at large. Two of the brothers had already been killed; the government was after the third. M.R. told me that four years ago he had been a classmate of this young Sepehri in Sari, near the Caspian Sea; he would hardly know the young man now if he saw him. But his torture went on, until we heard that Sepehri had been apprehended elsewhere.

H.A. gets the lice. He calls out to me, "What shall I do, Doctor? I've got lice."

He has one of the best memories I have ever come across. He recites poetry day and night. We have become friendly through poetry.

"I don't know," I tell him. "Recite a poem and they'll disappear."

"It's really serious, Doctor. They move all over my hair and face, and I catch them and kill them, but they keep coming back. I itch and scratch. I'm afraid I might get typhoid."

"Does Sh. have them too?"

Sh. is his cellmate.

"No, he doesn't. The lice don't find him sweet and good enough to eat."

"You should ask your interrogator for some *vadjebi* [depilatory potion, an Iranian folk remedy]," I say.

"I think I should ask Captain Qatri to give me and the lice

electric shock. The lice will confess to my crime before they die."

We laugh, but in less than an hour they come and take H.A. out, beat him up and bring him back. He doesn't know why he was beaten up this time. He was not interrogated on anything. He was simply beaten up by several men in one of the interrogation rooms.

The next day, when I go for interrogation, I tell Dr. Rezvan about the lice. He asks me how I know about it. I tell him one of the guards was talking to the prisoners in the neighboring cell and I had heard it come up. I ask him to do something.

For several days H.A. lives in fear. If he has a headache or constipation or diarrhea, he imagines it to be typhoid, and none of us really knows what the symptoms of typhoid are. Another complication is added. H.A.'s cellmate comes back crying from interrogation. We hear him through the wall. We also hear the guard walking in the corridor. I try to send a message. H.A. responds: "His brother." I try to get other messages through, but it is impossible.

I get up and yell, "Guard! I've got a stomachache. Let me go to the toilet."

"Wait until after dinner."

"I can't. It's diarrhea. I can't wait."

A prisoner from the other side of the ward, a man who started reciting a poem of mine when he came to know who I was, shouts, "Have pity on him, guard. He has diarrhea. Let him go to the toilet."

The guard says, "All right, shut up and I'll let him go!"

We all fall silent. H.A.'s cellmate is still crying. He is sobbing so loudly that everyone in the ward can hear him. The guard opens the door and sends me and my cellmates to the toilet. He doesn't have enough blindfolds for the three of us. I come back sooner than the others. They know they should take some time so that I can have a chance to talk to H.A.'s cellmate. The guard is standing by the toilet.

"What's wrong, H.A.?" I ask.

"His brother's heart failed under torture. They've taken him to the hospital. The interrogator has told him if he wants to see his brother ever again he should confess."

"Is he sure his brother's heart has failed?"

The young boy answers himself, sobbing. "He had a weak

heart. They gave him electric shock. He must be dead by now."

"What is your brother's crime?" I ask.

"Books."

"What kind of books?"

"The same books everybody reads. Al-Ahmad's *Westomania*, Gorky's *Mother* and some others."

"Did you have a group, or did only the two of you study these books?"

"We studied them together."

H.A. has forgotten about the lice and the fear of typhoid. He puts his mouth into the vent. I see his mustache going up and down through the hole. "What shall we do, Doctor?"

"His brother couldn't be dead, otherwise they wouldn't want to take him to see him after he confesses."

"But there's nothing more I can tell them," the boy sobs from inside. "There's nothing more to confess."

The guard brings my cellmates. He locks our cell door on us and goes into the corridor.

We send a hundred messages that night, and we receive as many from the other side. I decide to talk to Dr. Rezvan about it when I am taken out. I don't know how I'll bring it up. But before long the boy himself is taken out. He comes back at night. A distant relative of the family, a general in the army, has mediated, and the boy has been taken to the army hospital to see his brother. The brother is alive. They only see each other and smile. They are not allowed to speak. The boy is so happy that he hugs lice-ridden H.A.

The following Friday, H.A. is given *vadjebi* to take off his hair. The blankets from all the cells and all the prison clothes are thrown outdoors to be washed, and the guards come in with insecticide.

Someone says, "There's a rumor that investigators from the U.N. are going to come to the Komité."

I doubt that. "Princess Ashraf was the president of the Human Rights Commission of the U.N.," I say. "No one from that commission will ever set foot in the Komité. The Komité is ours, the lice are ours, the heart attacks are ours, the torture chambers are ours."

They come and beat me up until I forget what I was thinking out loud. And later I am taken out to the interrogation room where an older man, Dr. Javan (Colonel Assar), gives me all kinds of advice on how I should behave in order to stay alive in prison. He speaks very slowly, like a man from his deathbed, and he removes his glasses, puts them back on, then removes them again for no apparent reason. I have heard something about his brutality from the other prisoners, but, sitting there, I think that this man would need help from the other torturers even to go to the toilet. But the prison authorities have pretended to be so many things at all times that I think perhaps one way or another he must have a brutal character hidden behind that soft voice.

On the way back they don't find the blindfold, and I am ordered to cover my eyes with my hands. We get into the ward with help from the guard. I see through my fingers five or six men leaning with their foreheads against the wall. What is this? I ask myself. Why are they standing in this inconvenient and awkward position? I ask the guard to send me to the toilet. He tells me: "Run and do your job and get back to your cell!" Once in the toilet, I turn around, pop my head back out and observe:

There are five men, forehead to wall. Their hands are held behind them. Their feet and legs have been spread-eagled at some distance from the wall. The two guards poke the prisoners in the side and stomach with their truncheons and shout, "Ass and trunk as far from the wall as you can. Come on!" When a prisoner has trouble assuming that position or holding it, the guards strike him with the truncheon hard on the back of the legs. Finally, all five prisoners stand silently in a position which pleases the guards. In less than ten minutes there is blood running from the noses of all of them. It trickles in drops and forms little pools by the wall. They try to make moves to stretch their feet and legs and get rid of the pain in their stomachs as well as the pressure on their noses which is, apparently, the cause of the bleeding. The guards threaten them with truncheons.

I come out of the toilet and walk toward my cell. The guard suddenly sees me.

"Where were you?" he asks, as if it weren't he who had sent me to the toilet.

"I was in the toilet."

"Go put your nose to the wall!" he shouts.

"I won't do that," I tell him.

I walk to my cell, open the door and go in and lie down. Today

I have had enough of all of them. Today I will resist being tortured by them. I recite a poem as loudly as I can, and H.A. joins me from the other cell. When the two of us reach the refrains, others join in, turning the refrains to a chorus. At dinner time we can see that the five men are not in the corridor any more. The guards are angry, but they have been frustrated and, for a time, subdued.

THE FIRST MEETING WITH MY FAMILY

My feet are swollen and infected. I ask the interrogator to ask the prison doctor to take a look at my feet. He smiles and doesn't answer. I insist, and he asks:

"How do you know they are infected? Are you a doctor of medicine?"

"No, I am not, but I think they are infected. The prison is not the cleanest place in the world. You could ask the doctor to at least take a look."

"So you are not sure that they are infected. Then they are not infected."

"But, still, a doctor . . ."

"We'll see what happens."

At night the hole in the door is opened and a few aspirins are thrown in. I didn't ask for aspirin!

I shout, "I need penicillin, not aspirin."

"Shut up!" the prison medic yells from outside.

At midnight on the seventh day, when I am lying on the floor, the door is flung open and a huge hairy man stands before me with a long needle in his hand. I am immediately reminded of the torture chambers of Reza Shah, where prisoners were given shots of air bubbles by a physician named Ahmadi. Later I find out that Reza Shah's prison was located on these very same grounds, and it was here that the air bubbles were injected and cushions placed over the faces of the prisoners to be sat on by one of the executioners.

The hairy man looks at me. "Penicillin."

"Are you sure?" I ask.

"Quite sure," he says.

I fear for my life, but I have to take the risk. "Shall I go lie down?"

"No, just pull down your pants."

I pull down my pants. He injects me and goes away. I wait.

I don't expect to be given air bubbles at this time, but so many unexpected things, so many gruesome things, have happened to me during the last few days that I wouldn't be surprised at their throwing antediluvian beasts into my cell to devour me whole.

Yet nothing happens. The next day I am called out. I limp into the interrogator's office. I see Dr. Hosseinzadeh, Dr. Mostafavi and Dr. Rezvan.

"Why are you limping, you son of a bitch?" asks the first "doctor."

"The soles of my feet are still sore. They hurt when I put them down."

"No, you are pretending. Can you walk without pretending to be lame?"

"I am not pretending to be lame. At present I am lame, and that's all there is to it."

"Which means that you don't want to see your wife," says the second "doctor."

"My wife? What has she got to do with my sore feet?"

"She is coming to see you at five," says the third "doctor." "If you promise that you won't pretend you are lame in front of your family, we'll take you to see them."

"I promise. I won't limp," I say immediately. In my mind I say that I will even dance if you sons of bitches will let me see my wife and family.

The joke is over. I go back to my cell. The guard comes after me at five o'clock. He puts the blindfold on me. We walk out the door into the room of the Captain of the Guards, where they handcuff me, and then out from the prison area to a place which I later discover to be none other than the Central Department of Police. We stand at a door. The handcuffs and blindfold are removed. I see Dr. Rezvan by my side.

"Don't tell them about the torture," he says, "and tell them to reject all foreign correspondents. If you do otherwise, this will be the last time you see them."

I promise that I won't do otherwise. But I know very well that this will not be the first time I will break my promise to the Iranian Gestapo, nor will it be the last.

The door is opened. I enter and stand just inside. I see my wife, my mother, my wife's step-mother and my older brother. They look at me, but they don't say anything. What has happened? Is this the welcome I was expecting? Why are they so indifferent? I don't walk, fearing that they might see I am limping.

Suddenly, my mother shouts out, "But it is Reza! Don't you see? He's only changed!"

The interrogator does not know my mother's language. It is because of that language that I have been tortured.

My wife gets up. I walk, pretending that there is nothing wrong with my feet. We sit down. My brother shakes hands with me and sits down with the interrogator. My wife is by my side.

"But why has this happened? Why? What have you done?" She is crying and questioning me at the same time. "Have they hurt you? Who is this man? Are you being kept in one of the rooms in this building? Is it because of the articles you wrote or because of the things you did and said in the United States? Have they tortured you? If not, why are your hands swollen? What happened to your beard and hair? Did they shave you by force or did you do it voluntarily?"

She immediately makes me conscious of all the things that have happened to me. I try my best to answer her. I cannot tell her about the torture now, even if I want to. I tell her that I had my hair and beard shaved because I thought they needed a rest.

"But why are you so pale? Why did you lose so much weight?"

Who cares for his weight here and how do I know what color I am in prison? I cannot tell her about my feelings about prison. Instead, I ask her a question:

"Are you pregnant? You were going to go for the tests."

She is crying. I never knew that she was capable of crying this much. "I think I'm pregnant, but I'll know for sure tomorrow."

"That's great, don't you think?"

"What's the problem? Why have they got you?"

"It's because of my article. They didn't like it."

I ask my mother what is happening outside. She was not in Teheran when I was arrested, and she tells me that she heard about it from someone who came from the small city of Marand to the north of Tabriz, our hometown. My wife tells me that someone has just come from Berkeley and has told her that the Iranians in that city know about my arrest.

"So quick?" I ask my wife.

The interrogator and my brother are so deeply involved in

conversation that I think they will go out and dine together. The interrogator turns to me:

"I think his excellency, the Doctor, should tell the ladies that he is comfortable and that they shouldn't worry."

He is using his second language with us today, and my brother's politeness has given him a sense of pride and respect which he does not anticipate from the relatives of those he has hurt.

I tell the members of my family that they shouldn't worry about anything. They should never talk to a foreigner, and if anyone asks about my whereabouts they can say I am on a trip abroad and will be back soon.

I think I have satisfied the interrogator. He smiles and says a few things about what a great and learned man I am, and how proud he is that he has made my acquaintance, and how he hopes that the friendship between the two of us will not be limited to my short presence in prison. My mother, who doesn't understand any of these words, turns to my wife's stepmother. "What is this gravedigger saying in Farsi?"

My wife's stepmother gives a passing smile and says, "He is talking about Reza's greatness and goodness."

My mother curses the interrogator in her typical way: "May the liar's tongue turn into iron and stone and get stuck in his throat."

Dr. Rezvan asks, "What does the lady say?"

My wife's stepmother says, "The lady says, 'Bless you and yours!' "

I never thought Dr. Rezvan could be sociable. He tells my brother that he looks younger than I do, although he is the older of the two of us.

My brother, who has already sensed the factuality of my torture, says, "He takes life very seriously. I don't."

My wife tells me she has brought cigarettes and towels and pajamas for me. Dr. Rezvan says very politely that she can give them all to the guard and can be certain they will be given to me inside the cell. My wife hands them to the guard. None of us will ever see any of those things again.

"Are you going to grow a beard again?" my wife asks me.

"I don't know. It depends on the Doctor. If he gives me permission, I might grow a beard again."

"I wanted to bring you a razor," she tells me, "but I didn't know whether you needed one or not."

The interrogator blurts out, "No, ma'am, there is no need for a razor. The barber comes in every day, and if the Professor wants, they will shave him right away."

Not only razors, but even shoelaces are forbidden in the prison. The authorities are afraid the prisoners will kill themselves before they confess. One of the prisoners told me that one night a young boy chewed his veins open at the wrist before he was taken to the torture chamber. He pulled the blanket up over his head and bled to death. When they came to get him, they found his lifeless body. Now you are not allowed to put your head behind the cell door when you sleep, or anyplace where the guards or torturers cannot see it when they look through the door vent at night. You put your head on the floor, opposite the door, and you never cover it. At night you hear the guards shouting, "Get up and sleep properly!" You hear this on your very first night of imprisonment.

Dr. Rezvan gets up. Then we all get up. I say goodbye to everybody. They all go away before I do. We wait for a few minutes. The guard walks briskly in, puts the blindfold over my eyes and ties me to himself with the handcuffs. Then we go back the way we came.

That night, when M.A. is brought back from the torture chamber and I tell him that I have been to see my family, he immediately asks, "Did you tell them to send a telegram to your daughter so that she won't come back until you're out of prison?"

"Oh, my God, no!" I say. "How could I have forgotten something that important?"

AN AGENT IN MY CELL

A young man is thrown into dungeon cell 17. He tells me that he has been in Qasr, one of the oldest prisons in Teheran. But he doesn't look like a prisoner. An Iranian prison produces very serious effects on the face and the eyes. The face yellows in a few days, and the eyes become frenzied out of fear, morbid dread and insomnia. Nothing of this transformation is evident in this man. He also appears to be extremely brash and reckless compared with the rest of the prisoners.

He talks incessantly of revolution, of the situation of the

Iranian nationalities, of language and culture and their relation to imperialism, of the Arabs and Israel, of the Palestinians and their connection with the Iranian opposition. He ends every ideological discourse with a leading question: "What do you think?" He also seems to have read some of my work. I give him very vague answers. He pretends to be perplexed that I, "a revolutionary," should give such uncommitted and ambiguous replies. I tell him that my feet hurt terribly and that I want to rest. He says he might be taken out any moment to be tortured and he wants the "benefit" of my knowledge and specific opinions on all these matters since he might not see me again.

I tell him that because of my physical condition I cannot think properly. He talks about the death of the famous wrestler at the hands of the SAVAK torturers. He describes the process step by step, and in minute detail, as if he was present when the wrestler died. I have heard about the death of the wrestler and simply nod when this apparent impostor speaks. He is disappointed. That same night he is blindfolded and removed from my cell before supper. I will see him two months later, sitting at the side of one of the interrogators.

The next night the following events occur: I cannot sleep, nor can anyone else. An infant is crying in the cell by the ward door. It screams incessantly, and whenever its voice dies in its throat, the mother speaks, always in the same pitiable voice: "The electric prod has dried up my breasts. Get me some milk or my child will starve." But her pleas have no effect. One of the guards shouts, "Shut up, you whore!" She becomes silent for a while, but the child continues to scream and again she begins calling for milk. I saw her when the vent on my door was left open by mistake. She had on her veil and was carrying the baby to the toilet. She had the serious face of a professional Iranian mother.

Suddenly, the door of my cell is flung open and someone lands a heavy fist on my chest. This is followed by kicks and blows from other assailants. I start to yell, but the unknown attackers continue pounding and kicking. Then I am blindfolded and taken out. I am dragged to a room on the third floor. I have been there several times by now, and I can tell, even with the blindfold on, where I am. I stay there for half an hour before someone comes in and tells me to leave. When I reply that I cannot see with the blindfold over my eyes, he comes over, takes me by the arm and leads me to the balcony.

Then the ritual of intimidation starts and goes on in the same way it went on, apparently, for the famous wrestler, as reported to me by the spy. A cloth is thrown over me and another person. The blindfold is taken away by the same man who is with me under the cloth. At first, I cannot recognize the huge face next to me. Then it dawns on me. The man is none other than the famous Azudi. Our faces are so close that we could easily kiss or bite each other. A combination of onion, garlic and some cheap cologne fills the air beneath the cloth. The huge black eyes which I saw on the first day of my torture now have a doubly demonic quality. They are sinister, shining from the depths of this ghost hidden here with me beneath the cloth. This man becomes almost an evil spirit. He strains to invade my soul. A mixture of black magic and sheer nightmare overtakes me.

"Why don't you tell me who told you to write that article on the nationalities?" the ghost asks, seizing my right cheek in his hand and squeezing very hard.

"I wrote the article myself," I say.

He grabs hold of my sides and begins pressing. "Tell me! Tell me!"

He keeps repeating and squeezing. I become short of breath and start panting. He gives up squeezing and starts kicking me hard in my stomach, groin and testicles. I fall down; the cloth is dropped, and we are there on the balcony in the open moonlight.

Now the beating begins, with the help of others, and goes on for what seems an eternity until I faint. When I open my eyes, I see the torturers whispering to each other. Someone tells me to get up. I try and fail. Then I try again and succeed. The blindfold is put on. The whispering resumes.

"Not tonight," Dr. Azudi says. "Mr. Hosseinzadeh isn't here."

This is the man in charge of all the torturers, but the whispering goes on in spite of his absence. Later, when it seems they have all gone away, I try to lift the blindfold. Someone slaps me hard on the face, and I give up. It is early morning when the man who slapped me is told to take me down for interrogation. But when we go downstairs and the blindfold is taken away, Dr. Rezvan hasn't yet come.

There in front of me stands the huge Dr. Shadi, who always

goes about the prison with a whip in his hand. His great expertise is in ripping out fingernails. But this early in the morning he doesn't like pulling nails.

"Open the palms of your hands!" he shouts.

He starts flogging my hands like the dutiful torturer he is, and he doesn't stop until my hands have become two hunks of painful flesh.

A NEW PATTERN OF METAMORPHOSIS

A young man is brought to my cell fresh from the Faculty of Science and Industry. We all have on our dirty uniforms; he is wearing tight-fitting pants and a clean, colorful shirt. He is quite sure that he will be released within the hour. Mustapha, a prisoner from Isfahan, asks me to tell the young man the ugly truth. Already I have become an expert in the habits of executioners and torturers. I tell him that they will come after him and take him out to the torture chamber. I tell him that fear is pointless; we have come out alive, and so will he.

The boy objects: "But it can't be true. I haven't done anything."

I tell him that most of the people I have seen here have done nothing, but they were tortured in spite of that. He sits in a corner and waits until they come for him as predicted. He goes away with the dirty blindfold over his eyes.

The door of the cell is opened, and a heap of broken bones is pushed in by the guards. The young man has been given electric shock, tortured by the pressure device and beaten all over. We can hardly recognize the face, the body, the pants, the shirt. When the door is closed, I stretch his legs out straight to the wall, put his head on my knees, take his face in my hands and pour the luke-warm soup we have kept for him into his mouth. I use the bowl itself, because forks and spoons are considered to be dangerous and we are not allowed to have them. Later, I carry him on my back to the toilet.

I have carried several like him in the past. I have told them that it was all right for them to take a crap while they hung from my back. I have only asked them not to piss at the same time. But I know it is very difficult in their condition to hold in their piss when they are shitting. I have washed them afterwards as a Moslem washes himself. Then I have carried them back to the cell. You don't learn humility in schools. You learn it in an Iranian prison.

I THOUGHT YOU WERE DEAD

"It cannot be you, Reza Baraheni! Outside there is a rumor that you were killed under torture. Everyone believes this rumor. I cannot believe my eyes. What happened to cause the rumor?"

These were the words of a prisoner from cell 18 on the first floor, spoken when we met by accident in the toilet.

I tell him, "I am still alive!"

TWO GIRLS

For the second time they take me out of the Komité area, blindfolded and handcuffed, to the Central Department of Police to see my wife. The station is attached to the prison. I can hear the autumn wind rustling through the trees of the large station courtyard. We go up the stairs and walk through long corridors. We stop. The handcuffs are locked. The blindfold is removed. The door is opened. I walk in and sit down by my wife.

A girl is brought in, barely thirteen years old. She sits down across from us. Dr. Rassouli comes in and sits behind the desk. Guards are seated all around us. Then a man walks in. The girl gets up, stands on tiptoe and kisses him. The man is tall and resembles a schoolteacher. The girl is crying. The man, her father, tries to console her. But she goes on crying. I can hear everything she says.

"That man sitting there is Dr. Rassouli. He is my interrogator. He is the one who raped me."

Now the father is crying, too.

After my wife goes away, I am blindfolded and handcuffed again. Back in the small courtyard of the prison, I am taken upstairs to my interrogator's room on the second floor. The blindfold is taken off. Dr. Rezvan isn't there. But there are screams coming from the torture chamber on this floor. My handcuffs have been unlocked, and the guard has gone away. I walk to the window. A little girl, scarcely six years old, has been placed in front of several men in handcuffs. My interrogator is there. Hosseini, the professional whipper of the Komité, asks the girl questions about the identity of these men. The girl is having difficulty understanding what the torturer is talking about. She is beaten on the face, and her ears and hair are pulled. When the questions are repeated, the girl is terror-struck. Hosseini beats her again.

This goes on for some time until one of the men in handcuffs can stand it no longer and gives away his identity. The girl is taken back to her cell. The man is taken to the third-floor torture chamber. I go back and sit down until my interrogator returns.

THE MEANING OF INTERROGATION

The interrogation moves on from my days as a student at the University of Istanbul, Turkey, to my military service in Teheran, to my visits to Egypt, the United States, Britain, Greece, then back again to Turkey and Teheran. The faces of my family members and acquaintances and those of men and women I have known, be it in my private or social life, rise from the abyss of my memory and tell me, "Forget us! Say you never knew us! Don't get us into trouble! We've got kids and family obligations; we can't afford to lose our salaries and our jobs; we can't stand torture! We don't want to accompany you to hell! Now that you are in hell, save your skin by any means you can, but without mentioning any of us!"

If only I could erase the memory of the past from my existence! I wish to tell all of these remembered men and women: It is not I who wish to speak of you; it is you yourselves, almost by your own doing, breaking through the stronghold of my memory, falling into trenches where the draconian enemy awaits with a thousand mouths. The name of a friend leaps to the surface almost of its own free will, invading my senses, and I try to hide the colors and the lines and the sounds. As soon as I have subdued one, another leaps up in its place, and another and another. Memory! My curses on you! I spit on you! I try to hide my memory, those images and faces and words, the patterns of illusion and disillusionment, in the dark recesses of another subconscious—recesses I have discovered as the interrogation has proceeded. I take these memories out of my usual human consciousness and conceal them in the depths of this subterranean subconscious. I do this with some skill, with the archetypal expertise of an omnipotent Satan —after all, am I not facing the questions of the omnipotent interrogator?—and I go on doing things which even a Freud or a Jung would not dream of exploring.

I know that I am dealing with a crisis of conscience; I am also dealing with a crisis of consciousness and the subconscious, be it individual or collective, familial or social. I am dealing with the distortions of faces, names, memories, languages, patterns and colors. I distort them first, and then I transport them through the invisible channels of my mind into the pockets of my sub-conscious. I have a huge fist, a clenched fist in which everything is hidden. It has grown like an enormous tumor in my spirit, and no "doctor," including this Dr. Rezvan, will be able to descend far enough to extract it or perform an autopsy. He will never be able to open the fist; therefore, he will proceed with amputation of the arm. I try to eradicate everyone from my memory, and in so doing I subject myself to the danger of being eradicated by Dr. Rezvan. But the satanic miracle takes place. I face Dr. Rezvan without my memories. I never believed that I would be able to lie with such skill. The interrogation moves at a rapid pace.

In one of my books I called the novelist "the scoundrel of the depths." Now, facing Dr. Rezvan, I have become that "scoundrel." Dr. Rezvan is the "scoundrel of surfaces." Now two hypocrites face each other; two liars embrace each other; two syphilitics copulate in the same bed of filth. And the outcome? Page after page of distortion in the name of interrogation. If these pages could rise vertically as incarnate species of things, you would see headless children or children with double heads, blind, dumb and mute figures of unknown beasts defiling the world with their foul breath.

WARD 1 AND WARD 3

One afternoon toward the middle of the second month we hear the doors of the cells in ward 1 open one by one. What is going on? We hear the orders: "Take everything! Pull something over your head!" (When they don't have enough blindfolds, they tell you to throw something over your head—a blanket, a jacket, a shirt. No one sees you, and you see no one. You see only your feet, like an animal grazing.)

They come to our cell and open the door. The torturer Dr. Rassouli and another man I am seeing for the first time stand in the doorway. They write our names on a piece of paper. They tell us to get up and cover our heads and walk out. I throw my jacket on my head and walk out of the cell with my blanket tucked under my arm. I can see polished shoes and boots from under my jacket. Someone throws a cigarette stub on the floor. I try to smell out what is happening. When the boots and shoes stop moving around us, we start to whisper.

"There's been a coup, perhaps," someone says.

"Perhaps it's a general amnesty," whispers another.

"Maybe they're going to shoot all of us," a third voice says in despair.

Boots appear ominously; they pass by, and someone says, "Who will ever know that we're here?"

I try to raise the jacket a bit. At the other end of the ward by the door I see prisoners with blankets over their heads being led out. One of the guards is using his truncheon, poking a prisoner in the side to get him to move faster through the door. I also see Dr. Azudi on the other side of the entrance. Dr. Rassouli turns toward us, and I pull my jacket back down over my head. Then we are told to move out, each of us holding the hand of the prisoner in front of him. It takes more than half an hour to reach the door. All of us smell the same—a mixture of blood, pus from wounds, sweat and piss, combined with an aura of thousands of frustrated instincts, repressed desires and whispers of hope and prayer.

We pass through like blind bulls being herded through an enclosure. I lift my jacket for just a second to see what is happening in the courtyard. I see the short and shining barrels of machine guns in the hands of guards on the balcony aimed right into the midst of the crowd of prisoners in the courtyard. Before I pull my jacket back down, I feel the burning pain of a truncheon at the back of my knees, and I fall down helplessly and suddenly into a mélange of heads and feet on the floor. I am in the middle of a large clump of crouching, cringing, dehumanized bones and flesh. None of us knows what is happening. We sit there, the torturers all around us, their machine guns aimed at us. We wait. For a coup? For a revolution? For amnesty? For a massacre? None of us knows, but I believe that all of us are ready to die rather than stay suspended in this horrible vacuum.

> There is no door
> > no road
> There is no night
> > no moon
> Neither the day
> > nor the sun

We stand
            outside time
with bitter daggers
        at our backs[2]

But we don't even stand; we squat, heads bent forward and covered, the machine guns on the balcony aimed at our vitals.

I think we all suffered during those two hours more than we
had suffered ever before in our lives, even during torture. Physical
torture cripples the back or the teeth or the soles of the feet or the
genitals; you know that your nails are being pulled out or the soles
of your feet are burning under the cable whip, and you say, This
is it and nothing more. Here in the courtyard we didn't know what
was going to happen even in the next minute.

A friend of mine who never confessed under almost all the
forms of physical torture told me that there was a moment in that
courtyard when he was about to call out to his interrogator and
make a very honest and full confession. I really don't know
whether the interrogators were aware of what they were subjecting us to. If they wanted a collective confession, they could have
had it right there:

"Yes, if you want us to tell you we are all communists, terrorists, antimonarchists, if you want us to tell you we were planning
to blow up the palace of the Shah, you are right. Here is our
confession. Come and take it. Let us go back to our cells."

If only you could confess to what they believed you believed,
they would somehow let you go away, back to your cell and then
to a place where "every dawn is pierced with the chorus of twelve
bullets."[3]

We wait in silence. Then from under our covers we see boots
thrust among us and hands coming down as fast as they can and
digging into the sides of the prisoners. The torturers lift the covers
off, look at our faces and tell us to get up. They actually pull us
up one by one out of the squatting crowd and take us away. We
still don't know where. They separate us from each other like
butchers separating sheep to take them to the slaughterhouse.

A hand lifts my jacket and a froglike face with a mustache
bends down to my face; it is Dr. Rassouli, and I sense his hurried

[2] Ahmad Shamlu, *Abraham in the Fire* (Teheran, Zaman Books, 1973), p. 5.
[3] *Ibid.*, p. 8.

breath under my nose, and I get up. One of the guards pulls me out from among the heap of men, and I am taken to a corner of the yard where there are no prisoners. I stand there waiting. Then I hear approaching footsteps, and in another few seconds I can see from under the jacket the dilapidated end of a red tie, a thick leather belt and the protruding of the crotch of someone's trousers.

"What is your name?"

"Reza."

"Family name?"

Are we going through the same process? I answer exactly as I always have before:

"Baraheni."

The man bursts out laughing. Then he lifts the jacket and looks into my face.

"What has happened to you," he says, "that you have fallen down from the heights of power into the ignominy of our clutches?"

A nice attempt at literary parody, but I still have no idea what I'm supposed to do. I don't remember having seen the face anywhere before, nor will I see him later. He repeats the question in the same jovial tone.

"The world is a very tricky place," I say. "It has its ups and downs."

"Then I'll send you to the second floor, and from there to the top of the gallows, and from there up and up and up, to heaven."

The guard takes me to Ward 3.

THE WOMEN IN WARD 3

Here I stayed in cell 9 and cell 16. I got no light in cell 9. I saw three men in the cell, not all at once but at different intervals.

The first man was F.R., whom one could reasonably call both a coward and a sexist. He had not been arrested on his own. When they arrested his nephew, M.F., a man reputed even among the torturers for his resistance, F.R. told the guards and their chief that they could not arrest him that night and should come in the morning rather than at midnight. Dr. Rassouli slapped him on the face and told him to dress and come along. F.R. told them he had nothing to do with politics; he had just arrived home late from a cabaret, and they should leave him alone. They blindfolded him and put him in the second car and brought him to the Komité.

He told me, "If they shave my hair, my fiancée will kill herself. I have just found her. She is rich, pretty, from a very fine, noble family, and best of all, she has an ass this big."

He opened both his arms wide and clasped his fingers to show the size of his fiancée's ass. Then he suddenly turned and hugged the wall, pressed his penis hard against it, gasped *"Akh joon! Akh joon!* [Oh, my dear!]" and pretended he was coming on the wall. In the next cell, number 10, there were three women, all of whom had been tortured, and sometimes they lamented their lot, crying out about their suffering and pain. F.R. saw in these lamentations an invitation to love. He immediately jumped back at the wall to repeat his ritual.

His mouth smelled horrible. I asked him if he was constipated, and he said yes. Then he asked me how I knew about it, and I told him I could smell it from his mouth. He said, "I don't like to force myself too much when I defecate. Hemorrhoids will destroy my lovely walk." He smoked too. He borrowed cigarettes from everyone. And even when someone was in the torture chamber or the interrogator's office, he would eat his food or at least the best parts.

He considered me so dangerous that he told me, "If you see me in the street after we come out, pretend that you don't know me. Don't be surprised if I don't say hello to you. How can you give up those big asses and tits out there to come to die in this hole?"

But the fear of torture lay deep in his heart. He plucked out his beard, hair by hair, with the tips of two fingers. He looked like a chicken, bald from the bill down. We made an agreement that anytime he reached for his beard, I would slap him on the hand. "Like you would slap the hand of a child who has stolen cookies from his neighbor," he said. I slapped him more than fifty times a day. In almost a fortnight, i.e., his entire stay in the Komité, he became completely beardless.

He never forsook his inhuman attitudes toward women. "I wish I were their torturer," he concluded one day. This time I slapped him hard on the mouth. He shut up.

Two days after that he was released, the only person I ever knew to be released in such a short time. Months later I saw him standing in the street waiting for a cab. I walked up to him and said hello. He looked at me. He didn't believe his eyes. And then something happened which was much more ridiculous than anything he had said or done in prison. He turned away and started to run, not like someone escaping from a dangerous person but rather like a professional runner trying to make a new record in an international race. Although other people ran away from me after my release, in their various ways, F.R. was the manifestation of their attitudes, the best actual runner of all of them.

I never met any guerrillas in the prison. The closest I came to anyone who was even vaguely connected with arms was H.R., a tiny twenty-seven-year-old man who had been in the Shah's Literacy Corps. He had been apprehended for selling a sixty-year-old gun to someone who was supposed to have used it for something about which H.R. either knew nothing or was not willing to talk. He had gotten five hundred toomans for the pistol, and later it had been returned to him by the man who bought it. It hadn't even been used. H.R. had given the pistol to his mother and told her to hide it, and she had thrown it into a ditch. H.R. had been badly tortured after he was apprehended. When he was taken to get the pistol from his mother in a village in the north, the man in charge of the mission had fallen into the sewer ditch, which was full of the villagers' excrement. H.R. would tell me how the captain's stars glittered over the surface of the sewer water, and we would laugh.

The other person thrown into this cell with me for a short time was M.M.A., who had been arrested once before in 1963 when he was a student in the University of Teheran; he didn't know why he had been arrested this time. He and I would recite poetry to each other, and once he imitated the ritual religious breast-beating of the Arabs in the Iranian port of Booshehr on the Persian Gulf. I found it to be a mixture of modern dance and old ritualistic rhythmical patterns, which I really loved.

Both H.R. and M.M.A. were tortured very severely by Dr. Tehrani, a tall, dark, athletic man who tried to rape H.R., without success. He also suggested that H.R. become a member of SAVAK, his first mission being to check on poor old Baraheni and find out what he had to say. I had long discussions with H.R., and he weathered the storm, but only at the cost of being sent back to the torture chamber once more.

It was here that I first came to know about the women prisoners of Iran. The three women in cell 10 were tortured by a woman who walked into the ward as though she was wearing iron horseshoes. She would call down to the guards in an extremely virile voice and tell them to take good care of "her prisoners." She possessed them in the same way the Shah possessed the whole nation. When the women refused their food, she would slap them hard and make them eat it while she stood there. I saw her once from the hole in the door. She had a very bony, donkey-like face, smeared with too many cosmetics; even all dolled up she looked ugly. H.R. told me that he knew her. She had an apartment in the southern sector of the Niavaran Palace in northern Teheran, and she would always shout at the shopkeepers and the streetsweepers: "I'll have my men from SAVAK tear your fucking ass open!" But in prison she had nothing to do with the men.

One of the women sang beautifully. We exchanged messages, one of which was "Sing!" and she sang generously, knowing that even the guards loved her voice. Sometimes the refrain was picked up by the rest of the ward, and everybody joined in with a word or two.

There was nothing superficial in her voice. She explored all the sadness of a Persian song with her voice, and the words moved from one delineation of deep frustration to another, turning humanity's bitter vision of itself into a yet deeper vision of sorrow. Almost all Persian songs concentrate on the theme of separation. Studied in the light of this one major theme, humanity has been separated from the sea, the rain, the sky, the plants and vegetation, from beauty and freedom and love and the beloved. All these various aspects of alienation rise into waves of wistful song, and the prisoner feels his own predicament more and more deeply in the presence of this alternate form of expression of alienation:

> I swear by the swallow
> > whose wings have been cut
> by the deer
> > whose forefeet and back
> > feet are bound
> by those doves
> > sitting all around the shrine
> do not go away, do not go away!

Or:

> Kiss me
> kiss me for the last time
> for I walk towards my destiny

Or:

> Morning bird, begin to lament!
> Turn my wounds into fresh ones!
> Break this cage with your sighs
>   of flame!
> Turn everything upside down!
> Oh, wing-tied nightingale,
> Come out of the cage,
> And sing humanity's song of
>   freedom!

It seemed that she knew we all needed her songs, and she went on singing, taking us deeper and deeper into our own subconscious, reminding us of our waiting loved ones and that we should not forget them or the world outside.

The guard sometimes opened the door of the women's cell, and they were allowed to come out and walk in the corridor. As soon as they saw that the guard had gone to the other end of the ward for a moment, they opened the vents on the doors of the neighboring cells and we had conversations. I put my mouth to the opening and spoke; then I put my ear to it and listened; I repeated this several times until we came to know about each other's past, our alleged crimes, the names of our interrogators and what we could do for each other should one of us get out sooner than the rest.

When the guard came close, one of them would ask for permission to go to the toilet. And just who would be the guard not to indulge her? While one of them went to the toilet, the other two would walk arm in arm, as if they were strolling in a park. They didn't talk to the guard if they had something they wanted to say to us. The guard sensed their cool and indifferent attitude and moved to the other end of the ward, waiting for the third woman to come back from the toilet. We would go on whispering through the vent.

One day, when one of them had just returned from seeing the members of her family, the vent was suddenly opened and two eggs were thrown into my cell. I caught them in time, one in each hand, as if I had been expecting them all along. Two hard-boiled eggs. I hadn't seen an egg for more than seventy days. I looked at them. I fondled them. I compared the generosity of these women to F.R.'s selfishness and avarice. The only thing I could do was send them a message of gratitude by knocking on the wall.

When I was taken to cell 16, on the other side of the ward, if the vent was opened I could see three girls coming out of cell 5. One of them appeared ill. B.E., my cellmate, told me she had been a student of mine years ago, had been in prison once before and had a heart problem.

"She started having problems the last time she underwent torture."

"How do you know all this?"

"She is my girl friend."

"Does your interrogator know this?"

"He does, and he is exploiting that."

When B.E. went to the toilet, one of the guards, an obvious homosexual and a real thug as well, told me, "He is much better than a woman himself. I wonder what he sees in that ugly, sick woman! Whenever I see him, I get horny!"

The woman would scream at night, startling everyone awake, and B.E. would rush to the vent and listen. He was helpless to do anything. He would ask the guard to take him to the toilet, but the guard knew he was in love with the sick girl and he would shout, "There is nothing wrong with her. Don't worry! Go to sleep!"

B.E. hated the sarcastic, insinuating tone of the guard's voice. He cursed him, loudly enough for me to hear but not enough for the guard. He would come back from the door, huddle in a corner of the cell and go to sleep.

On Fridays we were taken to the showers, which were located to the left of the wards on the first floor. We were ordered to throw our jackets over our heads and hold someone's shirttail from the rear. The guards watched us—belts, whips and batons in hand. They used these indiscriminately on everyone they considered to be doing something wrong.

It would take the inhabitants of each cell only three minutes to occupy one of the shower booths, wash themselves under the cold, pressureless showers with rock-hard soap and dry themselves with towels of red cloth which were already wet. On the way to the showers, peeping from underneath our jackets, we would see hundreds of copies of confiscated books stacked by the walls. We faced the walls, so that others passing behind us would not recognize us nor we them.

B.E. was a handsome young student of metallurgy at the University of Teheran. He had been offered membership in SAVAK and had accepted out of fear for his life. He did not tell me this at first. Then, one night, he woke me up:

"Listen!" he said. "They offered me the chance to become a member of SAVAK, and I accepted. What can I do?"

The offer had been made by Dr. Tehrani. I tried to talk the boy out of it. He was convinced that he should do something about it before it was too late. Finally he asked the guard to take him to the "doctor." He went away and came back a few hours later, beaten up. I was convinced that this meant he had rejected their offer.

He and I went to the same booth in the showers. The door was left open. The guards loved to ogle his behind. They pointed it out to each other and giggled passionately. Sometimes they came even closer and touched his buttocks with the tips of their belts or batons and said suggestive things. I could see that they had hard-ons, and saliva glistened on their lips.

At these moments B.E. would ask me to help him. I stood by the door with my hairy back to the guards, obstructing their passionate erotic vision with my own behind. It seemed they didn't fancy mine. Rhythmic blows of whips and batons fell on my wet back while B.E. finished washing himself. Then he stood by the door in a loincloth while I showered. With our jackets covering our faces, eyes on our feet, we walked back to our cells. On Fridays this was the only form of torture, going to the showers.

The guards took the women to the showers before they took the men. We didn't know what happened in the showers. It must have been very difficult for the women, washing themselves within an inch of the curious eyes of the sex-hungry guards. But knowing what was happening in the minds of these women—their sweeping radicalization within the opposition, their enormous capacity for learning the tenets of modern ideologies, their increased participation in circles and meetings of oppositionist nature—one can be sure that they could do things far more difficult than endure the eyes of the guards while they showered.

Iranian women were first radicalized at the end of the nineteenth century and the beginnings of the twentieth as a result of the great social upheaval which culminated in the Constitutional Revolution. They even took up arms and fought beside their men against the rule of the tyrant. They would petition in the streets for the release of their husbands or leaders of the revolution.

The second wave of radicalization came in 1946, when they won for the first time equal rights with men in all affairs of the state of Azarbaijan. The first truly democratic women's organizations were created in this state and gave rise to the increasing consciousness among women in other parts of the country. However, the abortion of the government in Azarbaijan resulted in the suppression of both men and women in this as well as all the other states.

Iranian women from 1953 to the present have been able to nourish their consciousness from two sources: the cultural tradition of Masculine History, which trains them as males rather than females and thus alienates them from their own nature, giving them an identity as passive submales, and the abundance of rubbish (Hollywood stuff) imported from abroad and imposed upon them as ideals. Add to this a third element introduced recently by the Shah's court and its spokeswoman, the Shah's twin sister Princess Ashraf: a woman's liberation movement instigated and developed from above, by the elite. Politicized Iranian women revolt against all three, trying to form and maintain their own identity in the struggle against Masculine History, against the flow of hogwash from the West, against the imposition of the court women's liberation movement. The third of these elements is considered by the majority of the educated women in the country to be the most hypocritical of all, for they ask, "How can a woman like Princess Ashraf, a tyrant herself and the sister of a dictator, posit herself as the liberator of women in Iran, especially when both men and women are being tortured in Iranian jails on the orders of these so-called 'liberators'?"

Thus the finding of a feminine identity for Iranian women is a responsibility that rests on the shoulders of the women themselves. The reason that Iranian prison cells house an increasing number of women is that they, these women, are in search of an identity on the basis of equal rights with men in everything, and the government is aware that the politicization of women will lead to an even further politicization of men, which in turn will eventually lead to still greater tremors in the domain of Iranian monarchy.

It is no wonder, then, that all of the women I saw in the cells of ward 3 in the Komité prison were educated women: university students, teachers, intellectuals and artists.

PARVIZ SABETI: THE PUPILS OF THE SHAH'S EYES

My wife tells me on her third visit to the prison that according to Dr. Hooshang Nahavandi, chancellor of the University of Teheran, one of these days Dr. Parviz Sabeti is going to come to see me. She tells me that she is supposed to be present at this meeting. I ask her whether she knows what the topic of conversation is going to be, and she says she doesn't know but adds: "The chancellor told me that after he talks with you, the two of us can go home together."

"How so?" I ask.

"I don't know," she says.

I have once seen Sabeti on television, when he was reporting on the alleged capture of a large cache of arms belonging to the Iranian guerrillas, but I don't remember exactly how he looked. I remember how he talked for more than three hours on the operations of SAVAK, saying that his informants were everywhere and that every organization in the country was infiltrated.

My interrogator also tells me one day that very soon I will have an important visitor and that my fate will be decided in that meeting. In the meantime my interrogation goes on as usual.

I am in cell 9 of ward 3. I am mostly alone, and when the guard comes after me one afternoon and tells me to dress and come out, I have a premonition that this time I am being taken out to see Chief Parviz Sabeti, called by many of the torturers "the pupils of the Shah's eyes." Apparently he is the most trusted civilian in the Shah's SAVAK, and since he has come to power there has been a consistent pattern of recantations on the part of Iranian intellectuals delivered on national television. The intellectual is taken to prison, tortured and forced to recant; as a consequence of recantation he is isolated from the mainstream of the opposition and considered a traitor. Sabeti is the Shah's expert on dealing with intellectuals.

When the guard removes the blindfold and the handcuffs, I find myself in the corridor of the Central Department of Police. I stand there for a few minutes, and then a door is opened and Dr.

Azudi comes out. He tells me to remember what he has said about my wife and daughter.

"You should listen carefully to the Chief and do what he says. Otherwise, your wife and daughter . . ."

He goes away, and then the door of General Zandipour's office is opened and Dr. Hosseinzadeh pops his head out to call me in. I enter and stand by the door. General Zandipour is standing at the other end of his desk. A younger man is talking on the phone. He puts down the receiver, turns around, sees me, walks toward me, stretches out his hand and shakes mine, asking me in a rather affectionate tone of voice, "How are you, Doctor?"

"Very well, thank you, Doctor."

We will continue to call each other "doctor" all through the conversation, but later, when I am out of prison and see Dr. Nahavandi, chancellor of the University of Teheran, I will speak of Sabeti as a doctor and the chancellor will interrupt me: "You speak of Sabeti as a doctor, and that angers me. He is no doctor, and you know it."

I will find out later that the chancellor and Sabeti are very good friends and, in fact, colleagues in what they do for the Shah —one in the University of Teheran, the other in SAVAK.[4]

"Why didn't you have his beard shaved?" he now asks Dr. Hosseinzadeh.

"I had it shaved on the first day, but there were contradictory orders later, and he himself insisted on keeping it."

"I didn't insist on keeping my beard," I say. "It was Dr. Rezvan who told me that I should keep it. I obeyed his instructions." I look at the pupils of the Shah's eyes.

"Who the hell is Dr. Rezvan?" Dr. Sabeti asks.

"He is my interrogator," I retort.

"The one you have been fooling for the last month and a half," he says.

I don't say anything, and he turns to Dr. Hosseinzadeh: "Have you caressed him?" he asks.

"Yes, sir! And what a caressing we gave him. He loved it so much that he fainted several times in the middle."

Dr. Hosseinzadeh leaves. I am invited to sit down. Dr. Sabeti and the General sit opposite me on the sofa.

[4] At the end of 1976 the chancellor became personal secretary to Queen Farah.

Dr. Sabeti is tall and handsome, with hazel eyes and a white and reddish skin. He is extremely well dressed. Compared with him the haggard General looks like an old man of the ancient world dressed in a suit and tie. I have my jacket on over my prison-issue pants. Dr. Sabeti has long, strong hands, and at present he doesn't know what to do with them. The voice of authority speaks:

"I've read your article several times and received a report on your *Masculine History*. I've also received reports on your activities in the United States, both from our own sources and from our American friends, and we have come to the conclusion that you deserve nothing less than execution."

At this time the door opens, and a guard comes in with a tray and three cups of tea. He puts the cups in front of each of us and goes away.

"You are a separatist, and we know it! We have other documents besides your own writings, tapes, notes here and there, and we have witnesses, people with whom you have plotted against the sovereignty of the State. You want to cut the country to pieces, give some of it to the Turks, some of it to the Kurds and some of it to the Arabs. You are planning to become a second Pishevari[5] for the people of Azarbaijan. But this is only one of your crimes!"

"May I say something about this one crime?" I ask.

General Zandipour lifts his right hand and puts his long, black, thin index finger to his lips, motioning for me to be silent, as if we were all sitting around someone's deathbed in a hospital.

Dr. Sabeti continues: "Your writings are all against His Imperial Majesty, the Shah of Shahs of Iran. Your insinuations, your ironical remarks, most of the lines of your poetry and all of your prose are filled with incessant babblings against monarchy. You would like to destroy twenty-five hundred years of monarchy, all of our traditions, the name of our great civilization, our entire cultural heritage. You are anti-Shah and antimonarchy. This is your second crime, the punishment for which is none other than execution."

"May I say something about this one crime?" I ask again.

General Zandipour's index finger again.

[5] Seyyed Dja'far Pishevari, leader of the Democratic Party of Azarbaijan, founder of the first autonomous Azarbaijan government. Forced eventually to flee to the Soviet Union, he was eliminated by Stalin around 1948.

Dr. Sabeti continues: "The White Revolution of the Shah has transformed everything in the country during these last ten years. All foreigners, whether on the right or on the left, admit the great progress we have made during this last decade. The Russians admit it; the Chinese admit it; the Americans admit it; the Europeans admit it; the whole world admits it. But you, Dr. Baraheni, you don't admit it. You forget that these days are the brightest days in Iranian history, that the Shah is the greatest king history has ever seen. The villagers are happy; the workers are happy; the merchants in the bazaar are happy; the university professors are happy. Only you are not happy. You have a personal grudge against the State. And we here don't give a damn for people's personal grudges. You have written book after book, but there isn't even one word in all of them in appreciation of the Shah's White Revolution. Here in prison, we don't ask you why you haven't written about it. We punish people for having kept silent about our great progress. And the punishment is nothing less than execution."

"May I say something about this crime, too?" I ask.

General Zandipour's index finger.

Dr. Sabeti speaks like someone programmed to repeat the same things over and over. There is something of the savage animal in him. It seems as though someone has instructed the animal to attack, and now he is doing what he has been ordered to do. His voice is strong but naïve, unintellectual, unsophisticated. He is straightforward in the manner of a bull in the ring.

"All these years you have felt that you were invulnerable. You went on as the perfect opportunist, the perfect demagogue, listening to no one and attacking everybody—in the press, in the university, in the streets—like a dog you attacked. Living in the greatest period of the Iranian people, you lamented the plight of the people. But behind this crust, there was something which you tried to hide from the public. I mean your inner being. And how well we know that inner being of yours! We have a whole file here on that inner being of yours. You seduced other people's daughters and wives in the university. You slept with your students, one after the other. You were not ashamed. We kept silent, thinking that one day you would correct yourself, would learn to behave. But you didn't. You became even worse! We could not tolerate it any longer, and we got you."

"Can you tell me the names of those women I seduced in the university?"

The General is about to raise his index finger, but Dr. Sabeti all at once opens a thin file placed in front of him and produces a sheet of paper. He looks at it and says:

"Here is a name. Sanaz."

"Well, I'm very sorry about that seduction, sir. I couldn't help it. The seduction was mutual. After all, she happens to be my wife."

"Oh?"

"Can you give me other names, sir?"

"Shahin, Mahin, Soosan and many others. We can always produce as many women as we want to testify that you seduced them."

"The point is, you *have* to produce them. They don't exist yet."

The telephone rings. The General goes to his desk and picks up the receiver. Then he turns to Dr. Sabeti.

"It's for you, *qorban* [my lord]."

The General switches off something on the desk before he comes back and sits down. I try to see the object on the desk. It is a tape recorder. So they have been recording. So they have just begun to get documents on me. Or perhaps they are trying to trap me. I have to be very careful with what I am saying from now on. Maybe they are going to take the recording to the Shah and let him listen to the interrogation of one of his victims.

I hear Dr. Sabeti: "Yes, I have him here with me. I am counting his crimes one by one . . . Well, I cannot promise anything yet. I will let you know after I finish talking with him . . . Thank you."

He puts down the receiver. The General goes back to the desk and switches on the tape recorder.

"It was the chancellor of your university," Dr. Sabeti says, sitting down, "He needs a professor for your classes, but I told him he should be able to manage without you. You are our guest for good."

I didn't hear him say anything of the sort on the phone, so I know that it is a lie.

"We return to our discussion," he says. "We believe that it is demagogues like you who have filled the Iranian prisons with all these students and writers and intellectuals. You are the one who radicalized them. You and Al Ahmad and Ali Shariati—another fool whom we are going to keep in prison until he rots. If we had eliminated you years ago, we wouldn't have had to arrest all these people. All the interrogations show one thing: the prisoners all read your works, the works of Al Ahmad, Shariati and Sa'edi. Al Ahmad is dead and gone. You will have the same fate."

"If you think I am a criminal, why don't you send me to court, according to the constitution of the country, prove that I am a criminal and shoot me!"

"We just proved that you were a criminal. We don't have to go to a court to prove the already proven thing. You are a criminal. We start from there. The rest is mere ceremony."

I look at him. Which of us is confessing here? I push on:

"Then why do you speak of the constitution in the press every day? Why open the parliament with all the ritual involved? Why does everybody in the government speak of the country's laws as if they were divine decrees?"

"The laws, the parliament and the constitution are for those who obey them, not for traitors like you. In the case of criminals like you we start with the crime already proven and settled and then, before we shoot you, we have a little show, a trial by military tribunal. When I decide that you will go to the court, you will know that you are as good as dead."

I look at him more closely. He is so well-dressed, clean-shaven, neat and handsome that if he asked for one's sister's hand one would feel extremely proud and encourage the sister to marry and cherish him. He is like Dorian Gray, ugly inside and handsome outside, until one day the internal ugliness invades the entire visage, which would then put the devil to shame.

I know that he can't prove I have written anything against monarchy and the Shah. *Masculine History* in its Persian edition deals with the cultural disintegration as a result of monarchy, rather than with monarchy itself. As for the poetry, it is always very difficult to turn metaphors into pure political talk. It is through cultural corruption that I have sought to illustrate the socioeconomic roots of corruption. To prove that I am a criminal in the eyes of the Iranian constitution would be a most difficult task.

"You see, sir," I say, "you have to prove that I am a criminal and a traitor. In order to prove this, you have to have documentation. You must present this documentation to a civil court. You have to select a jury composed of members of the press and the publishing profession, men and women, because I am a writer, and a writer is entitled under the constitution to such a jury. If they say in open court that I am a criminal and a traitor, then I should be dealt with as such. Until then I am neither a criminal nor a traitor.

"I abide by the constitution which you claim is the foundation of all the laws in the land. You also try to abide by what you claim to be the right thing, i.e., the constitution. If you do so, you will find that all the torture I have suffered here, all the beatings and terrorizing and threats on my life or threats of raping my wife and daughter are illegal according to the laws which you claim outside of this prison to abide by. According to *your* laws, if a person tortures someone, he should be considered a criminal or a pervert and dealt with accordingly. I am not a criminal; only those who are torturing me are criminals. I have been coerced to fill out pages and pages of answers to illegal interrogation. If we act according to the laws by which you say you abide, your government itself turns out to be a criminal government, and all political prisoners should be acquitted overnight and all the interrogators go to prison. According to the constitution, a torturer is a criminal."

I have told him all I know of Iranian law.

Dr. Sabeti suddenly gets up. He unbuttons his jacket and tries to reach out from across the table in the middle of the room to attack me. The General jumps up and puts both arms around him, pleading:

"Forgive him, he is foolish, he doesn't know what he is talking about! If he were not a fool, he wouldn't be in prison in the first place!"

What a performance!

Dr. Sabeti says to me:

"You know what I've done, you son of a bitch! I've pissed into the mouths of all your martyrs in prison. I've killed men ten times greater than you! I am not going to pity you, and I am not going to let fools like you disgrace the country's name all around the world. Our American friends have told us what you said in America about the Shah. We will not tolerate this kind of shit from you or anybody else!"

I remain silent. They both sit down, one calming the other. Dr.

Sabeti's hazel eyes are full of blood. He is trembling. Is it genuine trembling or fake? I cannot say. He turns to the General:

"Tell them to bring in his real file."

The General rings the bell. The tall and athletic Dr. Tehrani comes in and stands at attention by the door.

"Get his file," the General says.

"Yes, sir!" says Dr. Tehrani, and he goes out.

In another minute I see something I cannot believe. Two files, each half as tall as Dr. Sabeti himself, are placed on the table between us. I can hardly see the General and Dr. Sabeti. I notice some of my books among the files and tapes and all kinds of papers. Dr. Tehrani walks out.

"These are your files," Dr. Sabeti says. "Do you want me to go through all of them with you and prove your crimes to you?"

"Hand the files to a civilian court, and let us abide by the constitution."

"Shut up and listen!" he says, picking up the first newspaper which is on the file nearest him. "This is the copy of the article which you published in *Ettela'at,* the one you call "The Culture of the Oppressor and the Culture of the Oppressed." Your picture is prominent in the file on intellectuals who are against the government. Your article is the feature article! The others don't say much, but you write three full columns on how you want to introduce a new meaning for the word 'culture,' insulting our sacred institutions!"

He goes on reading, ridiculing, laughing, showing parts of the article to the General, who joins in the laughter. Finally he looks at me:

"Do you agree?"

"With what?" I ask.

"With what the article says."

"Certainly I agree with what the article says. I wrote it."

"So you confess."

"Confess what?"

"That you are a traitor."

"I confess that I wrote the article, but as for the traitor business, it has to be proven in a court of law, in a civil court. If you are so sure that I am a traitor, send me to a court of law and prove it!"

"There is no other court, you fool! You are in the court right now, and we are all there is to a court! I am telling you, you are a traitor. The General knows that you are a traitor. You know yourself that you are a traitor."

"I know very well that I am not a traitor. If you know that I am, take me to a court of law and prove it!"

"I have already proven it. These two piles of documents show that you are a traitor."

"Traitor to whom?"

"Traitor to His Majesty, the Shah of Shahs, the Light of the Aryans."

"What is your proof?"

"Your being here is all the proof we need."

"Then, by the same token, you and the General must also be traitors to the Shah of Shahs, because you are here, and your being here is the proof!"

"I have never come across a tongue as long as yours in prison. Don't you know that we are going to kill you?"

The General interferes at this moment with great rational advice: "I think, as a first step, we should tell the University of Teheran to fire him." He looks at me closely to see what the effect of this threat has been.

"If you give me a piece of paper," I say, "I'll resign from the University of Teheran this very minute!"

But the subject is still the same. "The Pupils of the Shah's Eyes" does not leave it so easily, and he wants to show his intelligence. "If you say that you are not a traitor to the Shah of Iran, come out openly and say that you are not a traitor, that you have done nothing in opposition to His Majesty."

"First you must take me to a civil court and bring all your documentation to prove that I am a traitor; then it will be my turn in court to prove that I am not a traitor."

"The court is a formality; I mean, the military court is a formality. We never take political prisoners to the civil courts. When you are sent to a military court, everything has already been decided. If a person is going to be killed, he will be killed after the formality; if a person is going to get fifteen or ten or five years, that also is decided beforehand. The General and I will decide what to do about you. That is all there is to it."

Then he comes up with the proposal he has been skirting. Just as all conversations in prison have become branded deep in my mind, his proposals, verbalized in total solemnity, become a part of my memory, indelible and forever with me:

"We will hold a live interview with you on television with foreign and Iranian correspondents present. I will be there and the General will be there and Parviz Nik-Khah.[6] Farhang Farrahi[7] or, if you prefer, Iradj Gorgin[8] will ask you questions, and you will answer them. Five things should be included in your answers: one, that the White Revolution of the Shah is an excellent undertaking; two, that monarchy is the only form of government suitable for Iran; three, that the language of the people of Azarbaijan is not Turkish but Persian with Turkish as a mere dialect; four, that you recant what you have written in 'The Culture of the Oppressor and the Culture of the Oppressed' as well as what you have written in your prose and poetry; five, that you testify to the fact that in the past you agitated among the youth of our country against the state and that now you understand that you have made a mistake and from now on you will encourage them to understand the programs of the government and respect them. What do you say?"

I look at him and at the General. Their eyes are fixed on me; the devil watches me through their eyes. The stench of the disgrace of recantation fills my nostrils. I knew it was coming. They get you on some small pretext; they torture you, and the only way they leave open as an alternative to death is recantation. You recant and you stay alive; you don't recant and you rot or die in prison.

Those five statements would mean the end of my political, literary, academic and public life, not to mention my life as a human being. How can one say that his poetry, his prose, his national identity, all have been a mistake? I identified with these aspects of my life more than I did with my own face, my height, my hands and feet. How could I say that my whole life was a mistake? One makes mistakes here and there, and when he does he may be willing to announce it to the whole world, but how can one make the statement that he himself, his entire identity, has been a mistake, thus recanting his own existence?

[6] A former recantee and an apologist for the Shah's government.

[7] A SAVAK agent with the Ministry of Information.

[8] A highly placed official with National Iranian Television.

I sit there, thinking, staring at these two men who are waiting for an answer. There is a certain urgency in their look. It seems that they want my answer right here and now. It seems that if I tell them I will recant, they will take me to the television station this very moment and gather all the men and women of the press and their own scoundrels together and run the show on the air this very night. And if I tell them I don't accept their offer, they will execute me tomorrow morning. My life seems to be oozing out of me like some kind of foul-odored vapor. Now I have several beings, one sitting here sweating, the other recanting, the third facing the firing squad—not to mention others living far away from here, in another place. One of these beings sits with me there looking at the authorities of SAVAK; the others are outside, somewhere else—my *beings—there.* I am disintegrated, decomposed, parts of my being scattered all around the world without my knowledge or will. I have lost my horizon, the horizon of my being which spread about me in every direction with its own peculiarities, like a small garden that one makes for himself in his backyard and that he can tend while calling all the plants by names which he alone knows. This horizon of mine was not some ideology that I had acquired from my reading. There was nothing abstract about it. It was real, the experience of life, the entirety of one's experiences in the world, and now it weighed down upon me heavily. In the old days this horizon was part of a huge balloon that carried me everywhere, and I would land on the blank pages of the books I was writing like a weightless bird. Now the balloon had been filled with lead and iron, and I was trying to come in for a landing on the waves of the sea, knowing that the sea floor alone awaited me. I saw my own death staring at me through the eyes of my adversaries.

"Well?" one of them asks.

"What?"

"Are you ready to attend this interview?" Dr. Sabeti asks.

"No, sir, I am not. You may torture me to death, but I can never denounce my past."

There, I have said it in full. The words jumped out of my mouth as naturally as my breath. How is it that I am not thinking of death? I don't know. Perhaps I am thinking of something that matters before the fact of my death: my life, the way I am, the way things have accumulated in the fiber of my experiences throughout long years of toil and sweat and thought. These things mean life to me. They are real. They are mine. They are me. They mean more to me than my death.

"Is this your final decision?" Dr. Sabeti asks.

"Yes, sir, my final decision."

"Do you know about the rumors outside?" he asks.

"No, sir, I don't."

"There is a rumor that you are dead," he says.

"I have heard that from someone in prison."

I don't really know what I will do. If they start to torture my wife and daughter before me, or if they try to rape them, I know that I might accept all their proposals before it happens. But I will have to see what the next few days bring.

"Don't you love your life?" the General asks.

"I love it. I love it very dearly."

"Then why don't you accept the Chief's proposals?"

"Because I love my life; I love it dearly."

"We will keep you in prison for anywhere from ten to fifteen years," Dr. Sabeti says.

I am not the only one surprised at hearing this; the General registers surprise as well.

"How so?" I ask. "I thought you said you would kill me."

"We don't need another stupid martyr in our history. But we can kill you any time we want. You are always in our clutches."

He rings the bell. Dr. Tehrani appears at the door.

"Send him back to his cell," Dr. Sabeti says.

I get up. The guard comes in. I am blindfolded and handcuffed, and we go back to my cell.

Sometimes at night Dr. Azudi comes to visit me with the same threats and the usual beating. At other times I am told that the next day my wife will come to the prison, but I am never taken out to see her. Or if I am taken out I don't find her there, and they tell me that she doesn't want to see me any more. When I finally see her a few days later, she tells me that nobody told her a meeting was to take place. I don't let her know of the threats.

One day Dr. Hosseinzadeh calls me to his office. He lights a cigarette, offers one to me and tells me to sit down. Dr. Azudi walks in and sits on my left.

Dr. Hosseinzadeh is bald on the crown of his head. He tells me that I should accept Dr. Sabeti's proposal. It is for my own good. I am not like the other prisoners. I am a professor at the University of Teheran, and I should respect the laws of the country.

"I respect the laws, Dr. Hosseinzadeh," I tell him.

"I am not a doctor," he says abruptly.

"Excuse me, General," I say.

"I'm not a general, either," he says.

"Then what are you, sir?" I ask.

"I am only a former student of yours," he says, laughing.

"Oh. I didn't know that," I say.

"Ten years ago I was your student and you gave me a D," he says.

"You certainly deserve more than that," I say.

"I do. I do."

He lights another cigarette and looks at Dr. Azudi. I turn and look at him, too.

"You know, Dr. Baraheni," Hosseinzadeh continues, "there is a group of people in our country who have grown up and become public personalities without leaning to the right or to the left. These are a bunch of rootless bastards who think that they can do whatever they want with the people of our country. These rootless bastards are all around us. They don't care about the Russians or the Chinese or the Americans. We know only two things about them: that they are rootless and that they are also bastards. You, Dr. Baraheni, are one of those."

"Thank you, sir," I say, "thank you."

I am blindfolded and taken away.

Sa'edi, the playwright, will tell me later that he had been told the same words a few months before by this very Hosseinzadeh in the presence of this very Dr. Azudi. Sa'edi had told him, "You are a bastard, Dr. Hosseinzadeh, not I."

In a second the huge, beastly Azudi had risen and come over and beaten Sa'edi to a pulp, and the two torturers had walked out of the room.

For the next three weeks I think about recantation. Under what dire conditions would I do what Dr. Sabeti has suggested? Perhaps under further unthinkable tortures. You never know what is going to happen to you after torture. The next step is never known. I know many people among the Iranian writers who recanted, but I always think perhaps they were tortured more than

I was. I know one writer who developed a heart condition in prison and whose feet and the calves of his legs Hosseinzadeh burned with his cigarette stubs. He recanted under torture, but when he came out he never did anything for the government. Writers are lonely people. They write everything alone, and when they recant it is for what they have done alone. Their confessions are the confessions of lonely men and women. One seldom has an accomplice in the writing of a poem, a story, a play. Creation is a lonely process. A writer hardly exposes his friends when he confesses or recants. He exposes his work, and for that he can always find an excuse:

"Listen, I wrote those books. They have the record of my convictions in them. Now that I have been tortured, I believe that those convictions were of no worth. It is not I who should be incriminated. It is the torturer who has tortured me and forced me to tell you that I don't believe in my convictions. You as my readers can take it or leave it."

I know that this is not always the case. One thinks of his following in society, his prestige, his rivals, the members of his family and all of his acquaintances. He thinks of himself, too. But he can also be very rational about it. He wrote with pleasure, and now he has to vomit that pleasure up under torture. Those who incriminate such a writer are wrong. The writer here is a victim, someone who has been poisoned. The criminal is the person who poisoned him, not the writer, who retches his heart out in the middle of the public thoroughfare.

Perhaps I might have surrendered to Dr. Sabeti's proposal if my wife and daughter were taken to the torture chamber to suffer the way Dr. Azudi suggested they should suffer. Do I have the right to let others suffer for my ideas? Even my wife and daughter?

Let us reverse the question. Am I ready to suffer for someone else's ideology, even if I feel that he is right? Is he not trespassing on the sanity of my rationality when he sends me to the torture chamber to suffer for the ideology he embraces? Doesn't he, in fact, turn me into the prisoner of his ideology in the same way the torturer has turned him into the prisoner of the government's ideology? Doesn't he, in fact, become the accomplice of my torturer?

There were moments in my life in prison when my mind was divided between what I thought was right for myself and what I thought was right for my wife and daughter. How could I let a thirteen-year-old girl, whose present emotional condition and future ideology I could not possibly fathom, suffer for my ideas? Perhaps she would suffer such a psychological trauma that she would never recover from it. Wouldn't she have every right in the future to curse me for what she was subjected to because of me at one point in her life?

Or my wife? What right do I have over her to let her suffer for my cause? Isn't it enough sacrifice on her part that she became my wife? Marriage itself is the greatest torture a woman can suffer in Iran. Why should I subject her to additional torture at the hands of others because of an article I have written on my ideas?

I can tell the Shah of Iran now that there was a moment during my prison life when I was willing to lick his feet so that nothing might happen to my wife and daughter. I have never voiced it, but this is the truth. The right that the Shah thinks he has over the lives of others I don't somehow fancy myself as having. I would be quite ready to degrade myself rather than bring injury to innocent people because of myself. I own no one in the way the Shah thinks he owns people. If my revolt has a meaning, its first and foremost meaning is myself. If I do not wish to have the Shah of Iran enslave the people of Iran, it means that I myself do not wish to own or enslave anyone, and that includes enslaving my wife and my daughter, objectively, subjectively or ideologically. I don't want them to suffer for me. If the Shah had known what I was thinking, he might have instructed Dr. Azudi to carry out his threats.

But I have heard of a religious poet in Iran whose wife and daughter were raped in front of him and who simply lost his sanity. I have no idea what happened to the wife and daughter, but I don't think they could have had much of a life after that.

The fear of rape is in the back of everyone's mind in prison. F.M., a laborer, was one of those men who was raped by Dr. Ardalan. He thought of it as part of the ritual which necessarily takes place in prison. He told me about it in an interval of thirty minutes, the total amount of time he spent in my cell.

But this was the rape of the man himself, not anyone related to him. For my part, I decided that if my wife and daughter were brought into the prison to be tortured or raped, I would recant the moment I saw them. My wife was pregnant.

WHAT IS IT THAT RELEASES ME?

Toward the end of November I sense a change in the atmosphere. Dr. Rezvan smiles sometimes. He tells the guard to get me a cup of tea while I write the answers to his questions. But he never forgets his foul words to me; he never stops beating up others in front of me. The ritual is worthy of notice. When he doesn't want to take a prisoner to the torture chamber, he simply tells him to lie down on the floor of the office. "Give me a ninety-degree angle," he says. The prisoner raises his legs, forming a perpendicular angle with the middle of his body. The interrogator gets his cable whip, stands to the right of the victim and brings down the whip on the soles of his feet. The prisoner screams, but he keeps his legs in the air, the soles of his feet at the disposal of the torturer. The ritual ends when the torturer gets tired. He throws the whip onto the nail driven into the wall, comes and sits down, opens his tin box, takes a pill, swallows it, then writes his question on the paper and puts it in front of me.

One early morning I am called to my interrogator's office. He seems to be very angry and serious. Something is wrong somewhere. He opens a drawer and hands me the following:

HIS EXCELLENCY
AMIR ABBAS HOVEYDA
PRIME MINISTER OF IRAN
TEHERAN, IRAN

YOUR EXCELLENCY:

THE AMERICAN CENTER OF *PEN* CLUB, REPRESENTING 1600 LEADING
AMERICAN POETS, PLAYWRIGHTS, ESSAYISTS, NEWSPAPERMEN, AND
MAGAZINE EDITORS, PUBLISHERS AND NOVELISTS IS GREATLY ALARMED
BY THE CONTINUOUS ARREST OF DR. REZA BARAHENI IN TEHERAN AFTER
HIS RETURN FROM TEACHING POSTS IN AMERICAN UNIVERSITIES IN TEXAS
AND UTAH. IN VIEW OF THE RAPIDLY GROWING CONCERN FOR
PROFESSOR BARAHENI IN THE UNITED STATES WHICH MIGHT AFFECT THE
FRIENDLY RELATIONSHIP BETWEEN OUR TWO COUNTRIES, THE AMERICAN
CENTER OF *PEN* WOULD WELCOME YOUR EXCELLENCY'S INTERVENTION ON
BEHALF OF REZA BARAHENI'S RIGHTS AND LIBERTIES, AND INFORMING
AMERICAN *PEN* AS SOON AS POSSIBLE ABOUT PROFESSOR BARAHENI'S

STATE. *PEN* AMERICAN CENTER, WILL MAKE YOUR EXCELLENCY'S
STATEMENT AVAILABLE TO THE AMERICAN PUBLIC.

RESPECTFULLY YOURS,
JERZY KOSINSKI
PRESIDENT, AMERICAN CENTER
AND MEMBER BOARD OF DIRECTORS, THE INTERNATIONAL LEAGUE FOR
THE RIGHTS OF MAN
NOVEMBER 23, 1973

Dr. Rezvan looks at me. "Can you give me an exact translation
of the telegram?"

I translate the words into Persian. I know that it must have
been translated by others for others and that it must have taken
a long time to reach a minor figure like him. But he wants his lion's
share. He doesn't know English, and I really pity him for this
because he has to degrade himself to ask me for a translation. He
hates me for all the trouble I have given him through my work in
Persian, and now this.

"We want you to write a letter to this man," he says, "and say
that you are not in prison and that you are safe and happy and that
it's none of his business to interfere with your life and in the
internal affairs of our nation."

He knows that I have turned down the offers of men greater
than he, and he won't be able to coerce me to do things that I don't
want to do, but he still insists. I know that there is great hope for
me in this telegram, at least hope for some kind of better bargain
than the original offered.

"As you can see, Dr. Rezvan, the telegram is not addressed to
me. It is addressed to His Excellency the Prime Minister. I cannot
answer for His Excellency the Prime Minister."

"It's none of the Prime Minister's business. SAVAK is responsible only to His Imperial Majesty, the Shah of Shahs, the Light
of the Aryans."

He relays these titles to me as if they were three different persons: (1) His Imperial Majesty, (2) the Shah of Shahs,
and (3) the Light of the Aryans. Presumably, the listener is supposed to inquire which one of these great men is in charge of
SAVAK.

"You are quite right that SAVAK is only responsible to the
Shah of Shahs, but, as you know, I'm not a member of SAVAK.

The telegram has nothing to do with me when it comes to the business of answering it. It is addressed by someone I don't know to someone in this country who is not I. It deals with me, yes, but I am only a prisoner, and prisoners don't have the right to answer letters or telegrams."

"The government will make an exception in this case and let you answer the telegram."

"No, sir, I cannot lie to this man. As a prisoner, I could not write to him even if he had written to me."

"You will have problems. We know that it was your wife who wrote and told these people that you were in prison. We will get her right away."

I can guess what the situation is, but I don't tell him. "My wife doesn't meddle with politics. She doesn't have anything to do with it."

"You will see what will happen to you and your wife."

But there is an air of despondency in his tone which I really admire. I am blindfolded and taken back to my cell.

A few days later they start allowing me newspapers, books and even additional cigarettes. Before this they gave me one cigarette a day; now they give me three. The first book they let me have is Steinbeck's *Grapes of Wrath* in its Persian translation; the second is a collection of poetry by Mirzadeh Eshqi, the revolutionary poet put to death by Reza Shah. All the books are among those suppressed by the government. They have a whole collection of these books in the Komité. The next book is Nikos Kazantzakis' *Christ Recrucified* in its Persian translation.

One day, when they give me the paper, I see a news item in a corner about the trip to Austin, Texas, of Ardeshir Zahedi, the Shah's ambassador to the United States. From there he is to proceed to Salt Lake City, Utah. These are two cities in whose universities I have taught. Something must really be going on for me over there.

I am told that my wife is coming to see me. They take me to a room by the office of Hosseinzadeh. My wife is there. I tell her in English that the interrogator has spoken to me about certain letters, and that she should deny the whole thing completely. Then Hosseinzadeh walks in, followed by Dr. Rezvan. The former is extremely angry.

"We told you that there is only one way you can get out of

this prison, through showing your allegiance to the monarchy in writing and on television."

I don't even answer this statement. He doesn't insist that I say anything. He moves to other subjects.

"Oh, so now your wife is here. By what right," he asks her, "did you write those letters to enemies of Iran?"

"What letters?" she asks.

"Don't pretend that you know nothing about the letters!" he shouts. "We have copies of them at our disposal."

"Could you tell me which letters you mean, sir?"

"The letters you wrote to your husband's friends."

"Which of his friends?"

"The ones in America."

"I never wrote any letters to his friends in America," my wife tells him as coolly as possible.

I have seen the typewritten report about my wife having written to the United States. Dr. Rezvan has shown a letter to me, saying very proudly that the SAVAK agent from the University of Utah in Salt Lake City wrote the letter. But he hasn't shown me any letters written by my wife, so they must not have them.

Hosseinzadeh delivers all kinds of threatening statements to the effect that one day my wife will be brought to the Komité under less pleasant circumstances. But it seems that for now they can do nothing.

Several days pass with no one knowing what is going to happen. I am now alone in my cell. I read the books which come to me almost daily. Anytime I see Dr. Rezvan, he says something about my wife, something about recanting, and I ask for more books.

Around the middle of December he shows me the following letter from Jerzy Kosinski, whom he now calls "an enemy of the people of Iran":

December 2nd, 1973

The Secretary to
His Excellency Amir Abbas Hoveyda
The Prime Minister of Iran
Teheran, Iran

Dear Sir:
   On November 23rd, 1973, the telegram, a copy of which is enclosed, was cabled to His Excellency Amir Abbas Hoveyda. We

have taken the liberty of stressing that the concern about Professor Reza Baraheni is growing in the United States, and that a great number of distinguished scholars, writers, journalists, playwrights and novelists and poets have expressed profound interest in his situation. We feel that it would be to the mutual interest of our countries if we could inform the American public about the actual state of Professor Reza Baraheni at this time, and to prevent any harm that might have been (perhaps by mistake) done to Professor Baraheni upon his return from the lecturing posts in the United States.

We are most anxious to hear from His Excellency Hoveyda as soon as possible, as the matter is indeed that of great seriousness here.

"Who is this Kosinski, anyway?" Dr. Rezvan asks me.

"I don't know, sir."

"His name is strange. Is he an Armenian?"

"I don't know, sir."

"Then why does he send all these letters and telegrams for your sake?"

"I don't know, sir."

" 'I don't know, sir.' For the last three months you have been repeating, 'I don't know, sir'!"

We are silent for a time, and then he asks, "Has this Kosinski been to our country to see our progress?"

"I don't know, sir."

"We have all the money in the world. We can buy everyone, including this Armenian Kosinski of yours."

"You know better. I don't know, sir."

He changes the subject. "Did your wife tell you what was going on in the States for your sake?"

"How could she know, sir?"

"She knows everything."

"How could she?"

"She knows it, and the two of you will suffer the consequences. You have made everybody terribly angry with those letters."

"I didn't write them. My wife didn't write them. I cannot be responsible for letters written by someone else."

I want to push him further, to have him say more about what is going on in the United States. But he says little else.

They come for me at noon on December 22, 1973, and tell me to bring everything I have with me. I am blindfolded until we reach the room of the Captain of the Guards. There I see Dr. Rezvan and the Captain. But the big shots are not present. I am handed a bag with all my belongings. Are they transferring me to another prison? I don't know. I put on my socks. I string my shoes with their laces and put them on. Then I put on my belt. They hand me my money—ten tomans, or a dollar and a half—and give me the contents of my pockets. I see an article on the theater which the censors suppressed. I fit everything into my pockets. They tell me to sign a paper. They refuse to show me what it says. I refuse to sign. Dr. Rezvan tells the Captain to show me the paper. It says that if I leave Teheran, I will have to pay around ten thousand tomans, or thirteen hundred dollars. I sign it. Am I really going to be released? I don't believe it. What has happened outside!

Dr. Rezvan says, "Follow me!"

I obey. I want to say, "I am not accustomed to this kind of generosity, Dr. Rezvan," but I don't think he would understand or appreciate what I mean. We walk through the curving alleyways of the prison. He stops at the gate.

"Go away," he tells me. "You are free."

He turns back and goes into the prison. I am in the compound of the Central Department of Police. I walk slowly and carefully, looking back every now and then. Maybe they are watching me from invisible holes. Maybe they will shoot me and say I was running away. I pass through the gate of the compound and step into the street. I cross over and turn to my right, in the direction of the Ministry of Foreign Affairs. I still look back now and then. On my left is the Customs Department; on my right, the southern wall of the Central Department of Police. Vendors are all over the place. The tumult of the city engulfs me. Now I stand again in the street, facing the grounds of the Ministry with my back to the Department of Police. I call a cab. I jump over a ditch with joy, a suspicious kind of joy. When I am settled in the cab, my heart is beating fast. I am no longer the young man I once was. But I am free and heading home, where hundreds of letters of support await me and faces of kindness and love, and a son who will set foot into the world in a few months.

The government chases me, changes my speeches in the news media, pretends that I made concessions to get out of prison, slanders me and threatens me that it will apprehend me anytime I dare to write anything against it. But now I intend to promote exactly the kind of device that made my release possible: international pressure. I leave Iran about nine months later, believing that I do not have it in me to bow to the pressures of living under the Shah's dictatorship; to denounce my ideal of self-determination for Iranian nationalities; to denounce myself and become a poet who will laud the tyranny of the Shah.

My mission is simple: to force the kings, the autocrats and the fascists to release their political prisoners and their prisoners of conscience.

MEMOIRS OF OTHER PRISONERS OF THE PAHLAVI PERIOD

What follows is a very short selection of accounts from the lives of other prisoners in Iran during the last fifty years of the Pahlavi regime. The full story of the prisoners during this period would come to thousands of pages. In the few examples cited here I quote from both Persian and Western sources: newspaper accounts, books, court proceedings and documents published by various oppositionist journals. I am concentrating only on recounts of the torture procedure and torture instruments.

I WAS INSANE FOR NINE MONTHS

To the Editor:

I humbly plead with you to publish this short note as a token of your sympathy with a tyrannized, innocent man. Let all freedom-loving people of the world know how helpless prisoners suffered in the prisons of the Pahlavi regime and how they were not ready to exchange their honor for earthly wealth, how they did not fear to lose their lives but held to their honor.

I was arrested without a warrant, without a charge, without there being any reason whatsoever offered as to the reason for my arrest. I suffered twelve years of incarceration and torture in Teheran, Ardebil, Zanjan and Abadan. They kept me hungry for forty-eight hours, my hands cuffed behind me, my body hanging upside down from the ceiling in a dark dungeon. The handcuffs and the position of my arms put unbearable pressure on my wrists and chest and shoulders and arms. Once a pistol was held to my temple while someone screamed in my ear, "Tell me! Confess! Or else I'll blow out your brains!" I screamed, pleaded with them, asked them to tell me just what it was that I was supposed to tell them; I swore by God and by my honor that I had nothing to tell them. But the torturer said, "You must confess that you have been sent from the Soviet Union and that the Soviet Consulate keeps you on its pay list; you work for them."

I told them, "I'm a poor, illiterate man. I never knew anything about the Soviet Union in my whole life. I don't know what you are saying. I don't even know what politics is! If you can find anyone who has ever heard anything from my lips about politics, then you can hang me or shoot me!" After a long period of pleading and moaning, they gave me some 400 to 500 blows of the whip on my head and hands and entire body; then they started threatening me with all kinds of horrible torture devices so that I might confess to the crimes they wanted me to confess to.

After subjecting some of the prisoners to all kinds of torture, the torturers decided to pack their heads in ice for a lark. Some of the prisoners died with frozen heads. The torturers killed Hassan Ziya Mededov and Vedadzadeh Ardebili with electricity; they put Karbalai Ebrahim Kasamai before the firing squad. They killed Zarreh Tehrani, Hessabi Tehrani and Mohammad Bagher Ranjabar Ardebili. It was only later that they told me they had found out that killing the last man was a mistake. "Now that you have seen the deaths of these people, are you ready to make your confession?" When I swore to God that I still had nothing to tell them, they gave me a severe electrical shock in the head."

Signed: Ali Farrokhzadeh
(*Khandaniha,* Second Period,
Ninth Issue, 1941, trans. by R.B.)

THE WEIGHT CUFFS

The weight cuffs [*dastband-e-qapani*] are one of the ordinary torture devices in Iranian prisons. Javanshir (a torturer) has denied ever having even heard of them. I won't call him a liar. He used to employ this device all the time, but maybe he had a different name for it: "right-left handcuff" or "back handcuff." I think that if one puts weight cuffs on someone and asks Javanshir if he has ever used it, showing him what they mean, he will say that he has used weight cuffs a thousand times.

This is how they employ them. They pull the left hand up over the head and the right down around to the back, handcuffing them to each other in this position. After some time in this position the shoulder bones begin to ache horribly, and the increasing pain becomes so intolerable that the victim begins to scream, and if the hands continue to stay in that position his arms just might become paralyzed. The chest of the handcuffed victim is thrust forward, and sometimes Abbas Kadkhoda, a fat-bellied interrogator, punches victims in the ribs or uses a hammer on the victim's shoulder bones, shouting and swearing all the time. Then Javanshir asks the victim to confess."

(*Khandaniha,* Third Period, Eighth Issue, 1942, trans. by R.B.)

INTERROGATION UNDER TORTURE

Bozorg Alavi, one of the outstanding novelists of Iran, was tortured with weight cuffs during the Reza Shah period. Following is his account:

E.Y. wrapped a rag around my wrists and put the left wrist above my head and the right around my back into the steel rings of those German- or Swedish-made handcuffs and brought the connecting links of the two chains together with some kind of device of which I know nothing. Thus my two wrists were cuffed close together, and my chest was thrust forward. At first I felt no pain, but after a few minutes I felt a numbness in my shoulders, arms, hands and fingers. An extraordinary pain had taken hold of my whole body; I couldn't stay motionless. I would get up, sit on a chair, fall to the floor, hurl myself at the chair, the desk, scream, swear, sit and rise, and finally stop breathing, but the pain continued to increase. How long could one tolerate this pain? One doesn't know. . . . the agents were changing places. Two people stayed with me, and others went to have lunch, and everyone who came in told me to confess and free myself from the pain I was in.

"Tell us! Tell us! And get rid of the pain!"

"Poor thing! In the end you will confess!"

"What is the use? We already know everything."

When it was the turn of the pockmarked E.Y., he gave me two blows with his fists. The convulsion was so painful, it seemed that thousands of needles had been stuck into my flesh at once.

Once J.R. entered the room and rained angry blows with his fist and open hand on my face and head.

Finally F.Y. told one of the other agents quietly, "He can stand it no longer. Go and get the key from J.R."

F.Y. opened my hands. Naturally, one wants to stretch his arms and return them to their normal position. But it seemed such an action would be dangerous. F.Y. slowly moved my hands forward, but when I managed to touch the edge of the desk with my hands, I was shocked because I simply felt nothing, as if the muscles were entirely dead.

Even after a week, when I pushed a needle into the side of the first knuckle of my thumb, I felt nothing.

(Bozorg Alavi, *The Fifty-Three*, anonymous publisher, pp. 28–29, trans. by R.B.)

THEY BROKE MY TEETH

First he [Dr. Hosseinzadeh] lifted me from the chair and told me to put my nose to the wall. One of the guards kept his bayonet on my neck so that I wouldn't move my head. They kept me on one foot in this same position for fifteen minutes, and afterwards, instead of letting me sit on the chair, they let me sit on a high stool from which my feet dangled without reaching the floor. Two SAVAK agents started squeezing the hard veins in my neck for a long time. Then they asked me a question, insisting that I answer it according to their wishes, i.e., lie; and when I refused to do so, they repeated what they had done before several times; when this proved useless, they forced me to lie down with only my undershirt on. One man sat on my head, another on my feet, and the rest of them tore at the flesh all over my body with whips. . . . The torture [on another day] changed from whipping to kicking or the use of brass knuckles or rifle butts, in the process of the latter of which three of my front teeth broke. . . . Even the guards wept for me.

(Original text of Alijan Shansi's defense in the second court of the Military Tribunal in March, 1965, from the Publications of the Society of Iranian Socialists in Europe, March, 1966, pp. 4–5, trans. by R.B.)

HOW I FACED THE FIRING SQUAD

After they arrested me on January 8, 1969, I was immediately taken to the SAVAK station of Khorramshahr (a southwestern port of Iran). Three men stripped me naked with punches and kicks for the purpose of so-called physical inspection. From 8 P.M. to 1 A.M. the next day, the interrogation went on accompanied by more punches and kicks. . . . The next day I was transferred to the police prison of Abadan and imprisoned in one of the toilets there. I spent one whole week in this toilet with only an old army blanket, one meal a day and no clothes at all. On the eighth day I was handcuffed and transferred to Teheran in a SAVAK Land Rover, to the Evin prison. Interrogation began upon my arrival, combined with torture. Two men, Reza Atapour, known as Dr. Hosseinzadeh, and Biglari, known as Engineer Yoosefi, beat me for nearly an hour. Then they sat me behind a desk and told me to write down that I was a Communist and was engaged in espionage. When I refused, Reza Atapour ordered two sergeants to come and force me to lie down. They began flogging me with assistance from Biglari, using a black cable whip. The flogging and the beating and the punching and the kicking went on for more than three hours. My torturers were taking turns and resting. I fainted twice in the course of all this. My whole body had turned blue, and blood streamed down my back.

The interrogation on January 21 ended here; on the next day, the same things were repeated, with the only difference being that they put the weight cuffs on me several times. They forced me to stand on a stool with the cuffs on, with one of my feet held free in the air. Then they knocked the stool out from under me several times, causing me to fall onto the floor with my full weight. The following day, as a result of slaps I received from Atapour, my ears started bleeding. The eardrum of the left ear was torn. My left ear has lost its hearing faculty. You can examine it for yourself.

On that very day, at about 10 P.M., they took me out of solitary confinement of the horrible Evin prison and led me blindfolded across the grounds of the prison. They pushed me along for some time, and I could hear Atapour and Yousefi whispering about me. The crowing of the ravens, the cold weather, the welts from my flagellation, the pain from my left ear, and the ominous voices of Atapour and Biglari, who constantly addressed each other as "Doctor" and "Engineer," were a horrible combination. They tied me to a tree. The footsteps I heard and the orders that were being given convinced me that they had put me up in front of a firing squad. Atapour read the verdict. "Shokrollah Paknezhad has been condemned to death for making attempts on the life of His Imperial Majesty and for his connection with a hostile foreign government." Then he told the squad to make ready. He reminded me in the meanwhile that since I had been caught on the Iraqi border and nobody knew anything about my arrest, and since everybody thought that I had gone to Iraq, hardly anyone would know that I had been executed. After the rifles were bolted and the order "Fire!" was given, I heard a voice and then much whispering. Atapour shouted, "What is this? Why do you give an order and later cancel it?" Then for a time he swore at me.

Finally, they untied me from the tree and took me back to solitary confinement. All this play-acting was intended to frighten a confession out of me according to their wishes. During later interrogation sessions they pulled out the nails of my left index finger and of the little finger of the right hand. They knocked me down many times, using karate techniques, using their hands and feet on me. The obscenities these executioners used on me during their interrogation were suitable only for their mouths and the mouths of their overlords and will not bear repetition here by me; I would be ashamed to repeat them. Three times, and each time for forty-eight hours, they kept me awake. I don't even wish to talk about the long periods of hunger and the torture by increased light, to which I was subjected several times. All in all, my torture lasted 18 days.

(The defense of Shokrollah Paknezhad in the Third Normal Court of the Military Tribunal, a publication of the World Confederation of Iranian Students Abroad, February, 1970, place of publication unknown, pp. 14–15, trans. by R.B.)

THE HOT TABLE

> An iron frame, rather like a bed frame, covered with a wire mesh, which is electrically heated like a toaster. Prisoners would, it is alleged, be strapped to the table while it became red hot.
>
> (Philip Jacobson, London *Sunday Times,* January 19, 1975)

This device was used on Mass'ood Ahmadzadeh, a Teheran engineer who was finally condemned to death in 1971. When his case reached the Court of Appeals in February, 1972, two international observers, Nuri Albala and Henri Libertalis, managed to observe the hearing; Albala described Ahmadzadeh's chest and back:

> "The whole of the middle of his chest and his stomach was a mass of twisted scars from very deep burns. . . . But I estimate that they were months old. His back was even worse. There was a perfect oblong shape etched into it, formed by a continuous line of scar tissue. Inside the oblong, the skin was again covered with tinier scars from burns. I would estimate that the width of the table marks on his back was at least nine inches."
>
> (Quoted in Jacobson's article above)

Albala and Libertalis interviewed Nasser Sadegh and Ali Mihandoust, engineers awaiting trial on political charges.

> "Albala asked Sadegh if he or his colleagues had been tortured. An interpreter conveyed Sadegh's long reply as: 'No, only beaten when we were first arrested.' By facial gestures Sadegh indicated that this was not what he had said. Albala then asked him directly in English, 'Were you beaten?' 'No, toasted!' Sadegh replied."
>
> *(Ibid.)*

> "As SAVAK agents hustled the lawyers out of the room, Sadegh yelled out, 'Let them know that I saw Behruz Dehghani[1] die near me in the torture room.' "
>
> *(Ibid.)*

Nasser Sadegh and Ali Mehandoust have since been executed.

---

[1] A well-known translator and folklorist from the city of Tabriz.

CHIEF SABETI URINATES
IN A VICTIM'S MOUTH

I myself was under torture for fifteen days, and my blood pressure had gone down to 5, and I had lost 20 kilos. To make me ready for the trial, they had to keep me in the hospital for a month. They burned me with an electric heater. I could not walk, and I had to crawl on the ground, on my chest. Your agents (one of them Sabeti) took out their penises and urinated in my mouth. Aren't you ashamed of yourselves? This is the nature of the regime against which we have revolted. The regime of criminals from top to bottom. It is a disgrace throughout. Do you mean to pretend that you know nothing about these tortures?

> (Text of the defense of Mehdi Rezai in the Military Tribunal, undated, from the publications of Organizations of the National Front of Iran, Middle East Section, March, 1972, trans. by R.B.)

REZA R.: A FREE POET

Teheran: The room is minuscule and the floor is cluttered with a mattress, piles of books in Persian and French, foreign newspapers yellowed by time and a low table strewn with rough-draft manuscript sheets around a half-empty bottle of vodka.

Reza R., slumped among the cushions, has lost the carefree vitality of his student days when I knew him in Paris. Stupefied by my unannounced night visit, he immediately asks whether I am "absolutely certain" that I have not been followed. At first reticent, Reza R. outlined in personal terms his entanglement with the Iranian authorities. "My story is nothing unique. Thousands of Iranian intellectuals have seen an analogous fate with slight variations." [Footnote: To preserve his identity I have deliberately changed certain features of Reza R.'s portrait; with his concurrence, however, I have retained the essentials of his trying experience.]

Formerly a literature professor, he made no reference in his courses to the Shah's "White Revolution," and was thus judged a nonconformist. He learned later that one of his colleagues had filed reports on his "suspicious" attitude with

SAVAK (the political police). Anonymous tracts denouncing him as a traitor circulated until one day he was stoned by a group of students "indignant" over his "subversive" teaching. He was asked to resign but refused.

A few days later the police came to his residence at dawn to haul him off. For months his family could not determine where he was detained. The SAVAK agents, protected by regulations governing "military magistrates," and accountable only to the Shah, can incarcerate and interrogate a citizen as long as they find it necessary, without obligation to try him before the military tribunals. Abusing their powers, they detain even those who have been released after serving a sentence legitimately imposed by the normal judicial system. SAVAK has its own prisons throughout the country, sometimes ordinary-looking apartments or houses where it conducts some very unique interrogations.

Reza R. calmly described the atrocity of the torture that he suffered in these detention centers and showed me the resulting scars on various parts of his body. [Footnote: The Shah once stated that the torture practices in prisons are not physical but psychological and thus more "refined." A detailed study over a two-year period, revealed by the London *Sunday Times,* January 19, 1975, shows that one such refinement consists of mistreating children while their parents observe.]

"My suffering was all the more unbearable due to the fact that for weeks at a time I was not informed of the reasons for their inflictions. My torturers probably were unaware of my offenses as well, as in carrying out their task they only swore at me and threatened to kill me. No specific allegations or accusations were made against me. And for good reason, as I am neither a terrorist, nor a clandestine militant, not even a Marxist." Subsequently, Reza was asked to "frankly and publicly" declare his allegiance to the Shah's "revolution," which he finally refused to do. When he finally expected the worst, he was released following "high-level foreign intervention," whose origin he did not specify.

Reza R.'s prolonged mistreatment didn't end there, however. SAVAK, which can impose "economic sanctions," prohibited him from working until he repented. His passport revoked, he cannot build a new life abroad where his wife and children have already taken refuge. His friends no longer dare visit him, and his isolation is all the greater since he has given up reading newspapers—"What good," he explains, "since the censors have turned them into propaganda sheets?" Pointing to the table, he adds, "I have taken to drinking; in my more lucid moments I write poems for my own pleasure, since the three collections I submitted were rejected in spite of their apolitical character. In the end, we must pity the censors; they have no grasp of poetic language, and when in doubt, they prefer the safety of rejecting the manuscript. They too live in terror."

(Eric Rouleau, *Le Monde*, October 5, 1976, trans. by and reprinted in *Swasia North Africa*, October 29, 1976)

MASKS AND PARAGRAPHS
Poems in English

In this hot night
My light will be on till morning
I intend to build a better wall
Around the house of the blind

One blind man puts his finger on the wall
"There're so many things wrong with it," he says
A second chides me with questions:
"Why do this, and why do that?"

I go on putting one brick over the other
Around the house of the blind
I intend to build a shade for them
To fend off the sun's fierce heat tomorrow
                                        — *Nima Youshidj*

With no consideration, no pity, no shame,
They've built walls around me, thick and high
And now I sit here feeling hopeless.
I can't think of anything else: this fate gnaws at my mind—
Because I had so much to do outside.
When they were building the walls, How could I not have noticed!
But I never heard the builders, not a sound.
Imperceptibly they've closed me off from the outside world.
                                        — *C.P. Cavafy*

The Mask of the Other

There's something in me that doesn't think of me
Is it my beard or my eyes?
Is it my gray age reaching the future page?

Is it the sugar in my blood?
Or the uric acid in my brain?
Or my knees touching your knees in my heart?

It's like thinking in a language I don't know
About a woman I don't know
Who happens to know me in a language
She doesn't know but she thinks I know

The archetypes of my fingers rise in the mirror
Like Shiva dancing somewhere else
In Athens, Burgundy, or Sudan
What is it in me that doesn't think of me?

Dwarfed commas move from me to me
Separating me from me
Each hand is a canto unrelated to the other
Each step a bird flying in a different continent
Each eye a distant century, a blind entity

Someone is writing me in words, flying me in birds
Someone is gravity, pulling me down, pulling me down
Who is it in me that doesn't think of me?
Or doesn't think of me when he *does* think of me?

The Mask of Li Po II

Once in a distant concentration camp
Where he was raped by a man with myopic eyes
He wrote a poem with the blood running from his asshole
On injustice, smelling of man's entrails
His manicured asshole was his pen
For paper the old tiles of his cell
Li Po came to his mind, Rumi, Rilke, and Heidegger,
Passing in parade through the prostate of his time

He knelt and drank his poem

A Double Mask
Our Mission in Arras[1]

For Samad Behrangi and Mustafa Dzhemilev

The snow is melting in Julfa[2] now
Our mother sits on the southern bank
Watching the easy flow of the river
Our bones pass in the undercurrent
Our mother knows this and smiles

A dissident poet from Russia whispers to me
I whisper back
We smile. We depart
Soft pieces of ice pass between us
Sheets of wave cover us
Our anchors pull us to the bottom of the river
Our mother watches us and smiles

—Where shall I go, Comrade? I ask
I was killed once in Turkestan in 1935
A second time in Georgia in 1952
A third time in Tabriz in 1953
And a fourth time in Teheran in 1973
Where do our bones meet again?
When do our ankles whisper again?

—Is it the time or the place that counts?
You mention both, but I wonder
Don't you think we had better forget
Both the Shah and Stalin, and let our
Grinding bones rest in peace?
Night is falling, tell me, or if you cannot,
Let's have another appointment,
Give our ankles another chance
To whisper each to each?

[1] A border river between Iran and the Soviet Union where dissidents of both countries are rumored to have been drowned.

[2] An Iranian town on the border.

—Keep your voice down
The water is recording our voices
Our testicles are tapped
The movements of our shoulders are being taped
Be hermetic, so the police won't understand

Our mother watches us and smiles

The river has a sound when you are far away
When you are in it the river is silent
It runs over you like a poem without words

—Let's forget the dictators for a second
And think of poetry, comrade!
I want the words of a poem to think about the poem
When *I* think about the words
Dictators walk in; when the words think about
The poem poetry walks in; I like the sun
Thinking about the sun; the tree thinking
About the tree; and they both thinking about
Both of us; whisper on brother, whisper!

—They shot me after I was dead
Did you know that?
They pretended I didn't die under torture
Did you know that?
I offered to recant
They thought I was even too dangerous for that
Did you know that?
Only the river knows I'm here
My bones speak to the river
As your words speak to the poem
The river runs through me
As the poem runs through you

Our mother watches us and smiles

A shadow has passed over the world
The fish know the meaning of the shadow
They are rushing away to the sea

—Are they building a dam over our bones?
Is there a joint project to get rid of language?

Are we the mice they use for future discoveries?
Perhaps ages have passed
They're drilling a well over our hearts
We'll suddenly leap to the sky
Catch fire in the sun
And burn the earth to dust
And burn the earth to dust

Our mother watches us and smiles

—Let's have another disappointment
Or rather
Let's have another appointment

The Mask of the Poet

Poetry is the better name of silence and the
Better name of language. In between
There stands the rose that speaks
And doesn't speak

The syllable is a condition of silence
The long-legged fly from Ireland
Was a quiet beat in Africa, between
The shallow and the profound beats
The Hindus spoke in silence. The unravished
Bride of the forest is a language. Homer is
Not the beginning. Both Pound and Eliot
Were wrong. Homer is the middleman,
The equator, the gap between the two
Hemispheres. The gap is the gap of silence:
The lost syllable between the East and the West

Not Heidegger but Rumi is my master
—I will demolish the letter, the sound and the speech
I will speak unto you without these[3]

A syllable speaks to a syllable
As stone to another stone. The stones move
Together; downhill, uphill, downhill, uphill;
Up and down they go in silence. Morning eagles
Fly in silence. The Orient is in their guts.
To dig it out you have to learn to fly. Not there
Into the space outside; but to the space
Here and inside. All the leaves of the Orient
Have fallen inside, and the world has become
Weightless; the world is silent; the wine
Has returned home; the vineyard and the grapes

Scientists have changed the world!
Deceive yourself, my Western brother!
The unconcealed is concealed, still there. The giant's fist
Resists. Even the colonial ax has turned against
You. To conquer, doesn't mean to win. You destroy

[3] The translation of a famous couplet from Rumi, the classical Iranian poet.

The world's silence. Listen once more to the sound
Of your action. The surface reaches your ear
The seed returns to the home of its mystery
You are drunk on an empty bottle
And, what am I to learn from you,
When your language doesn't tell you what I say?

I'll go back to my rare language;
The Mother, my main language
I'll go back to her womb;
I'll mate with my own silence

The Mask of the Writer
Facing the Police

I come back from the city
Where I have shaken hands with the police

The ritual is worthy of historical remembrance
He puts his rifle on the floor
I put my pen on the paper
He takes off his cap
I take off my pants
He takes off his pants
I take off his jacket
He takes off my shorts
I take off his shirt
He takes off my jacket
I take off his shorts
I remove the label: "Up with the king!" from his penis
He removes the label: "Down with the king!" from my ass
We shake hands solemnly
Like a general surrendering to another general
Then we dress:
I put the label: "Up with the king!" on his ass
He puts the label: "Down with the king!" on my penis
I put on him his shorts
He puts on me my jacket
I put on him his shirt
He puts on me my shorts
I put on him his jacket
He puts on me his cap
There's a mistake
I take off his cap
I put his cap on him
He picks up my pen
I pick up his rifle
There's a mistake again
He gives me my pen
I give him his rifle

He follows me
I run

I come back from the city
Where I have shaken hands with the police

The Mask of Your
Limping Murderer

One day a middle-aged man
Will follow you down the stairs
You won't notice him
Only when he puts the bullet in your lungs
Through your burning ribs
You will think you should have looked back
But had you looked back
You would have found him an old man
And perhaps you would have pitied him
For the cancer in his right lung
And the weak eyes that can hardly see
The stairs, the bridge, the fences, and the doves
Playing around his limping legs

There's a moment of loneliness in everything that counts
Or in the man who mounts the hill
To look beyond the river to the forest
Where a cottage stands like a white limpid bird
You would have loved to die there
And in the right moment
But no one dies in the right place
Or in the right hour
And everyone dies sooner than his time
And before he reaches home

Death is the limping legs of the criminal
Who runs faster than the victim's blood
Your flesh remains behind those legs
Like an envelope emptied of its fragile check
The world forgets you
Reminding you of a sky
That shoots its hasting meteors
Out of its darkening thighs

The Unmasking of the Mask

They're cutting me to pieces now
They've removed my kidneys
Like a pair of old shoes, newly polished
My hernia shines in the alcohol
Like the tanned skin of an embryo
I'm like a fart hidden under heavy clothes
My decomposing flesh is beginning to be felt
My stomach has been scooped out
My surgeons are getting ready to fuck me

Bearded physicians whisper around my body
As if I could hear and get up
And have them all shot
I'm responsible for the death of 2 million people
And the fall of a revolution
What do I care for the lives of 32 terrorist physicians?
2 million forms of cancer dig into me
With their malignant miniature cocks
And I simply don't care

What are these machines attached to my body?
One is attached to me as my prick
The other as my ass
The third as my ears
The fourth as my nose
The fifth as my heart
Into which the people of Spain will fart
The sixth as my kidneys
God! This word reminds me of donkeys, monkeys,
And Mrs. Franco's bikinis
And the seventh as my mouth
I had false teeth; now I have a false mouth too
They're replacing my brains with some mechanical crap
That works, they say, like the bowels
Of a six-day-old mouse (Science has improved since Hitler
     died)
I think I'll simply get up
With all the cats and the mice

And all the machines attached to my bones
And have all the bastards shot
Then send a message to the Shah of Iran
On the occasion of the anniversary
Of his 26553rd birthday, to be exact,
And prove to the world
I'm Generalissimo Francisco Franco
The Dictator of Spain
And unfortunately, I'm failing all of you
And I'm dying

The Mask of the Dictator

Last night my general came to see me
We agreed on everything
He said the number I had given him was correct
I told him the number he had given me was also correct
I asked the general about his wife
He told me she was always ready
I thanked him
His wife tells me about the general's bed habits
We laugh till we come together

The general stood at attention
I told him to undress
He did like an obedient soldier
Naked, he stood like a hairy pig
I told him to turn around
His hanging buttocks sneered like a double chin
I invited him to play checkers with me
I had all my ribbons, medals, stars and crowns on
The general's shoulders were naked
When I won I told him to get up and fart
He hunched up his shoulders
He squeezed his bowels
He pressed the weight of his crimes on his rectum
He failed
"Your Majesty, I don't have one this time
Forgive me, Your Majesty!"
I have never forgiven anyone
I have read and unread the books of my enemies
They are dead
I am depressed like a big bug that cannot walk
"General! Come and poke your nose into my ass!"
I want him to see the galaxies there
With his myopic eyes
But half-dictators have no vision
I throw him out
Ring the bell
And ask for my naked cabinet to walk in
When the birds sing outside

I ask all of them to speak at once
"Not less than a hundred words in a second, you sons of
    bitches!"
They chatter on things that don't matter
Everyone fails nowadays
Where are the old ways
When rhymes flowed like melted honey
When I gave my eunuchs and poets
tons and tons of money?

I stand by the mirror
My country is a large mirror
It shows only me, only me
The people, the filthy people, have departed
I am past, present and future
Bury me standing, if you must
Bury me standing, if you must

The Mask of Our Ancestor

The man with the two mouths
Has been our ancestor for a long time
We cannot dream of changing him
If we do, we will change ourselves
That we cannot tolerate
Neither can our sons

He sits by the river
Each mouth facing each direction of the water
The river runs both ways, he knows it
The sun shines on his blue rings
His fleshy tongue hangs out
His bald head sweats in the sun
He watches the world through eyeless holes
Unaware that he is rooted to the ground
And is laying golden eggs in the bowels of the earth
We move round his huge face
We file on his tongue
As flies on a donkey's tail
We embarrass him
Asking about the number of his wives
But we observe the rules of decency
We never ask him about his slaves
Or his mistresses

The answer never comes
He cannot speak
Only the wind blows the sand into our eyes
The owls screech through the humid summer day
He is covered and uncovered a million times a day
Still he knows that we are watching him

We go away from him as ponies from their mare
We go back to him as bees to their queen
We pity him, he doesn't understand
We cuckold our lovers to him, he doesn't notice
We offer him our cunts, pricks and asses, he doesn't care
We recite hieroglyphs, he doesn't nod
He simply sits there, the huge primitive asshole
He has been our ancestor for a long long time

Stupid questions should never be asked:
Does he have a soul? Do we have a body?
Don't make him laugh! Don't make him laugh!
He won't get angry! Don't make him mad!
Only at nights we cannot see him
He departs in the form of a black cloud
Or sinks into the river washing his double mouth
Or brushes his rotten teeth with stars from the milky way
The divine asshole is too big for us to see

Our women bake bread sweating in the huts
His images fuck our women through us
In the morning when we wake up
He is sitting by the river
Laying eggs for the future of our sons
We are vultures watching the beast in agony
We need him
We will cut him to pieces when he dies
But the divine asshole never dies
The river runs in both directions

My Father

My father
The classless man
Sits in his inferno
Watching me use
Words which he
cannot understand

There is a singular
Subterraneous fire
Between his fingers, in his armpits
Around his ears, and
Certainly, deep in his eyes

"Look at me, you son of a bitch!"
He shouts. "If you want to be
A great poet, behold this shriveled
Parchment on my bones
And then write. A man without an inferno
Will never mean what he says.
His poems will *only* be modern
Nothing else!"

I am looking for the torch of his burning bones

The Mask of Our Blind Man

I am the blind man who has walked all over the East
The road from Balkh to Marv is dangerous
Swords clash in the intestines of the warriors
And horses walk on the faces of fallen men
There the highwaymen thought I was pretending
They opened my eyes with the tips of their daggers
And then left me alone
In the city the children
Pelted me with stones hidden in snowballs
I hardly knew where to go
The sky they said was blue like a yankee's eyes
Then someone smelling of radish
Pressed a coin in my hand
So small that I could lose it in the wrinkles of my hands
A woman gave me a long shirt
"It belongs to my dead husband
He died in the desert
Pray that his soul may rest in peace."
I prayed
A cobbler gave me a pair of old shoes
I couldn't understand what he said
He had a thousand nails in his mouth when he spoke
The shoes were small
I tucked them under my arm
To use them as a pillow in the mosque
Then I walked into the desert
With the sun burning the scalp into ash
The pebbles melted like tar
I put one foot down raising the other
And began to dance in the heat
To the beat of burning inside
Running and running I danced
I learned to dance in only one afternoon
The desert as my school
My legs my teachers

Then the evening of the world cooled the earth
I slept with the earth impressed on my chest

The stars shone on my back
Like the wings of butterflies on the march in the light
A caravan picked me up in the morning
I sat on a young camel
And sang all the way to the sea

The Mask of the Sultan's Slave-Boy

In the winter of that year (399 Hegira)
The coldest winter of the world
The clown and I shared a room
In the outer palace in the city of Balkh

In the summer the news had come from China
Smelling as usual of dove's eggs
India moved in the Sultan's bowels that year
As an ibex swallowed in full by a snake
But not yet digested
The Caliph had sent new titles to the Sultan
The Northern Turks had been subdued
The River Oxus ran on,
Brimming with beheaded corpses, our victories
Young slaves were castrated daily, happily
And the Sultan walked to the mosque
With his learned ministers, scribes and poets following

My friend the clown had been castrated by the late Emir.
In the year 369 Hegira
The Sultan entrusted me to him and him to me

"Now that we share our room, let's share our beds, too,"
The clown said on that first night
Naked, we slept in each other's arms
Not knowing what to do with each other
He pressed his fragile ribs on my chest
His thighs were bashful
I hugged him
Our chins touched
I loved the smell of his mustache
Had he been a full man, he would have slept with me
Not knowing what to do, we shared our minds

The Sultan loved my black hair and small penis
He sometimes let me do it to him
But even then it seemed that he was doing it to me
We kissed and parted
The clown took me to our room

The clown did not die
He gradually froze stiff in my arms
Our chins touching
The frost in the River defied the Sultan's sword
Dead animals smelled of ice
And the Turkish nomads could not move
They peeped like Eskimos from their huts
Ice shone as the devil's dark eyes
Historians record pneumonia as the cause of the clown's death
They were wrong
I record it as frustration in love
And failure in duty

The Sultan died 19 years later
Now, the clown's body lies
At the foot of the Sultan's grave

I am a free man with a long white beard
I pray in the mosque among other free men
What is written in the chronicles will happen to me
My eyes can hardly see the young Sultan's face
Those who slept with me are all dead
When I die I will be buried
At the foot of the old clown's grave
The chronicles are correct
The year of my death is: 426 Hegira
The fourth night of the third month of the year
The moon will be crescent as usual

An Empty Mask Speaking

The rose grown between us will fade
Of the sky nothing will remain
The gates of the city will be closed
Gods will be thrown down from the walls
Old armies will defeat the young ones
Decrepit bats will fly through the city of Shiraz
Human balls will be squeezed into puss
Poison will be served in wineglasses to the guests
Coffins will be carried in the air in Tabriz
The desert will stretch itself to the capital
The earthquake will break the capital's back to pieces
Snakes will run through the spines of the earth
The martyrs will sneak away from ancient shrines
The Caspian will go dry
The fish will swallow whole villages with beasts and men in
    them
Burning stars will shoot out from the Southern Gulf
Piercing the eyes of Persian cats, sitting behind windowpanes

Then a shriek will summon the kings waiting for their turn
Whole kings will walk on the earth,
Greeting each other with daggers in their teeth
In nails
In smashed pieces of glass
In men as small as atoms
In sands
In fists in gloves
In sediments of piss and puss
In wolves and jackals
In dry trees and ruddy autumn leaves
In vultures and blades of beaks
In beasts equally unknown to men and beasts
In lepers scratching each other with nails and knives
In lips of blood and mouths of hell
A new country will be born
Persia will be reborn[4]

[4] "Persia will be reborn in ten years' time," the present shah reports.

The Mask of the Traveler

For Willis Barnstone

There was a tree
There was a lake
There was an abstract horse
In the dangerous process of tumbling down
From a rising mountain
And the queen of birds
Watched the scenery blindly

It was here we shook hands last time
I wanted to kiss you
But I was ashamed of your daughter
We spoke of things that didn't count
And parted like people who had known each other
For only a moment

China doesn't count
Neither does the rest of the East
The roots of the trees of th world
Were in my palms
When I was with you
In the world's empty pocket
Now I stand
Dry like a match

The butcher across the world is walking toward me
Each day is a step
My exiled shoulders move away from lights and stars

I'm the defeated satrap
Revolving
In the fire of his nakedness
Accept my bones, my friend!
As tokens of a traveler's farewell

A Mask for Further Confusion

Birds have come in; no!
Mr. Bird has come in; no!
I said, no! birds have come in

You know what birds are?
They're things which fly; no!
They're things which fall when you shoot them

Not American birds, not Indian birds; no!
Birds on Persian wings, Arabic,
Turkish, Hebrew wings;
Dream vultures,
Spinning above the shoulders of a desert sphinx
No menagerie of Oedipus, Orestes, Menelaus
No sphinx with American shoulders in decline
Facing shining walls of China;
Dream birds on real shoulders;
Not Dante, or Jung
But hell, upheld on fingertips of form
Like a Shakespeare on tiptoe
Walking back to Macbeth

Birds have come in; no!
Mr. Bird has come in!

The Mask of the Exile

I want to get up and go see her again
The woman as familiar as the desert
She sits there by the window
Her hands smelling of turnips and the sun
The sun that makes her old,
The sun that kills her
The sun that forgets her

Her pygmy eyes know the meaning of exile
She knows the corridors of immigration by heart
Cars and camels and flies pass
But no flowers pass
She knows the meaning of her hands
Throttled by the veins on her wrists
Her share is a wrinkled heart
Her feet are weightless
Like empty slippers
Her womb is a balloon
Deflated, its sons gone out

What am I doing here?
She sits there, a year before or after her death
A year before or after her funeral
Round like the word Orient
Round like the O in the word or the world

I want to get up and go see her again

The Woman's Mask

The day I gave birth to the apple
The Americans came
It was long ago

I measure time with the length of a camel's neck
Time is curved as the camel's neck
I don't think
I simply watch

Birds pass carrying scorpions on their bills
Do birds have ribs like human beings?

My husband holds his penis in his hand
And cries
His tears fall over his wrinkled face and prick
He is impotent like a four-year-old boy

We try to make love to the memory of our son
He died in prison
He was raped
I tell my husband about the rape of our son
He comes in his mind
His memory is ageless like the stones in the mosque
Horses cough in the cold chambers of his memory
His penis is a beheaded penguin
We speak about it
Reminding ourselves that it was the prophet
That had failed

I watch everything and wait for the day
I will not watch anything

The Mask of Enemies

I begin to forget the names of my enemies
These unpaid bills

It was difficult to live without them
Now it is difficult to live with them

Their daggers have turned into paper in my heart
Their bites have healed
My soles are as smooth as they were
My knees are healthy again

The trees from the forest have thrust out their fists
A face has drawn closer
The face of a leafy beast
The birds have stopped singing
My enemies have gone away
And I am here already with that animal
The trees from the forest
Are withdrawing their fists

The Mask of the Unknown

I put the light out
I sat down and watched him
His nose was taut
—an arrow in a drawn bow
The eyes swam under the bridges of the eyebrows
Into the channels of eternity
His chin was a fallen kite
His card shone from his pocket
—an obscene sign

He defied the machine guns of the world
Holes travel through his shoulders
He has a thousand hearts now
Silent as stones in a sick bladder
Hamlet is here? or Che? or both?
Or neither?

We should ask the man himself
We should read the card and find out
We should ask the men who shot him

The men have left
The card is blank
The man is no more

Or perhaps we should read the books of the world
And find a name for the mask
But first let's bury him
And then get back to the task at hand

The Mask of the Runner

Oh, fuck it all!
Let me hate the self-pity
I've cherished so long

One day I'll leave it all
Leave them all
I'll rush to a new continent
Crush countries under me as eggs
And drop my skin on the shore
My bones in the sea
I'll appear nowhere and disappear
Everywhere
I'll crown myself
As the king of my limbs
And be proud of my decent ignominy
And think of my toes in my knees
Of my knees in my heart
And my heart in my mouth
Springs will bloom with the birds of my cock
My words will shine like fried testicles
I'll shoot into me
Like the lips of masturbation
Fuck it all!
What else do I want?

The Mask of the Revolutionary

The spirit of the glass is broken
The blood is already in their hands
Pimps and kings sit together, answering questions
The cameras of the revolution move on their faces
The end of the joke is here
The beginning of seriousness is here
The task is a river
We should swim in it
Even the birds have forgotten they had a class
They all sing together
The dream touches our shoulders
We move in to write the future

Several Masks for the Lover

1

She writes everything into me
As a notebook
Leans on my hands until I wake up
In public we walk naked
In private we dress each other
In kisses
I hate leaves falling
And the birds
When they're not there

I hate all the bridges we will not cross

Like a child
The world is embarrassed it contains us
My palms are wrinkled as an old man's face

Making love, we
Go blind; we cover each other
In snow; we forget the meaning of metals
And stones; we speak like the fish; we
Smell like the sea; and think like the moon

When the beasts of our hands
Eat each other, and the hips of the
World move in the hides of the sun
We speak in the tongue of our ribs
We forget that the world is poor
And we're rich; we only remember
That we don't remember
Or we don't remember that
We don't remember

2

Like warm bread in the morning I take you
Do sharks pray when they embrace in the water?

Like a cold shower in the morning I take you
Do wolves make love with their teeth bleeding?

Like a road of flowers in the morning I take you
Do lions make love with crowns on their cocks?

Like the silk of a breeze in the morning I take you
Do gods make love burning each other?

3

If only I could translate
The moods of your limbs into words
I could see the repetition
Of trees in bloom,
Holding the cunts of their flowers in the rain
I could see the repetition of
Stones basking their buttocks in the sun
I could see a nation of orange testicles
belonging to millions of twelve-year-old boys
Hanging in twins from the thighs of the trees
I could see the spine of the Nile
Scattered into ribs of villages
I could see the shoulders of the desert
Moving in the direction of the ocean
Ringing in the armpits with the bells
Of camels
I could float into the entrails
Of standing mares
And sink into the trails of arteries
Bleeding into the heart
Then I could come back with a huge shining china
In my arms
And translate
The moods of your limbs into words

4

Water runs over the apples when we meet
The dagger of flesh hangs in between
One anus speaks to the other unthinkably
Women are equal to men, no doubt
We fill in the crossword puzzles of eyes and ears
We speak in hieroglyphs of wrinkles around our eyes

Then the desert opens up and we enter
Speaking the language of lions and eagles
And pitying the sun and the moon
—Those innocent, impotent globes
Hanging from the balconies of the earth—
We exchange nothing
We stay intact
Love makes everyone a round, complete thing
A round thing with ends like eggs
Standing on round sides in the desert
Cooking unknowingly
Like one anus speaking to the other
Unthinkably

The dagger speaks to its natural sheath
Then tears its sheath
Speaking to it even more naturally
The apples melt into birds
The birds into their feathers
And water runs through the feathers
Then breasts bake like bread

As an egg from a chicken
Or a chicken from an egg
We separate
Water runs over the apples when we part

Before us lies the desert as a sealed earth
The lions and eagles wander in a wounded heart

5

When the man had stopped screaming
The city rose as a confusing dream
The fountain ran profoundly
On the shallow grass
The woman walked away softly
Like a bird kissed on the forehead
By the boy
By the fountain

I have hidden the wallet
Of my lips in exile
In her ankles, in the back of her knees
In the shade of her ribs
And in the pockets of whisper,
Her ears

Let the world smell as an empty icebox
When I'm gone
Now that she's gone
Let the world freeze as an empty icebox

Masks for a Woman in Prison

For Vida Hadjebi Tabrizi,
an Iranian woman, kidnapped,
tortured and still imprisoned
under torture in Iran

1

Sister!
Speak to me of your words when stars are not shining

Speak to me
Of your words
When stars are
Not shining

Sister!
Speak
To me
Of your
Words
When
Stars
Are
Not
Shining

Your fingers stretch in my hands
The petals of spring roses
You are decoded to me in roses
Through walls standing between us
Standing around us

Sister!
Shining
Stars
Speak

Speak to me of your words when stars are not shining

2

The body of a woman in prison
Is the body of the same woman
In the frozen lake of bitter waters

The walls stand and stand
The ice stands and stands
Nothing moves

Let me take you out
Let me warm your hair, your eyes, your frozen shoulders,
The snowballs of your breasts
And the icy fist of your heart
Let me carry you out to the sands
To the heat of the sun
Let me watch your rebirth from the ice
Let me see you walk and talk

Sister!
Shining
Stars
Speak

Speak to me of your words when stars are not shining

3

Darkness has a stench of its own
Not made for a woman
Standing as a young sapling in the dark

Your toenails are my roots
The soldiers are blind
Pulling them out, they make me go dry

Swim through the air toward the world!
The molecules of the air shine with light
Coruscate like the fresh cells of an apple
Every atom bursts out of its own free will
In the ended form of a round, female nipple

Sister!
Shining
Stars
Speak

4

Historical leaves fall outside
     garish yellow
Men walk on each other's shoulders
     clownishly
Birds gather together in conspiracy
Two men were shot today shouting:
"Long live the blood of revolution!"
Fleshy, cock-red bureaucrats leave the Ministry of Foreign
    Affairs
Indolent doves fly above their heads
The Queen, your old classmate,
Has miscarried another bastard
And you sit in your dungeon
Hugging your lonely knees
As if they were the only unbeheaded children
Left undiscovered in the world

5

A woman is more than a tree
And a tree
Beautiful in all seasons of the world
No shape is more soothing than the curves of her shoulders
Her crisp fingers cover the earth with kindness
You can sit on the soft benches of her knees
And sleep until you die happily
You can swim through her arteries
Into the lakes of motion and emotion
You can rise on the soles of her feet to heavens
And dive in measured transport into the earth
You can lean on the balcony of her hands
And still be symmetrical

A tree is the measure of one's climbing
Only fools aspire for more than the top of the tree
The tree is always taller than the child climbing the tree

A woman is a tree
But surely, more than a tree

6

I know you are counting your hopes in your mind
Like someone counting his coins in his pocket
But please add to your coins
The unacknowledged singing of future birds
—feathered virgin brides, who will step down
          coyly from the white staircase of their eggs

You know we will stop them from shooting you
Count that as one of your mysterious coins
And listen to the screams of other prisoners under torture
That's a human voice and a historical coin
Count that too

There's also the stale smell of your body
Your falling hair
And the stuffy stench of the cell
Count those coins too

And you might think you have become ugly
And men will no longer make love to you
Knock on the solid wall
The neighboring prisoner, just tortured,
Will hug you through the wall
Count that coin too

The dearest coins of our history are they
Hold them all in your hands
You are the treasure we buried in the ruins of history
We are the beggars of this world
We'll dig you out, find you
And raise on your arms
The richest continent of the world

7

The nimble hoopoe spreads its colorful fans
On the ugly crown of our alligator regime
Acromatic locks and bolts stand out
On the alligator's skin
In defiance of our liberty and small-arms fire

Reclining on the narcotic trunks of espionage
The slumberous animal dreams of all the fish it's swallowed
And of all the fish it'll swallow

But the bird stands on the ugly crown
Absorbing the sun into the texture of its feathers
Training its colors in the art of caressing our eyes

One day
We'll put the animal's carcass away in the museum
We'll step into the hoopoe's wings
And fly in collection over the shoulders of the world

8

When friends told me you had been
Kidnapped by the dogs
I wondered how the moon could have been
Snatched away by the wolves

I stand in front of a nonexistent statue in my room
And talk to you as if
We lived in post-revolutionary days
And we were to choose a suitable name
For a very rich wine
To honor the four years you spent in the Shah's jail
You said a peasant taught
Was better than a peasant untaught
I agreed that a worker unbought
Was better than a worker bought
Then we said Cheers!
And thought of all the good days
We could have spent together
Instead of rotting down there in jail

9

The sleeping horse will get up one day
And run and run

The dormant snake will raise its neck
And bite and bite

The bulging balloons of our enemy's rhetoric
Will be deflated
And fall and fall

Riding the horse, riding the snake,
Kissing the winds and the hills with your hair
You will arrive
Pure woman, and naked and milky,
As a full Oriental moon
You will nurse the stones of future
Female Daedalus, lovely architect of hearts
Yardstick of immeasurable acceptance
Unimaginable continuity
Cotton-like flexibility
Everlasting breeder and builder
Woman, synonymous with freedom
And open to the world's being
Mother of children and songs!
You will arrive
And only then we will all be free

10

Half of me and half
The rest of the world
What are you doing
In your cemented hexagonal grave
Granted to you
As a lifetime Imperial professorship
By the agents of dagger, rape and plague?

Half of me and half
The rest of the world
Home of hopes and female colors
From which we stand deported
Sailing ships and flying birds
From which we stand isolated
Feasting hands and kissing eyes
From which we stand separated
Birth, copulation, rebirth
From which we stand cut off, castrated

Woman!
Without whom we are emasculated

What are you doing
Half of me and half
The rest of the world?

11

Mother!
Shepherd of words
Sister!
Walking with trees on your shoulders
Sun-moon!
Commanding galaxies
Beloved!
Pregnant with stars
Woman!
Mother tongue of every man and woman
Banner of human identity!
Erected on classless continents of thought
Body!
Formulated on hills and forests
And in the corridors of style, speech and poetry
Come and release us from our prisons!

12

In the chambers of
Our inspiration
The poem and the poet
Are one and the same

The reader and the writer
The singer and the thinker
The player and the play
Are one and the same

The brother is the sister
The child is the father
The father and the mother
Are one and the same

No matter what the name
Everything in the world
The walking and the lame
Are one and the same

For the girl in the jail
Of the Shah, I offer
These words of solace
Let her name be the shame

Of the Shah and the rest
Of his crew. For the test
Of the norm is: Friends! we
Are one and the same

Paragraphs

1

A dictator is a beast
Who walks from himself to himself
In between
He shakes hands with beheaded ghosts

2

When the Queen shook hands with me
She looked at my throat
Too thin or too thick, she thought
I assured her that I was regular size
She nodded and we were finished

3

He was told never to look back
Ever since
He has not looked back
But he has never looked ahead either
Our double-headed Orpheus walks around himself

4

In the court he sits after the clown
The clown sits after the scribe
The scribe sits after the minister
The minister sits after the king
The king sits after God
God sits after no one
He smiles with one eye to the poet
With the other to the clown
The poet sits after no one
He doesn't even smile to God
The clown smiles to the crown
The minister smiles to the scribe
The scribe smiles to you

5

I've put the ladder against the wall
I've climbed the ladder to the last rung
Take the ladder away
I'll sit on the wall forever
And watch the camels of the young prince go by
Shall I report what I see?
The prince is blind
The camels are lame
The camel men are dumb
And the desert is endless
My wisdom shows me only this
And bells that don't ring
I'll sit on the wall forever

6

Rumi's eyes journey from city to city
His body squats by the gates of the big city
The eyes will go back to the body one day
Be patient
Don't let the young pony catch cold
Cover the doors and windows with rugs and blankets
Sit inside and wait
The eyes will go back to the body one day

7

The gate with the rotten wood is still there
The dog is frozen to stone
The wolf is bleeding wax and steel
Men pass, exchanging slaps
And I'm not ashamed to be here in exile
When women die in hell
And pimps shoot the stars in the name of poets
When houses refuse to stand
And the whole world is covered with sand

8

Poor General Zandipour[5]
He's dead and I live
He presided over the Committee of Rape
He smoked his opium in prison
His wife was fucked by other executioners
—The hand that gives is the hand that takes away—
Birds sing outside prison walls every evening
The torture chambers are full
He would have rejoiced to see his killers tortured
Poor General Zandipour!
He's dead and I live

9

There's nothing softer than the deer's neck to the panther
The reality of the struggle escapes us
We only see a picture and scattered entrails
On the road to the spring
The hunter knows only the road
The shining fur in the sun blinds him
To the identity of the animal
The name escapes him
He sweats and forgets, he sweats
And forgets his mission
While vultures reel around the carcass
And snakes escape from the smell
And the sun sets and the panther
Sleeps
And other panthers
Sleep

10

Whoever gathers the breeze
From the tops of the trees
Will find the same grace

[5] An Iranian general in command of the famous prison called Joint Committee for Campaign Against Terrorism in Iran (the Komité). The General was among the interrogators of the present poet when he was in the above prison in the fall of 1973. He was shot by the urban guerrillas of Iran in 1975.

God is supposed to have
Given to prophets and saints

For:
God is an abstract
Miser who doesn't give
Anything to anyone
A man collects his grace
From the knees of women
And the tops of the trees

Reality

The thought
That the flower
Should be ours
Should become a
Reality

The reality should become
A flower

Pattern

Architecture
Is the texture of
An arch
Erected without anarchy
And with
Structure

A sudden mixture
Of apparently
Unpremeditated parts
With art

Poetry is no
Less
Than the height
Of an arch

My Only Bird

The one-winged
Eagle
The abortive triangle
In the space
Is the only bird
I have created
In addition to other
Birds of prey
Created by others
Of clay, of colors
Of vision

The Planet

Two lines
One
As long as eternity
The other
As tall as eternity
They meet together where
The shade thickens into a planet
We live on that planet
Doomed to die
With others
And others

The Politicians

The politicians are effete
They give birth only
To hernia and prostatitis
"The strokes I had," says one,
"Make me eligible for the White House!"
"My bald head," says another,
"Requires a crown!"
"I will have a face-lift," says a third,
"Let the young generation
See in me their leader!"

What the young generation needs
Is a tractor, or maybe a broom

And then let's spit on the faces of the old politicians

Third World

The youth in the
Third World
Take hand grenades
For breakfast
Gunpowder for lunch
Blowing to pieces for dinner

They will switch to a
Diet of atom bombs
Tomorrow or the day after
When more calories
Are needed
To stand dying
Or die standing

The Winter of Our Discontent

A season of glass
And cold
Passes through
The leaves of the world

Birds flip through the pages of ice

The cattle breed
Frozen animals

Broken legs of starving
Horses
Hang in the space

A terrified neighing
Is heard
From the depths of a well

The world is a file
Stamped
Classified

Spies rain
Like hail
From the air

The regiment
Of sharks
Invades
Our neighborhood

Someone is cutting
Our cocks
Scooping out
Our cunts

We're all bridges
Falling down
Falling to pieces

Beheaded poets
On our saddles

Frozen heads
In our satchels

Dwarfed trees—
Dead fields
Naked landscape
Yawning horizon

The Mask of the Damned

The old woman at the gate
Was ready to tell us the names of the flowers
It was her duty to tell us the names of the flowers
But the old man came over to her
And stapled her lips to her tongue

Not knowing the names of the flowers
We dived headlong into the wilderness
Our books packed on the backs of our jackasses
And our coins for water and camel meat
Jingling in our pockets

Like an obedient son
I bought fifteen years of prayer
And twelve years of fasting
For my dead father
Mother had prayed and fasted all her life

We crossed the equator
Boiling in our skins as butter in a pan

All this happened a long time ago
We needed the punishment
Whoever doesn't listen to the words of the old woman
Will suffer as we are suffering
He will die in exile in the other hemisphere

I Used to Be Innocent

And then I used to be so innocent
With the nightingales at my elbow
And the springs snapping their fingers
At the end of my arms
And an entire school of birds climbed above my shoulders

And there were women too
With armpits full of clusters of golden grapes
And with round mouths
Who blew their songs into the reeds of my bones
Making me sing and whirl
Round all the deserts of the East
Planting white villages at every rise and fall of my feet
And thoughts appeared in my mind
As fresh and warm as the downy heads of newly born infants

Let me tell you my friend
I used to be innocent
Like a camel's face
Masticating his turpentine
And not even thinking for a second of his neck
Reflected in the sun on the dunes of the desert
And let me add that I used to be innocent
As racemes of stars, luminous, and almost eloquent
Cluttered on a couple oases in an oriental night

Imagine bread baking and rising like rivers swelling
Imagine grapes squeezed into wine by sweating, female heels
Imagine the ritual of drumming fingertips
On a man's vertebrae
Imagine throwing yourself on the grass and saying,
Take me
Imagine

I used to be innocent

What happened on a September day in 1973
Is already an old story
But imagine a sieve, or rather, a screen
Placed in front of your memories

And everything passing through it
The faces of all men and women you loved
The children you saw and spoke with
The grass on which you slept
The stars you watched, the camels you rode
The rabbits you followed
Imagine all of them and other memories
Passing through the screen
And changing and changing, constantly changing
And becoming things which are unrecognizable
Imagine all love and beauty kept behind that screen
Or memories distorted, standing upside down
Or swollen like decomposing flesh
Imagine a hell you recognize to have been your personal
    paradise
Imagine

I used to be innocent

Our Unfinished Mask

The three pieces of the horse squat in the square
Watching the statue of our ancient king
Erect and self-conscious
He stands in his mask of stone
Covered with the dust of coups
And the smog of assassinations
His sword more like a saw than a sword
Because he knows he is not a swordsman
He is the carpenter of human bones
He loves flesh ground to ashes
And blood vessels relieving themselves
Of their palpitating burden into the gutter
And the three pieces of the horse watch him
Each looking exactly like a separate horse
Only a bit smaller

Our class in ancient history started here
The ancient reflects itself into future
Time here is the echoes of a modern plane engine
Trapped between vertical gashes of an ancient mountain

We see first the ghost of the *biaban* (desert)
In the nightmare of our words
The desert is our stage
We try to make it modern
We cover it with chairs and desks and charts
We invite the ghost on the stage
Let the ghost of the dunes speak
Let him dramatize time and space and forms for us

But the ghost of the *biaban* is the ghost of the king
He passes above the chairs and charts
And above the crowd
In his armor of sable sands
Then he takes off in the dark
As a bird in a myth
He disappears in the folds of our imagination

We set the stage for the appearance of the *karkas* (vulture)
He loves carcasses
Out of the ancient catacombs and tombs
He flies out first vertically
Then horizontally into the desert air
As the wings of a bloody oblivion
He descends upon us
We withhold our hearts—cringed in our chests
As rotten seeds of bad almonds
But his iron beak digs into us
We are not dead yet, we are dying
An intoxicating twilight
The tiny moment before *marg* (death)
Holds us in its melting arms
We dissolve into the margins of the desert
As oil from dirty skin stretches threateningly
To the rims of a hat

The vulture invades us
Our hearts become the fibers of his bowels
He excretes our cheeks on the sands
We become him, flying in his wings
To the gates of our cities
We become miniature vultures
We place him on the throne made of our bones
We crown him as our unique master
We speak of him all the time
We sing songs on the sharpness of his tongue
We eulogize his appetite
We praise his stomach
That grinds tempered steel into soft flour
Our epics and odes intone the largesse of his rectum
Our lyrics flap in his wings
We are his victims
And we love it

He is our unfinished mask . . .

About the Author

REZA BARAHENI is an Iranian poet, novelist and critic. He was born in Tabriz, Iran, in 1935, and educated both in his hometown and at the University of Istanbul, Turkey, where he earned a doctorate in English literature. He is the author of more than twenty volumes of poetry, fiction, literary criticism and translation (in Persian), and he has taught and lectured in Iranian as well as American universities. His works have appeared in half a dozen major languages, including English.

The author now lives in exile in the United States with his wife and two children. He teaches creative writing and also lectures at college campuses on literature and on politics and oppression in Iran.